RENEWALS 691-4574
DATE DUE

**WITHDRAWN
UTSA LIBRARIES**

ON THE EVE OF 1917

ON THE EVE OF 1917

ALEXANDER SHLYAPNIKOV

Translated from the Russian by
RICHARD CHAPPELL

ALLISON & BUSBY
LONDON · NEW YORK

First published 1982
by Allison and Busby Limited
6a Noel Street, London W1V 3RB
and distributed in the USA
by Schocken Books Inc
200 Madison Avenue, New York, NY 10016

Translation copyright © 1982 by Allison & Busby Ltd

British Library Cataloguing in Publication Data:

Shlyapnikov, Alexander
  On the eve of 1917
  1. Munition workers – Europe
  2. European War, 1914–1918 – Economic aspects
  2. Work environment – Europe – History – 20th century
  I. Title
  331.2'042'340924   HD7269.M92E/   80–40641

ISBN 0–85031–376–7
ISBN 0–85031–377–5 Pbk

Set in 10/11 Imprint by
Alan Sutton Publishing Ltd, Gloucester.
Printed in Great Britain by
Biddles Ltd, Guildford & King's Lynn.

Contents

Introduction   vii

1. Russia   1
At a Banquet in Honour of Vandervelde   4
July Days   9
War   13
Attitudes to the War   16
Revolutionary Social Democracy Against the War   19
The Social Democratic Duma Faction and the War   25

2. Scandinavia and England   31
Our Revolutionary Work and Diplomacy by the Conciliators   37
At the Swedish Social Democrats' Congress   42
The Copenhagen Conference   47
Social Chauvinists as Servants of the Bourgeoisie   51
To England   53
Among the Russians in London   57
In Scandinavia   61
An Illegal Journey   64

3. Petersburg   70
War Industry Socialists   73
A Repeat Election Campaign   78
A Secret Meeting of Industrialists   80
The Ninth of January   84
The Situation of the Workers and Party Work   88
Organizational Plan   94
Gathering the Party's Forces   97
Insurance Work and the Chernomazov Business   103
Chernomazov and Co's Provocative Activity   107

4. Scandinavia and America   110
Among the Party Exiles   113
A Trip to America   115
Return from America   120
The Return to Russia   125

5. Back to Petersburg   133
The Central Committee Bureau and Party Work   140
The Social Movement and Social Democracy   146

6. **The Beginning of the End**   156
The Central Committee Bureau's Links with the Provinces   159
Relations with Other Parties   163
The Bourgeoisie's Struggle for Power   167
Support for the Fourth Duma   172
From the Activity of the Russian Social-Democratic Party (Bolsheviks)   181
The Sailors' Military Organization   190
The Government and the War Industries Socialists   197
The Activity of the Bureau of the Central Committee of the RSDLP (B)   200
The Food Crisis   203
The Food Question in the State Duma   208
Organizing Working-Class Action   211
The Underground and the International and Tsarist Okhrana   216
Before 9 January 1917   224

Index   227

Introduction

Shlyapnikov's memoirs open just prior to the St Petersburg barricades of July 1914 and break off on the threshold of the revolution of 1917. His experiences and subsequent researches on this period throw into sharp relief the contradictory effect of World War I upon the development of the Russian revolution. The imperialist conflict delayed yet deepened the crisis of the tsarist political system and the economic life of the country. Shlyapnikov was the key Bolshevik organizer throughout these years, acting as a roving liaison officer and contact man between the Bolsheviks' exile organizations in Scandinavia (and thence to Lenin and Zinoviev's Central Committee in Switzerland) and the fragmented and precarious local party organizations, presses and legal groups in Russia itself. The memoirs, being written in a down-to-earth, practical spirit reflecting the personality of the author, are unique in their first-hand portrayal of the complex interplay of the developing revolutionary awareness of the working class and the mounting predicament of the nobility, the bourgeoisie and the tsarist bureaucracy itself, in each case confronted with a political and economic impasse created by the war.

His brief but vivid sketches of incidents during the July days of 1914, the details of the economic demands of the tramway maintenance men whose victorious strike in January 1916 uplifted St Petersburg workers across a number of industries and the account of the Gorlovka miners' unrest and the ensuing massacre are in themselves historical documents of events rarely recalled today but crucial in the process of the Russian revolution.

We find on the other hand similarly perceptive choices of anecdotal and documentary material which give an insight into the state of the bourgeoisie and nobility. The encounter with an irate patriotic lady on a tram in the early days of the war has almost a Gogolian flavour as does the meeting of big industrialists with the police chief to devise ways of keeping key employees in the arms factories away from political activity. "Revolutionary patriotic" agitation against Rasputin and the tsarina and the connection between the court and the German General Staff, and the crisis in the Duma when the bourgeois and Menshevik "Progressive Bloc" are thrown out and Protopopov goes over to the side of the court, again highlight in concrete terms the break-up of the old régime.

Outside these two elements in society, the struggles of the sailors and the plight of the labouring population as a whole, oppressed in the course of 1916 by a collapse of food supply and distribution with its attendant speculation, graft and misery, are brought into focus that few other historical works attempt.

Alexander Shlyapnikov is most widely recalled today for his prominent role in the activity of the "Workers' Opposition" in the Russian Communist Party between 1920 and 1922. However, his revolutionary work had started back in 1901 at the Obukhov engineering works in St Petersburg. Born into a family of workers and artisans in the small town of Murom in Vladimir province around 1884 (the precise date is unknown as his Old Believer parents would not register his birth officially), he suffered material hardship from his earliest years and from 1900 made a living in engineering shops first in Sormovo (just outside Nizhni-Novgorod) and then in St Petersburg. The city which had introduced Shlyapnikov to Bolshevik ideas and organization was, in the crucial war period, to become the cradle of the workers' revolution and although Shlyapnikov's itinerant life brought him to work there only intermittently it is clear from this book that he was more intimately and practically familiar with the rank-and-file workers there than many another, perhaps more celebrated, Bolshevik leader.

His deep involvement in the gruelling day-to-day minutiae of reconstructing a tightly-knit clandestine organization under the fire of the tsar's security service and cossack lashes is evidenced by the numerous technical and organizational details of daily work in the underground. We are given a schematic view of the internal mechanics of a typical branch organization. Flexibility and local grass-roots initiative were indispensable in illegal conditions. As Preobrazhensky declared at the 13th Party Conference in 1923 when battling the rising apparatus led by Stalin: "What bureaucratism did we know in the old underground organization? None." The arrest of one branch general secretary would have meant total breakdown. The handling of political education, publishing and fund raising is also brought to light and the relationship between illegal and legal work. The latter was undertaken in the Insurance Council and the Hospital Funds which were the only worker-elected factory bodies still permitted to operate. Strict separation of personnel was necessary to avoid the wholesale destruction of the underground groups. The distinction between legal work in the popular elected insurance bodies and participation in the War Industries Committees set up to boost the war effort by top industrialists like Gvozdev and Konovalov in conjunction with Mensheviks is clearly drawn. Yet the subsequent outlawing of much of their activity by the end of 1916 emerges as but another symptom of the terminal sickness of the old society. How could these committees represent the interests of two antagonistic classes at the same time?

Party organization at the base in such case required exceptional initiative and resolve but also vigilance. Infiltration of agents of the security service (the Ohkrana) such as Chernomazov, Starck and possibly Shurkanov was an ever-present risk. On the other hand, "sympathetic" approaches with offers of finance, equipment and communications from unproven individuals like Keskűla or Kruse had to be responded to with great caution. Michael Futrell in his book *Northern Underground* (Faber, London 1972) has delved into the vagaries of the speculation and corruption, both for personal and political motives, that were rife in the First War especially with regard to the German General Staff efforts to enlist Bolshevik support for their own ends of defeating Russia, in the same way as they fostered Finnish nationalist "activism". Shlyapnikov's unconcealed qualms about many sympathizers and party members from the intellectuals arise primarily from the large-scale desertion of many of the more educated activists who were prominent in 1905. This fact is referred to in various connections and imposed an additional burden upon those struggling to rebuild the organization in wartime. Gorky stands out, perhaps surprisingly, as a distinguished exception. Several incidents involving Bukharin and Pyatakov shed a comic light on the author's generally guarded view of the practical and organizational skills of party intellectuals. Kamenev and Krestinsky among others are not highly regarded by him.

Russian history as a whole from 1914 to 1917 is not served well by the available literature, from whatever standpoint it may be written. Admittedly, studies of the economic and political impact and social complications produced by the war were put out by the Carnegie Endowment for International Peace in their series of monographs under the rubric of *The Economic and Social History of the World War*. Also, of course, there is Sir Bernard Pares's *Fall of the Russian Monarchy*. Largely based on reminiscences and papers of statesmen, generals and court figures and eschewing an analysis of the underlying social conflicts, it inevitably strikes an elegiac rather than historical note.

Likewise, the best-known available works dealing with the history of the Russian revolutionary movement itself tend to fight shy of illuminating proletarian struggles and Bolshevik activity inside Russia during the war with the impression resulting that Lenin engaged himself in dreaming up revolutionary fantasies and ingenious schemes in a Swiss village with no sound information and even less communication and organization links with Russia. This widespread misconception is belied by Shlyapnikov in his authoritative and detailed account of the Russian end of the Bolshevik organization and of the communication of literature, information and finance and of its contacts with the Central Committee abroad and the exile groups in Scandinavia. While the author in no way understates even the most bizarre practical obstacles and setbacks that were daily experienced, the reader cannot come away from this book still harbouring the notion popular in bourgeois historiography that Lenin, Krupskaya and Zinoviev had wholly lost touch with the intricate realities of life in wartime Russia whether for the proletariat and peasantry or for the bourgeoisie.

The traditional cultural values of nationality and religion, however pervasive in certain sectors of the population, were not in the end decisive. The war undermined their economic basis, and class consciousness won out. Lenin's strategy and tactics on revolutionary defeatism and of converting the imperialist war into a civil war which at its inception encountered the reservations if not open hostility of even many prominent people of the left internationalist wing of the socialist movement (notably Trotsky and Luxemburg) were derived as much from the study and the experience of Russian social and political ferment in those three years as from an overall assessment of the world imperialist crisis and the state of the International as a whole. The spontaneous defeatist moods exemplified by the St Petersburg graffiti — "If Russia wins, they'll squash us even harder" — bear witness to a contradictory response to the outbreak of hostilities; the subsequent course of the war ensured the growth of such attitudes among the working class. Through the small active organizations and links painstakingly built and maintained by Shlyapnikov and his comrades, a political programme based on the proven slogans of the "three whales" (the eight-hour day, the confiscation of landed estates and the democratic republic) but enhanced by the revolutionary defeatist approach to the war could be tested, refined and rechecked against the day-to-day work of the local underground and legal (insurance and hospital funds) organizations in Russia. However, this crystallization of a rebuilt and tempered Bolshevik network could not of course prove a passport to instant success and be rewarded with a blank cheque of full confidence from the workers and peasants when the revolution of February 1917 erupted. What it did contribute was a political and practical maturity demonstrated during the period of the Provisional Government: wartime experience of the role of bourgeois industrialists and of the Mensheviks showed that their attitude even to

INTRODUCTION   xi

the democratic element of the revolution would be other than in 1905. And it was this maturity of political tactics that brought success in October.

On the Eve of 1917 also includes an episodic but perceptive international commentary. Brief excursions into working-class life in England, Scandinavia and the United States and reminiscences of opportunists of the Second International such as Troelstra, Vandervelde and Stauning, centrists like Branting and, in the Russian movement, Larin and members of the left wing of the Scandinavian parties (Höglund and Wiik, for example) give an extra dimension to the book.

Shlyapnikov's memoirs appeared in 1923 and, to judge by their style and compilation, were written in some haste. Moreover, the pointed remarks and references to certain figures who had since the October revolution risen to positions of importance in the nascent party bureaucracy, particularly Larin, Schmidt and Kamenev, suggest that Shlyapnikov had a certain factional motive behind the publication of his wartime testament. Through it he could prove that his credentials as an "Old Bolshevik" were second to none. Upstart careerists hidebound to the administrative style of the tsarist bureaucracy had spawned during the Civil War and colonized the upper echelons of the party organization, and the social effects of the New Economic Policy fertilized the soil for the growth of a political bureaucracy. Leading members of the Communist Party (notably Trotsky, Preobrazhensky and Pyatakov in alliance with the former "Democratic Centralist" faction) launched a public challenge to the political and economic policies and power of the so-called "triumvirate" of Stalin, Kamenev and Zinoviev in the Party discussion of autumn 1923. Yet it was surprising to some that Shlyapnikov remained aloof from the 1923 struggle, making only one brief written contribution to the public debate in *Pravda* in which he described the whole conflict with the Opposition as an intra-bureaucratic struggle and maintained that neither side had any real link with or concern for the condition of the working class.

Although there is evidence of further, if spasmodic, demonstrations of hostility to the rapidly degenerating Stalinist political régime, Shlyapnikov finally with his old ally Medvedev formally surrendered to Stalin's Politburo in 1926 and dedicated himself to writing a four-volume history of the year 1917 which covers the period from February to July in considerable detail. As with nearly all the Bolsheviks of his vintage, political capitulation did not buy ultimate physical security. In the 1930s he was along with tens of thousands of others arrested and imprisoned, and unlike some of the most prominent Bolsheviks was not exhibited to make a public confession of criminal guilt at one of the notorious show trials of 1936–8. Like so many others, he simply disappeared from history in circumstances even more obscure than those of his birth. Various dates ranging from 1937 to 1943 are offered as that of his death, so that Leopold Trepper's anecdote of an encounter with a man purporting to be Shlyapnikov on a plane over North Africa in January 1945 though improbable cannot be conclusively discounted. Trepper maintains that Shlyapnikov told him he had been invited to return to Russia from France where he had been living in the thirties. He had been enticed back by a very cordial letter from his old comrade from the underground movement, Molotov, now of course in a position of great power. He had expected to be met by Molotov's car upon arrival in Moscow. Instead he was met by a police car and driven straight to the Lubyanka jail, and no more was heard.

* * *

This first English version of Alexander Shlyapnikov's memoirs owes a debt of gratitude to John Archer, Jane Ayton, Steve Carter, Martin Cook, Len and Les Dolphin, Paul Moore, Mair Owen, Anthony van der Poorten, Cathy Porter and Scott Spencer for their assistance, encouragement and constructive interest. As always, the staff of the British Library (Anwar Baba and Stan Jagdar foremost among them) and the School of Slavonic and East European Studies have also made an indispensable contribution with their consistently friendly and attentive service.

R.C.

I

Russia

IN APRIL 1914, after six years of wandering around the workshops and factories of France, Germany and England, I safely crossed the frontier carrying the passport of a French citizen, Jacob Noé, and reached Petersburg, my native city, now red and already a seething cauldron of revolutionary energy. It had just seen a political strike on the anniversary of the Lena shootings and was preparing to celebrate May Day.

I went round the working-class districts, the plants and factories, the same old walls and hooters which involuntarily aroused memories of the heroic period of the Petersburg proletariat's struggle between 1900 and 1907. I was drawn towards my native bench, and wanted to submerge myself in those toothed, cranked, noisy surroundings, so I decided to turn down an honourable and distinguished post as a party official "at the centre" and go to a plant.

I sought out the premises of the Petersburg Metalworkers' Union on the Petersburg bank. There I got to know the union's secretary and several members of the staff and presented my Paris Mechanics' Union card, asking for assistance in my search for work. I received some general information about opportunities for turners, and a few contacts. I deliberately avoided visiting the editors of our newspapers in person. My unusual illegal status — being a foreigner in my own country — required extra caution. My desire to live and work for a while in the very thick of the Petersburg proletariat barred me from visiting points watched especially by the Okhrana.

The need to find work as quickly as possible prompted me to make a personal trip around the workshops and plants. The engineers and foremen greeted me as a "foreigner" quite courteously, but the "alien" origin of my passport obliged me to break my native tongue and often, for the sake of appearance, to resort to the aid of a Russian-French dictionary which I always carried with me. Some knowledge of German allowed me to find work on the Vyborg bank in the first engineering shop at the New Lessner Works. The foreman, a Baltic German, quickly put me on shift work at a lathe.

The workers received me with undisguised curiosity but with good will. The only thing was that my relief proved to be a drinker and often slept on his shift, so I had to work the two. My workmates were a Finnish turner and a Russian milling-machine operator, a good workman and something of a womanizer. I stuck out the first days cautiously to wait and see. I could not keep up empty conversation, and when I had had enough of small talk I got out of it by my incomprehension of the language. But I would willingly answer any serious questions and a "club" of visitors, the most conscious workers in the shop, soon formed around my bench. Comrades were quick to give me a run-down on local life and party work. I was becoming a reference-book on the position of workers in other countries, and on the theory and practice of socialism and syndicalism. Some came to me inquiring whether I knew Lenin, Martov or other exiles who were well known at that time. Ticklish questions about my acquaintance with Lenin and others had to be evaded with general replies like "How could I help knowing them?" and so on. The Petersburgers were highly interested in the lives of their own people and I wanted to tell them, but this was risky.

The spring and summer of 1914 was the high point of our party's struggle against liquidationism. The polemics between *Pravda* and *Luch* had developed such acrimony that workers at the grass roots from both warring factions began to talk of the need for some control over their papers. A gathering of serious-minded workers from Ericsson and Lessner factories was held in the allotment nearest the works, where we started a discussion not about the tone but about the essence of the differences, and the "*Pravda*-ites" did not have much difficulty in demonstrating to the "Menshevik" workers the whole hypocrisy of the "*Luch*-ites", the liquidators of the party's revolutionary traditions, who had clad themselves in the shining armour of the "unity of the workers' party".

May Day was approaching. As opposed to West European workers, who would agitate for staying away from work that day and participating in open rallies organized by the party, the Petersburgers agitated for workers to assemble in the factories at the normal time, and then to walk out of them demonstratively in an organized fashion. On May Day morning the New Lessner proletarians came to work at the usual time but instead of starting work gathered in the yard amid the stacks of iron and steel. Everyone was waiting for something. One speaker got up and, his face hidden under his cap, made an excited speech on the significance of the day for the proletariat of all the world. I too wanted to get up and speak, to share my mood and feelings, but common sense stopped such an act. After the speech we went out on to the embankment in a crowd of several hundred, hoisted a red banner and moved towards neighbouring factories to the tune of the "Marseillaise". We ran into a mounted police patrol, and a skirmish and chase started. In the face of some well-aimed stones, the police, the defenders of "throne and fatherland", disappeared in search of reinforcements. The streets of this working-class district were unusually crowded; people, predominantly workers, walked along with set expressions and on their guard, ready to deal the enemy a blow or two or to make a getaway if those superb Cossack forces galloped in.

The following day all the talk in the workshops was about the May Day demonstrations. Everybody shared impressions and exchanged reports from other districts, plants and factories. As in 1912 and 1913 the young industrial district of Vyborg, where a considerable portion of Petersburg's precision engineering and heavy war industry was located, marched at the head of the movement. In the pre-war years, a significant upturn in industry was taking place; the plants were inundated with orders, the need for manpower was great and employers in the Vyborg district were attracting skilled workers with high wage-rates. This led to a concentration of the most advanced elements in these plants. The better working conditions and militant mood of the workers had given the district a revolutionary reputation, and the Vyborgers were proud of it. Enormous changes had taken place in the attitude of the workers as compared with the time that I was last working illegally, in 1907, at the "1886" power station. The absence of the timidity and submissiveness which even then was very strong in the plants of Petersburg, hit you in the eye. You sensed that the workers had matured considerably as individuals. However, the absence of trade-union organization was apparent. The internal, unwritten but effective regulations on the shop floor were extremely varied and differed not only from one factory to the next but were not even uniform among shops in the same works. The employers cunningly divided workers according to earnings. Workers in the same shop and in the same trade, turning for example, would earn anything from two to six rubles a day on tools and jobs of amost equal complexity and precision. Moreover, a curious phenomenon could be observed, though one that in wartime would become quite natural, whereby the roughest jobs that did not require a high degree of skill, such as work on shells, paid the highest.

The workshops, even the rebuilt ones, were notable for the lack of auxiliary gear — cranes, trolleys, hoists and so on — vital for servicing the smallest requirements of a workshop. The lifting of loads, setting crude jobs on the tools and lifting manoeuvres during positioning and assembling were performed manually by labourers nearly everywhere. Establishments run in this way required a great number of labourers, and all the Petersburg plants were overflowing with them. An uneducated worker from the countryside was paid extremely little. The pay of labourers in Petersburg workshops ranged from ten to thirteen kopeks an hour. The low cost of manpower was reflected in the level of technical installations. Employers were not interested in equipping the plants with auxiliary gear, as "forced" labour came cheaper. As compared with those in the west, the productivity of the shops was very low, and although individual workers might sometimes be even more skilled than their foreign counterparts the general technical and organizational primitiveness suppressed their personal talents. There were few mechanical aids, and management had no concern for the application of modern working methods.

Inside the plants a system of fines flourished. You were fined automatically for lateness, absenteeism and so on. Insults, harassment, docking of pay and petty pressures like opening your locker only when the whistle had gone and not before, as workers liked to, would now and again spill over, and a storm of indignation would break out. The direct lackey of capital, the foreman or engineer, would be wheeled out in a barrow. There was little experience of persistent day-to-day struggle, as the trade unions were too weak; they lived under the threat of being closed down, and could not nurture or discipline a trade-union type of struggle among the mass of workers. My New Lessner workmates exhibited great interest in the life of fellow metalworkers in other countries. Carried away with my tales I would often forget my "alien" origin and embellish my speech with Vladimir argot. My workmates were surprised at my ability to learn the language so quickly, and I had to explain this by saying I had practised talking Russian in Paris. They believed me.

I got into the swing of the job quickly, which pleased my relief no end. He now came into the shop only to sleep. I would be satisfied if he worked half his shift. But I found it extremely arduous doing the work of two, for as we worked on one pay-book the pay was shared equally. The more conscious workers quickly noticed this malicious exploitation of the "foreigner", and asked the manager that he sack the relief. I was left by myself on the lathe on one shift. Work became easier.

At a Banquest in Honour of Vandervelde

One evening in June party comrades in the Vyborg district sent a courier to the "Frenchman" to ask him to take part in a ceremonial banquet given by the Duma faction of Bolsheviks and Mensheviks in honour of Vandervelde, who had come to Russia. The banquet was organized semi-legally at the Palkin restaurant. There were quite a few guests in the small room. There were few Bolsheviks, but among them were comrades Petrovsky and Badayev. The Mensheviks were represented by Dan, Chkheidze, Potresov and other stars of *Luch*. After the appetizers, the speeches of welcome began. Petrovsky spoke for our faction, Chkheidze and Dan for the Mensheviks. The liquidators' speeches exuded diplomatic grief over the split in the ranks of the working class. I interpreted for Petrovsky and then, on our deputies' instructions, took the floor in reply. With the facts at my fingertips, I demonstrated that in its struggle the Petersburg proletariat was one. "In day-to-day struggle," I said, "the working class marches under the banner of our party's Petersburg Committee, in spite of the scheming by the minority, which can only form majorities at banquets. The workers' struggle here in Petersburg itself demonstrates, even though only a superficial study is available to you, comrade Vandervelde, for you cannot go out to our factories and see our strikes and mass meetings, that we have the majority behind us; and you, as an advocate of the unity of workers' organizations, should propose to the minority, the intelligentsia sitting here, that they submit to the majority. Take what aspect of the workers' movement you like: the trade unions are with us and the insurance organization is ours. Unity can easily be achieved, for we need only bind the minority to the wishes of the majority. If you would declare exactly that on behalf of the International Socialist Bureau whose president you are, we shall not push any of them out of the organization, and we shall not have a split."

My speech in French agitated the Mensheviks. Despite the presence of the eminent foreigner, they interrupted me and I only managed to finish thanks to the intervention of the guest himself, Vandervelde, who was listening and watching the gathering very attentively. After my speech he felt it necessary to reply to questions so bluntly put, and in his speech about unity, patience and other related matters, he did declare that the minority should submit to the majority.

We broke up as a milky morning was relieving the white northern night. In the morning I was at my bench again, but I did not speak about my night-time trip to the banquet in honour of Vandervelde to any of the proletarians. It remained known to only a limited circle of organized comrades and party workers.

Political activity in the workshops was carried out by workers belonging to the three Russian parties: Bolshevik social democrats, Menshevik social democrats and Socialist-Revolutionaries.* Most active of all were the Bolsheviks. Bolshevik workers would get up at workshop meetings, and a little military strategy was practised: workers capable of speaking on political subjects were spread around the district, so that the same worker did not always get up in any one factory, preserving the vital secret of the agitator's name from the

---

*The Socialist-Revolutionaries were colloquially referred to as Narodniks. —Ed.

Okhrana. A typical feature of the pre-war period of party work was its lack of intellectuals. The exodus of intellectuals that had begun in 1906 and 1907 meant that party workers, full-time staff and so on were workers. There was so little of the intelligentsia left that it barely sufficed to meet the needs of the Duma faction and the daily paper. The place of the petty-bourgeois intellectuals and student youth was taken by the intellectual proletarian with his caloused hands and highly developed head who had not lost contact with the masses. A very favourable impression was made by our insurance organizers G.I. Osipov, G.M. Shkapin, N.I. Ilyin, Dmitriev and others, and also the trade-union activists such as the metalworkers Kiselev, Murkin, Schmidt and others.

Working in the shops and being often at comrades' houses I met quite a few outstanding workers who were more highly developed than many famous European workers I had known well abroad. Bitter struggle, exile and prison crippled thousands, but they reared individuals incomparably better than the "peaceful" struggle in the west. In the workshops there were often collections for solidarity causes; for people in prison, exiles and convict labourers and their families, for example.

Propaganda was done in the plants and shops on an individual basis. There were also discussion circles, but they were joined only by the most conscious workers. Legal meetings took place on matters concerning the insurance funds, but this activity was skilfully integrated into the general struggle for the liberation of the working class. Illegal meetings were arranged fairly often in the plants during the summer of my stay in Petersburg. This was usually done on the spur of the moment but in an organized way, during the lunch or evening break in front of the exit, in the yard or, in establishments with several floors, on the stairs. The most alert workers would form a "plug" in the doorway, and the whole mass piled up in the exit. An agitator would get up right there on the spot. Management would contact the police on the telephone, but the speeches would have already been made and the necessary decision taken by the time they arrived. Frequently clashes with the police would ensue, in which the latter would put its "herrings" into action and the workers nuts and cobblestones. Mass rallies took place all round Petersburg. The Vyborg district gathered mainly at Ozerki, Shuvalov and Grazhdanka. Holidays brought crowds of visitors to these villages on the outskirts. This made it easier for workers to get to the mass meetings.

In the spring of 1914 the atmosphere in the factory districts was tense in the extreme. Every conflict, small or large, irrespective of its origin, provoked a protest strike or walk-out. Political meetings and skirmishes with the police were everyday occurrences. The workers began to make contacts among the soldiers at the nearby barracks. Revolutionary propaganda was also carried out in the army camps. An extremely active part in propaganda work was taken by women workers, the weavers and mill-girls: some of the soldiers were from the same villages as the women workers, but for the most part the young people came together on the basis of "interests of the heart", and thus kinship relations were established between barracks and factory. It was totally impossible to turn such troops against the workers.

Lessners ceased to satisfy me, and I started to think about changing to some other plant. This was very easily done. For my very first days there I had incited workers to fight against the management's dictatorial fixing of earnings. Right from the start I had begun to set a personal example in fighting for higher wage rates. I was deeply indignant at the unequal earnings for workers on identical jobs. Thus, when working with my drunken relief, I would clear some four rubles a day, while the turner working next to me, a Finn, would earn only two rubles fifty kopeks at the most, and with greater exertion. And this was not a unique example. For all the revolutionary fighting spirit of the Petersburg metalworkers, their trade-union solidarity and understanding were both poorly developed. This derived in part from the fact that our metalworkers had grown used to collective struggle "in a bunch", whereas the defence of a standard rate for workers in the same trade, like so much else in factory life, demanded a certain personal grit, stubbornness and ability to defend oneself as an individual, sometimes without general support.

I presented a personal demand to the manager for five rubles for a ten-hour day, even when the piecework given me could not yield such earnings either because of its quality (you'd get stuck with a bad casting) or its small quantity. The manager, with the equivocation customary in this type of person, half agreed, but when the pay-out came my wages had been adjusted to forty-eight kopeks an hour, i.e. twenty kopeks a day less. On seeing this I immediately resigned, and on 17 June left the shop. My workmates at Lessner and especially in the first engineering shop, were very sorry to see me go. But they realized that as a "foreigner" I was curious to move around and work a bit in as many shops as possible, to get to know Petersburg proletarians as widely as possible.

After the job at Lessner the search for another post was considerably easier. I no longer carried the dictionary around but went to see comrades who could introduce me to the foreman. Within a few days I had two offers: at the Parviainen Shell Works, and at Ericssons. I chose the latter, where I started on 26 June. My start was preceded by a trip to the doctor. The doctor at the local hospital fund permitted only absolutely fit men to work there. Workers worn out by prolonged unemployment or intense physical exploitation in their previous job were ruthlessly sifted out. The doctor was an old cynic who recommended such comrades to a high-calorie diet, a long rest period and other such delights, though it sounded more like a gibe at their hunger. The actual process of "certification" took place in an extremely slipshod fashion: hands were not washed after examination by the doctor or his assistant, instruments were taken straight from one body to the next, and so on.

But my health was found to be good and I was taken on in the Turning Shop no. 1, known inside the works as the "Third Floor", where I was set a highly exacting test. After completing it, I was offered a "shop rate" of twenty-three kopeks an hour. But I had already stated to both the foreman and those near him when I started that I would not work for less than five rubles a day, no matter what "shop rate" I was offered. Within the shop, however, the management permitted an output bonus system for piecework at double the "shop rate". I finished the first piece for four rubles sixty kopeks, and I demanded that the foreman raise the rate so that my pay would be equivalent to five rubles a day, otherwise I would not agree to stay on. The foreman gave way, and this became a precedent for me.

In the turning shop, as throughout the works, there were many politically highly conscious workers. All the Menshevik workers were concentrated on our floor. Their attitude towards management was impeccable, they were all in excellent standing and had the highest shop-rates, which gave them the opportunity to earn nearly twice as much as many others. Yet this workshop, for all its consciousness, was the same as the rest when it came to trade-union solidarity. The same incredible discrepancies existed in wage levels which were fixed arbitrarily by the section foreman and varied from sixteen kopeks an hour for the "novices" to thirty-five kopeks an hour for the "veterans" who had become well established and had the chance to double their earnings on piecework. I made a personal campaign for "levelling" earnings for the same trade and job. All those who had low wages were on my side, while those who had attained a privileged position were naturally against. Disputes arising from minor trade-union matters moved on to a political level. The Mensheviks, who had the upper hand in the workshop, decided to "give battle" to the French Bolshevik. The arguments and abuse brought a crowd together around my bench. It was only events of a greater significance outside our factory which rallied us all and for a while diverted us from our internal struggles.

July Days

On 4 July the story spread round the city's workers that a brutal police assault had been made upon the Putilov workers, resulting in the death of several. The workers' indignation was great, and it was clear that the inflamed atmosphere would lead to bloodshed. In a number of places work was halted earlier than normal in protest.

On the morning of the 5th people came to work at the normal times, but after only half an hour reports began to come in of stoppages at first one and then another factory. People were not starting work. The New Lessner factory was out, the neighbouring textile mill on the Nevka embankment was out and demanded that we stop work too. A meeting was organized in the factory yard, the police broke in, a skirmish took place and the workers smashed through the police cordon across the gateway and came out on to the street. Workers converged from all sides on the Bolshoi Sampsonievsky Prospekt, forming a crowd of demonstrators over ten thousand strong. Revolutionary songs began, red banners and kerchiefs were waved. The police locked themselves up in their station. Speakers got up appealing for armed struggle and the overthrow of tsarism. Trams in the Vyborg district were halted and for over an hour workers moved through the streets to the sound of revolutionary songs. Cossacks were despatched to the aid of the police and, whooping and holding their rifles at the ready, they burst among the crowds, lashing out with their whips and firing at the open windows of workers' flats. The workers dispersed throughout the district, through back gardens and orchards, showering the police and cossacks with stones. Though a foreigner, I escaped the cossacks' whips just the same as the Russians, and hid. Once reinforced by the cossacks, the police summoned up the courage to go hunting round the shops and back yards and even broke into flats. Several hours of cavalry charges were required to "impose order", but calm could not be re-established just like that. With the onset of dusk the police and cossacks decided not to probe any deeper into the working-class quarters, where until deep into the night the strains of revolutionary songs could be heard.

The action was led by groups from our party. The events were taking place just as the president of the French bourgeoisie, Poincaré, was arriving and the authorities were preoccupied with organizing his welcome. The police had mobilized the flat caretakers to act as a backdrop representing the "Russian people" on the day of Poincaré's arrival in Petersburg. Police and cossacks were tied down there, and on the bridges linking the outer areas with the city centre patrols were posted to prevent the demonstrating workers getting through.

The protest strike against the violence and arrests switched from the Narva and Vyborg districts to Vasiliev Island, the Kolomna district and beyond the Neva Gate, and flooded throughout the city. The newspapers spread the news across Russia, and a response to this powerful movement could be expected from the provinces. From 6 July till 12 July the strike was almost general, and the number of strikers reached 300,000. Meetings and demonstrations took place everywhere, and in some places barricades were erected. Workers sought arms everywhere, and bought up stocks of revolvers and knives to arm themselves somehow against the police and cossacks. Mounted forces moved through the city and the outskirts. Mass arrests started in homes and on the streets. Newspapers were closed down and their staffs arrested. The more advanced workers usually gathered at our *Pravda* office, bringing in reports, and members of the Petersburg Committee would also go there. In an unexpected raid the police arrested a large number of party workers and activists. These arrests decimated the leading ranks of the Petersburg proletariat, but did not stop the movement that had begun. Every day workers arrived at the plants and factories at the normal time, held meetings and demonstrated through the streets. This movement was especially militant in the Vyborg district. On the morning of the French visitors' arrival in Petersburg, nearly all the working-class districts had gathered in the Bolshoi Sampsonievsky Prospekt, filling the whole width of the street from the New Lessner Works to the police station. The sun smiled happily upon the twenty-thousand-strong crowd, among whom there were working women, wives, children and so on. Police and cossacks were absent. Here and there speakers came forward from the crowd calling for a demonstrative welcome for the visitors. "Let's tell them," said one worker, "that we've got trouble at home and can't receive visitors." The strains of the "Varshavyanka" began to sound, and the workers moved towards the city. But then a cry from behind: "Cossacks!" We turned and saw a cossack detachment galloping away from the Landrin factory. The working men and women took to their heels as best they could. Drunken cossacks rode into the side-streets and courtyards and beat up the demonstrators there. The police came running out of their ambush too. The roadway and pavements bore traces of blood many hours later. All this was in the Vyborg district, but the same thing also happened in the Kolomna district, where dockers and workers from the Franco-Russian factory were beaten up.

The clashes in the Vyborg district continued all day and shifted from land to water. Young workers clambered on to barges lying on the Nevka and started singing. The police tried to subdue them, but to the locals' great delight they failed to board the barges, as the workers had hauled up the gangplanks and were using the poles to keep the police at bay. Nor could the latter operate too safely on water, for this was really a job for the river police.

I took advantage of my "foreign" status to tour the city, especially the working-class districts. There was unusual excitement everywhere, and you could sense the depth of what had been experienced: it recalled the red years of 1905–7.

Workers in the Vyborg district decided to organize the defence of their quarter from cossack raids. Spades, saws, hammers and axes appeared, and they started knocking down telegraph poles and setting up barricades and wire entanglements. All along from the Wylie clinic to the Eiwas Works, poles were sawn up and the wires removed. All this was done on the instructions of some Moscow metalworkers who had been participants in the December armed rising in Moscow in 1905.

Towards evening the workers headed towards the wire entanglements in groups of several hundred. Near the Landrin factory workers stopped the draymen, unharnessed the horses and returned them to their drivers and then overturned the carts across the streets, making barricades of them and entwining them with wire. Only the odd worker had a revolver, and most were armed only with enthusiasm.

In the evening demonstrators gathered around the Wylie clinic, where two huge poles formed the base of a barricade while wire entanglements in the side-streets and in front paralysed the movement of mounted cossack and police forces. Shops, bars and restaurants were closed. In the gateways to tenements the caretakers were out on duty, with orders not to let in outsiders and to keep a watch on residents. The clash outside the Wylie clinic was almost an organized engagement; the defenders were virtually without arms and used the barricades and wire entanglements as cover from behind which they pelted the cossacks and police with stones. Collecting stones and pulling them up from the roadway was the children's job, and they carried them to the workers in the folds of their tunics. The police and cossacks succeeded in taking the barricade and clearing the square with revolver and rifle fire.

Returning late at night from my usual walk round the districts of the city, I ended up in Wylie Square several hours after the battle. There was an ominous silence in the streets. Neither residents, passers-by nor police could be seen. The square was strewn with stones, smashed lamp-posts and loose bits of wire, and across the road lay two telegraph poles still entangled in wire. There were bullet-marks on the walls of buildings. My steps echoed with a hollow sound on the flagstones. Suddenly there was a distant shout: "Stop, don't move!" I stopped and waited. Two white shadows strode towards me from the opposite side and pointed revolvers at me. *"Est-ce que je ne puis passer par ici?"* ("Can't I get through this way?") I asked. Hearing a foreign language, the policemen lowered their revolvers. I asked them in French once again, "What danger is there?" and so on. The policemen in the end said that they did not understand. Then I, in slightly broken Russian, explained that I was a Frenchman going home. "A Frenchman!" the policemen joyfully exclaimed. "Have you just arrived?" A couple of heavy arms descended upon my shoulders. I said that I had arrived some time ago and that now I was going home to my flat.

"Is it really dangerous to proceed?" I asked, without making any attempt at "Franco-Russian" fraternization. The policemen's arms fell from me, and pointing to their revolvers, they said: "Well, we do have these, see?" I decided to go on my way without "these", and made for the depths of the working-class twilight. I had scarcely gone a couple of hundred yards when I heard another shout: "Stop, stay where you are or we'll shoot!" And then the sound of several hundred steel horseshoes rang over the roadway, and from behind a home for war invalids a whole squadron of Don cossacks under the command of two officers rode out to block my path. I shouted in French: *"Attendez tirer! Je m'approche!"* ("Hold your fire, I'm coming.") The two officers hurried forward to meet me. I asked whether they spoke French: they did not. Again I used broken Russian and said that I was going home but could not make it as I kept running into drunken armed policemen. The officers assured me that the policemen were not drunk but tired, as the official welcome for the visitors and the disturbances had worn them all out. Towards myself they were most considerate, but they searched and questioned all other passers-by.

From the dark depths of the Bolshoi Sampsonievsky Prospekt wafted the sounds of an accordion, revolutionary songs and shots. Over there in the working-class quarters life and a readiness for struggle were seething, and the cossacks could sense it. They warned each other against approaching the walls — the outside walls of a sugar factory — and they were afraid of every rustle from the trees. The officers tried as best they could to dissuade me from going on into that "frightening hellhole" where I could be brought down with a shot. They suggested I stayed with them as they were ready to return to the city, where they promised to give me a room for the night and gladly help me back home in the morning. I thanked them for their kindness but thought it unnecessary to trouble such busy people especially as it was only a couple of streets to my flat in Maly Sampsonievsky Lane. In the end one proposed to the other that the whole squadron escort me to my house. I thanked them profusely but I felt that it might be rather unpleasant to arrive home under cossack guard. However, the other officer did not back the proposal to accompany me into the "hellhole", and stared diplomatically into the dark, noisy distance, warning the squadron to be at the ready. It was clear they had the wind up, and I was glad I could go home alone. A girl was running past. She was stopped but not searched. They asked her if she knew Maly Sampsonievsky Lane, and if it was far. The answer was yes, and the officer suggested that she accompany me. We set off into the revolutionary dark, and they withdrew from the area.

War

While the brokers of the imperialist bourgeoisie were drafting their final notes and the Triple Alliance was putting the blame on the Triple Entente, the Petersburg proletariat and the workers of many of Russia's other industrial centres were wholly engrossed in matters of domestic strife. The July events in Petersburg woke up the drowsing provinces and the strike wave rolled literally "from the cold Finnish crags to fiery Colchis".

The street rallies by the Petersburg workers finished on 11 or 12 July, but a considerable portion of the 300,000-strong army of strikers did not go back to work. The Association of Factory and Plant Owners decided to punish the "labour troubles" with a lock-out of their own. Many factories and nearly all the privately owned metalworking plants planned the complete dismissal of all their employees. However, the approach of a "critical turn of events", i.e. the commencement of hostilities, forced the government to introduce some "peace" into the life of the capital, to avoid "upsets". The announcements posted up about the lock-out were suddenly replaced, the factories were re-opened, and instead of threats the workers received polite invitations to resume working at their former posts. Many of them, foreseeing a protracted conflict, had gone out to the country for a while and did not learn of the reopening of the factories until considerably later. Some two days before the mobilization, working life in Petersburg had already returned to its normal pattern.

The mood of workers was very buoyant, in spite of the orgy of repression, the lack of newspapers and the fortnight's unemployment. Everyone was overjoyed and encouraged by the recent strike, which had united a huge army of labour in one vivid upsurge of anger. This solidarity could not be smashed either by the police, or by the "glorious" cossackry, or by the threats of starvation from the coalition of factory-owners. The first day back at work was spent exchanging impressions of the recent events. Everyone felt that a decisive and nationwide battle was just around the corner. The bloody operations on the Austro-Serbian frontier were a minor topic, although workers did follow the progress of the negotiations between the powers.

Pan-Slavist circles had, however, already set to work. The gutter and semi-liberal press was paving the way for patriotic demonstrations. These soon took place, springing up "spontaneously" in the central areas of the city and finishing at the Serbian Embassy.

The hard core of these demonstrations were caretakers, office workers, intellectuals, "society" ladies and secondary-school pupils. Flags, placards and portraits of the Tsar, concealed in advance, were "spontaneously" produced and a procession went round the allied embassies under the protection of mounted police. During the early days everyone in the city centre was terrorized by these patriotic hooligans. They took the "freedom" extended to them to its logical conclusion, i.e. to attacking the German Embassy and other private establishments on the advice of *Vechernee Vremya* ("The Evening Times") but they were not deprived of the right to demonstrate.

The Petersburg Committee of the Russian Social-Democratic and Labour Party had previously agitated among workers to turn patriotic demonstrations into revolutionary ones; such attempts had already been made and ended in clashes. The city governor then banned any further demonstrations. Before this ban there was no let-up. The slightest success at the front: a demonstration. The entry of a new country into the war: a demonstration. The philistines, white-collar workers and Petersburg intellectuals had a craven attitude towards hooligan patriotism. Democratically minded circles of Petersburg workers were interested in the events, especially after the German ultimatum to Russia. The special editions of the newspapers were avidly read. Of course, all the papers tried to use this ultimatum to prove the "honour" and "dignity" of Russia as a "great power". The next day the slogan of both right and left was "We have been invaded".

The journalists had already been tuned up in a patriotic key, and wrath against "villainous Germany" became the daily diet of Petersburg democrats. Among the jackals of chauvinism there was not a single voice to remind us that it was they themselves who had prepared for this two weeks previously, during Poincaré's arrival, when reactionary newspapers were already challenging the "Prussian fist" and saying that in two years' time Russia would be ready to settle accounts with them. For these "services" to the fatherland our honourable journalists got the Order of the French Republic.

Events developed so rapidly that organized workers were caught off guard. Although in principle they were all opponents of the war, the complexity of the situation was beyond the understanding of many, and many "private opinions" were expressed. General mobilization of the Petersburg zone (together with the whole of European Russia) was announced on 19 July, to take effect from six o'clock in the morning. Police stations worked all night distributing call-up papers. In the morning red mobilization posters were displayed throughout the city, along with white bills giving the rates of compensation for requisitioned articles like boots, bedding, etc. Knots of people stood in front of them, discussing the events from every conceivable angle; but an anxious mood united them. Hundreds of workers' families crowded round the police stations, which had now turned into recruiting offices. The women wept and cursed the war.

In the workshops and factories, mobilization wrought havoc. Up to forty per cent of the workers were taken away from their benches and tools. Feelings of helplessness and despondency were widespread. Factory-owners demanded from the authorities that their skilled workers be returned, otherwise they would not be able to fulfil their military contracts. Their request was granted: a few days later all mobilized metalworkers from factories with military contracts were sent back, but were regarded as "on the books" of the military governor.

When people arrived at work on the morning of mobilization, no one as much as thought about work. They gathered together around the workshops without changing, agreed on what to do, and went out into the streets to the sound of revolutionary songs. In some plants there were general meetings with conscripts, from whom the workers extracted oaths not to forget the workers' struggle, and to use their arms at the very first opportunity to "liberate the Slavs within Russia itself". Once again the streets were filled with thousands of people singing revolutionary songs and shouting: "Down with the war!" Often even the tear-stained women standing by the police stations shouted, "Down with the war!" through their tears and encouraged others to do so. The police, who were neither as numerous nor as rough as in the July protests, attempted to break the demonstrations, but on encountering the energetic protests of the reservists, they thought it wiser to disappear.

Around noon the first parties of conscripts, surrounded by a feeble escort of policemen, moved towards the central city assembly points. The crowd quickly attached itself to them and a demonstration was formed with red streamers and placards tied to sticks. During these send-offs there were clashes with the police, but with the reservists' active support the demonstrators always got the upper hand. Scenes like this occurred in various outlying areas of the city and even, within the city itself, in the Kolomna district. The demonstrations outside the Neva Gate and in the Vyborg district were particularly impressive. In the first case a crowd of several scores of thousands accompanied the reservists singing revolutionary sóngs and carrying a red banner as far as Znamensky Square, where they clashed with patriots and were dispersed by police. In various parts of the Vyborg district there were demonstrations nearly all day long.

Simultaneously with the mobilization, Petersburg was declared to be on a war footing. The railways, bridges, warehouses and other such establishments were guarded by military patrols. Post, telegraphs and transport served only the needs of the war. In the early days Petersburg was entirely cut off from the world and, oddly enough, more so from the provinces than from "abroad".

The city was full of alarming rumours. Sensational tales were passed from mouth to mouth that such-and-such a princess had been locked up in a fortress for treachery; talk had it that the ex-city governor of Petersburg, Drachevsky, had already been convicted and hanged for selling "important documents" kept in the Kronstadt fortress. People coming from Kronstadt maintained that three hundred mines stuffed with sand had been found among those ready for laying. Rumours of this kind greatly undermined confidence in the authorities and their ability to "organize defence". Patriotically-minded petty bourgeois, shopkeepers, white-collar workers and peasants who accepted the inevitability of the war considered that any shortcomings were to be blamed on the Germans, who had already taken power in the country: Rennenkampf and other such "true Russians" lost at one stroke even their colleagues of yesterday.

Attitudes to the War

From the moment of Germany's declaration of war on Russia until Britain's entry against Germany, the mood of the Petersburg bourgeois society was sombre. It was considered that, had Britain adopted a neutral position, the fate of Petersburg would have been sealed. People began to move out their valuables, and several museums started to pack up their treasures. It is not hard to imagine the joy with which the news of Britain's declaration of war on Germany was greeted. There was applause in restaurants and theatres, toasts were drunk, and in the evening a patriotic demonstration marched to the British Embassy.

In the first days of the war thinking workers were convinced that West European democracy, headed by the organized proletariat, would not allow the mutual destruction of workers and peasants. It was clear from the international situation that the German government had been the initiator and the first to pull the trigger. From this we drew the conclusion that the task of leading the way to a decisive struggle against the imperialists' bloodthirsty designs fell to the German proletariat. But when we learned what was happening, it struck us by its absurdity. Newspaper articles spoke about the leaders of German social democracy justifying the war and voting for war credits. Our first thought was that the government wire-services were false and that they wanted to whip us Russian social democrats into line. But opportunities to verify them soon came: hundreds of refugees from Germany, and people returning from other countries confirmed what had appeared to be a libel.

However monstrous this new turn, we had to reckon with it as a reality. Workers showered us with questions as to the meaning of the behaviour of the German socialists, whom we had always presented as models for ourselves. Where was all that world solidarity? It was particularly painful to hear that the German army, with so many organized workers in its ranks, was laying waste to Belgium, and that Belgian soldiers were defending their country to the sound of the "Internationale". Answers had to be given to all these questions, and it was essential to point out that the leaders of German social democracy had betrayed the workers' cause and betrayed international socialism. We pointed out that in recent years the German workers' movement had been led by reformists, or "liquidators".

"Burying the German leaders" did not come easily to us, as in the broad circles of workers supporting social democracy the idea emerged of "if the Germans have done it, we might as well too". It took a lot of effort to explain to thinking workers that betrayal by some must not lead to universal betrayal, as only the capitalists would stand to gain from that. It was vital to restore international contact between workers over the heads of the leaders.

As the conflict developed, the Russian government itself did much to "clarify" the confused situation. Hardly had mobilization in Petersburg been completed when a campaign was afoot against "the enemy within". More repression rained down on the working class in the form of arrests, deportations and the closure of those unions, clubs and trade-union journals still remaining. This was how the government had resolved to "unite all classes and nationalities". The workers who had been mobilized but remained at the plants were subjected to harassment. The employers decided to exploit their status by turning the workers into serfs, a sort of "conscript labour". At the Lessner works in the very first weeks, deductions from pay and the abuse of overtime working brought protests; there were protests too at Ericssons, the Vulcan works and other engineering establishments. Small-scale employers and contractors made wide use of the state of war to rid themselves of troublesome elements or to avoid paying wages, resorting to the police station for assistance.

The defeat of the Russian army at the Masurian lakes greatly encouraged all those who tended to favour suspending the struggle against the government. The working masses concluded from this defeat that the Russian government was so rotten and incompetent that it deserved simply to be swept away. The critical attitude towards the capabilities of the reactionary government had very much in common with the attitude that manifested itself during the Russo-Japanese campaigns.

From soldiers' tales of pilfering, bad food and poor organization, an unattractive and hitherto concealed picture of the true condition of our army came into view. These stories circulated even among peasants, and their mistrust of the "leaders of the Russian army" can be judged by their comments that it would be better commanded by Japanese generals, for then the Germans would be smashed.

When the letters by Plekhanov, Burtsev, Kropotkin and others appeared in the press calling for a temporary "truce" and support for the government in its "struggle against German militarism", Russian revolutionary democrats, including the patriotically minded element, were a little disillusioned, as they had expected that the appeal would be first for the victory of democracy and only then for a struggle against the external enemy. But the notorious "truce" with tsarism only strengthened reaction, while in no way raising the army's so-called "chances of success" — not to mention the damage that was inflicted on the Russian democratic movement by these proponents of "truce". Around them danced the chieftains of Black Hundred patriotism.

At the very start of the war persistent rumours began to circulate round the city and in working-class circles of reforms being drafted, an amnesty and a Kadet government. The source of these rumours, or rather "Kadet longings", some of which found their way into print, was the liberal circles. Having themselves renounced any struggle against the government and having got nothing in return, they grew most indignant and sought to intimate this to the government. But *Rech*, after paying a fine of five thousand rubles, fell silent and put about rumours that the British government had "advised" the Russian government to relax the régime. But time went on, and the influence of West European democracy was imperceptible, unless you count the acceptance of the "Marseillaise" as one of the obligatory anthems.

The Petersburg press did much to kindle popular chauvinism. They skilfully blew up "German" atrocities against Russian women and old men remaining in Germany. But even this hostile atmosphere did not drive workers to excesses of nationalism. One rare incident of a demand for the removal of a "German" from his post took place at the Bryansk locomotive works, and concerned an engineer in charge of a workshop. He was so "necessary" to the exploitation of the workers that the management had succeeded in obtaining him a permit to live freely in Russia. But the workers "picked their moment" to rid themselves of an enemy of their own, and demanded his removal. There might have been cases where workers had demanded the removal of Germans as known scabs who had been brought to Russia to replace strikers, but one could not conclude therefore that the Russian workers hated the Germans, as the newspapers claimed. This "literary chauvinism" considerably outweighed the actual mood even of petty-bourgeois circles.

The attitude of Russia's oppressed nationalities towards the war differed little from any other supporter of the theory of "the defence of national independence". The Jewish bourgeoisie in Petersburg held "pure Jewish" patriotic demonstrations. Prayers for victory were offered in the synagogues. The liberal newspapers *Rech* and *Den* tried to stress this, so that the powers that be could not reproach the Jews for lack of love for the fatherland. And indeed the powers that be, the Markovs and Purishkevichs, were so touched that they had only praise and affection for the Jews. In areas close to the war zones, however, the Jews had a tough time. They lived under the permanent threat of pogrom, as much from the mob as from the military authorities. In wartime conditions it was forbidden to publish anything about this, but the news did find its way indirectly to the press in the form of reports of arrests of thugs with stolen property. A patriotic demonstration in such areas bore the character of a "pogrom warning". The Moslem Tartar population was also dragged into patriotic outpourings of love for the homeland. There were services in the Petersburg mosque, and deputations were sent "on behalf of Mohammedans". Czechs, Poles and other Slavs were sometimes, through the police, called upon to form volunteer legions for the sacred liberation struggle.

The Petersburg patriots held a procession to the Winter Palace and fell on their knees cheering at the tsar's appearance on the balcony. The epidemic spread, threatening to swamp the pores of Russia's already meagre social life, and only the desire for "reconciliation" could be heard from the democrats. But healthy proletarian instinct saved the working-class element in the capital from this intoxication.

Revolutionary Social Democracy Against the War
The administrative and police repression that rained on the Petersburg proletariat in July had not smashed the illegal cells of the social-democratic party, but the mass arrests and searches did greatly weaken the quality of the party organizations. The Petersburg Committee was deprived of its best workers but still maintained its contacts and worked as normal.

There was acute need for intellectual workers. After the swoop on *Pravda* there was not a single person on the Petersburg Committee capable of writing a leaflet. I had to spend much of the first day of mobilization with the Vyborg representatives of the Petersburg

Committee and in particular with comrade Mokhovaya, who was lamenting the lack of forces and asked me to write a leaflet on the war. I wrote it and sent it into the district committee the same day.

Upon the declaration of war and in the very first week of the mobilization, our workers' organizations took up a hostile attitude to the war. Even prior to the convening of the State Duma, the Petersburg Committee had issued the leaflet I wrote against the war, in which I warned the proletariat against the lie that the government supposedly had declared the war in the name of the independence of Serbia and the liberation of Galicia. This leaflet, which I managed to find later in Police Department files, was set in an underground print-shop and ran as follows:

> Workers of the world, unite!
> To all workers, peasants and soldiers!
> Comrades!
> A bloody spectre hangs over Europe. The capitalists' greedy competition, the politics of violence and plunder, dynastic calculation and fear for privileges in the face of the rising international workers' movement, are driving the governments of all countries along the path of militarism, the path of expanding the military machine which crushes the labouring people of all lands and all colours with its expenditure. Over recent years the European "armed peace" has been many times threatened by the danger of passing over into a general war but the sabre-rattling capitalists and landlords have been compelled by the pressure of popular protests in Germany, France, Britain and other countries to regulate their affairs without bloody collisions between peoples. The International Socialist Labour League, standing guard over the interests of all the labouring people of the world, has been at the head of this movement in favour of peace and now calls upon the working class of all countries to protest against the war. "Down with the war!" "War on war!" must roll powerfully across city and hamlet alike across the width of our Russia. Workers must remember that they do not have enemies over the frontier: everywhere the working class is oppressed by the rich and the power of the property-owners. Everywhere it is oppressed by the yoke of exploitation and the chains of poverty.
> In the conflict that was coming the tsarist government had declared itself the "protector" and "liberator" of the Slav people but here we see now no protection but only a thirst for the seizure of new possessions. Displaced from the east by Japan, our irresponsible and bloody rulers are attempting, by means of secret diplomatic agreements, to fish in the murky waters of the Near East. The working-class press has been completely strangled and is unable to speak the truth in this "age of blood" and yet bourgeois and police-managed newspapers speak of a community of interests for working people. "Off with the mask!" workers and all labouring people must reply in the face of our bashi-bazouks. The government of oppressors of Russian workers and peasants, the govern-

ment of landowners cannot be a liberator. Wherever it penetrates, it brings fetters, the lash and lead. Without having time to wash workers' blood off the streets of Petersburg and only yesterday branding all of working-class Petersburg as well as all the workers of Russia as "enemies within" against whom savage cossacks and mercenary police went into action, they now call for the defence of the fatherland. Soldiers and workers! You are being called on to die for the glory of the cossack lash and for the glory of a fatherland that shoots starving peasants and workers and strangles its best sons in prison. No, we don't want the war, you must declare. We want the freedom of Russia. That must be your cry. Long live world-wide labour solidarity!! Long live the Constituent Assembly that will give all land to the peasants and working folk the freedom to fight for a better world and socialism where the peoples will live by peaceful labour. Down with the war, down with the tsarist government! Long live the revolution! Amnesty for all martyrs for liberty! Long live the equality of nationalities!

Petersburg Committee of the RSDLP.

The convening of the State Duma found the majority of our deputies away in the provinces, where a strike movement was developing. The Duma social-democratic faction had a few meetings before the Duma assembled, where the declaration, now familiar to all, was adopted. Two attitudes to this war were revealed in the drafting process. There were among deputies of the Menshevik right-wing supporters of the defence of "Russian culture". That is only a point in passing, for officially the SD faction *bon gré mal gré* marched together on this question. The declaration, bold and brief in form, was "Bolshevik" in content and landed amid the chauvinist yelping like a stone in a stagnant marsh. The right wing greeted it with whistling. But the working class learned of it with great satisfaction.

We were to learn of the attitudes of the other socialist sections of the International towards the war from the bourgeois newspapers. The first report from Paris, seized upon with glee by the whole bourgeois press, announced that "the French socialists and syndicalists have dropped their criticism of the Russian government's actions". The war censorship that banned news of pogroms, arrests and searches very graciously let through all the telegrams about the actions of socialists in other countries. We knew about the voting of war credits by the German "orthodoxists" of social democracy. We were well informed on the activity of the new socialist minister Vandervelde. *Birzhevka, Vechernee Vremya, Kopeika* and others devoted all their articles to this and carried his picture. The reorganization of the French ministry into a "cabinet of national defence" and the admission of socialists into the ministry was hailed by all our press as a stroke of genius. This provided only a superfluous pretext for sighs by the Russian liberals from *Rech* and other papers about how things were sadly not the same here as elsewhere, so everything would stay the same.

Minister Vandervelde's telegram to the Russian socialists was received by the deputy, Chkheidze, via the Minister of Foreign Affairs. Workers got to know of it via the bourgeois press and considerably later than its receipt. By then copies that had been handwritten or knocked out on typewriters had appeared.

In contrast to the fact that "European democracy" had given very poor support to the democratic movement in our country, Petersburg workers were very sensitive to the predicament of the Belgian proletariat. However few of those socialists would have excused Vandervelde's joining the royal bourgeois ministry. We considered that Vandervelde had abandoned his post and in the given situation that far outweighed the advantages of a portfolio in a clerical cabinet.

Nevertheless the war greatly inhibited Petersburg's "right to mass meetings" in the outlying woods: there were soldiers and spies everywhere. Moreover, many workers had been mobilized and this obliged them to work overtime — many were intimidated. The discussion of Vandervelde's telegram therefore took place inside the plants. To organized workers it was not so much the reply itself that was important as the related question of the attitude to the war. On the question of a "truce" there was complete unanimity. The social democrats — Bolsheviks, Plekhanovites and liquidators — all stood for the continuation of the struggle against the Russian government. On this question liquidationist workers parted company from their closest counsellors, the officials of the hospital funds and the patriotically minded elements. In the assessment of the war itself there were individual feelings of Francophilia, although on the whole the masses had a negative attitude.

Curious inscriptions appeared in obscure corners of workshops: "Comrades; we won't be any better off if Russia wins, they'll squash us even harder." One could judge by this the anxiety felt by the workers, whom everyone was trying to lull and "unite" with their sworn enemies.

The attitude to the war of the social-democratic intelligentsia was much more "complex" than the workers' negative attitude. They all started from the fact that they opposed the war on principle. But then came a string of qualifications starting with "but". The "literacy" which social democrats had usually displayed before the war disappeared as if by magic. The war was not seen in connection with the governments' previous policies, but as a "fact" with which we had suddenly been confronted. And it was towards this "fact" that the attitude of the intelligentsia was nebulous in the extreme and deflected many workers from positions they had firmly adopted.

The most widespread opinion was that this war would bring about

Russia's emancipation from political and economic oppression by Germany. In the event of victory for the Triple Entente, Russia would gain free access through the Dardanelles and new trading agreements would create the possibility for a rapid development of the country's productive forces. This "marxist" formulation of the question seduced few workers: their international solidarity could not be blunted by future "blessings" after the "victory". They would tell the intellectuals at meetings that for Germany the question was also one of "possible further development of the productive forces": the way out of this knot of capitalist conflicts would be found by workers acting in international solidarity. We spoke out on the need for international relations between workers' organizations. This was considered to be the factor that could really advance an active struggle by Russian workers against the war. News about the social chauvinists of Germany and their true estimation of the revolutionary movement, the active assistance of revolutionaries in the plans of the German General Staff and the infamous "struggle against tsarism" — the shooting of Russian workers and peasants upheld by the German social democrats — greatly hampered our propaganda. It all seemed to us a monstrous provocation against our movement.

However, despite this difficult situation, our organizations continued to conduct their anti-militarist work. At the beginning of August and in September the Petersburg Committee issued another set of leaflets against the war. News reached us that local organizations — in the Caucasus, Poland and the Lithuanian territory — had also issued leaflets against the war. The publication of the leaflets in Petersburg was accompanied by searches and arrests. Over eighty people were arrested.

In Poland, despite the promise that "there are no longer enslaved peoples", government policy remained reactionary. In several cities close to the theatre of operations, such as Lodz and Warsaw, the political climate changed according to whether the Germans were approaching or moving away from the locality in question. The German move on Warsaw brought "liberty" back to life — arrests ceased, the city administration fled and the city was left to itself. This brought "public-initiative" into being, in the form of a residents' committee which raised a militia. It also helped to set up cheap or free canteens for the unemployed, of whom there were a great deal in the district. We received a proclamation from Poland:

> *Russian Social Democratic Labour Party*
> *Social Democracy of the Kingdom of Poland and Lithuania*
> Fellow workers,
> The working class, in its day-to-day struggle against exploitation and

oppression, directs the weapon of the workers' organizations and working-class solidarity against its enemies. Only in the ranks of an organization can each individual worker become a force capable of triumphantly fighting shoulder to shoulder for the rights of the proletariat in one common upsurge; in the ranks of an organization the hearts and minds of workers blaze with the flame of common tasks; under the banner of an organization the consciousness of workers is born and common action forged. The higher the wave of the workers' movement rises and the more acute the general political situation, the more serious are the tasks that fall to the social-democratic workers' organizations and the more crucial its own work becomes. We are living at a time when historical events are demanding that workers closely unify their ranks, and when questions are posed to the proletariat which can only be answered by starting out from a working-class policy based upon the class consciousness of the proletariat and a precise explanation of its revolutionary aspiration to destroy the existing social system. In the chaos of political events and the fire of the social changes caused by the European war, the proletariat must enter the scene as a highly organized detachment and a community mighty with the revolutionary slogans of international solidarity.

Fellow workers, today every thinking worker, every proletarian to whom the workers' sacred cause is dear, must be in the ranks of a workers' organization. At a moment of great trials, when it is sought to divert workers from their revolutionary path and bring confusion into workers' consciousness, the stronger must be the influence of workers' organizations upon the masses. Let the efforts of workers be united along the path of creating powerful organizations, let the proletarian social-democratic flag be hoisted over the wide proletarian camp and let our revolutionary slogans ring out ever louder in working-class circles. Long live organization! Long live the revolutionary struggle! Long live social democracy!

Regional Board of Polish Social Democracy.

The questions of assistance frequently confronted Petersburg workers too. Employers agitated for the deduction of a fixed percentage for the Red Cross, but that institution enjoyed the confidence neither of workers nor even of "society". Stoppages from pay on the pattern of the Russo-Japanese War, made without the employees' authority, caused protests (e.g. at Putilov). Aid did not come for the "red" nor any other cross. Workers pointed out that the state must provide for the wounded and their families in the same way as it did for officers. But workers did find it necessary to aid the victims who populated the Siberian tundra and the jails of Tsar Nicholas, the "liberator" of European democracy. However, such a broad measure of aid could not be given legally, and many people began to think about organizing special factory cells "in aid of war victims", among whom would be included convicts, the unemployed, and families of workmates at the front. It was decided to contribute such aid through the hospital funds and on a city-wide scale. Collections had already been made at the Semenov works and the Neva shipyards, but with the exception of the Neva district which sent them to the local poor people's home, the funds were held back until the possibility of creating our own organization had been explored.

Among the "legalists" the idea emerged of using this "benevolence" to legalize party cells, but this idea never went beyond the desires of intellectuals. Members of the intelligentsia such as Finn, Dubois and company conducted patriotic sessions at the Free Economics Society. Our comrades tried to make use of this institution for the benefit of the local social-democratic organization, but the society was by the nature of its activities too far from being socialist.

The Social Democratic Duma Faction and the War

In the first weeks of the war I had a meeting with our State Duma deputies, comrades Petrovsky and Badayev. This was after their appearance on 26 July in the Duma and their demonstrative exit from the debating chamber. I remember how deeply they had been shocked by the behaviour of the German social democrats. The attitude of the French party saddened them less, as it was from the Germans that all social democrats of that time "learned" how to be socialists. I personally, after my illegal stay and work there in 1912 (as a Frenchman, Gustave Bourne), had substantially amended my "faith" in German social democracy.

The deputies and the few workers who were invited tried to find a key to the Germans' conduct. Several expressed the sentiment that the deciding factor was probably the threat of tsarism, and it was common knowledge that even Engels had, in his day, wished for a war against tsarist Russia. But whatever the reasons, it all amounted to one thing only: such behaviour was a betrayal of all the precepts of revolutionary socialism. At the crucial moment the German social democrats had felt that they were closer to their own bourgeoisie than to the workers of other countries. Nationalism had proved stronger than socialism.

The action of our deputies in the Duma had been welcomed by workers. But intellectuals reacted differently. Wavering had already begun. In the first weeks of the war a special gathering of marxist intellectuals was held in some club in Baskovaya Street. There were a few lawyers, literary figures and others there such as N.D. Sokolov, N.N. Krestinsky, A. Blum, N.I. Yordansky and others. From the exchange of opinions, characterized by their many shades and hesitations, the future social patriots could already be defined. However, the majority of those present were still ashamed to tie socialism to the chariot of war.

Lenin's theses on the attitude to the war, later elaborated in *Sotsial-Demokrat* no. 33, appeared in Petersburg in about August. They were brought, I believe, by the deputy, comrade Samoilov. They responded to the mood of party workers at the time, but the question of "defeatism" did cause perplexity. Comrades did not want to link their tactics to the army's strategic situation, but at the same time nobody wished Nicholas II the smallest victory, as it was clear that a victory would strengthen the vilest reaction. At the end of August our social-democratic (Bolshevik) organizations began to revive and recover from the blows dealt by the July arrests and the mobilization. The Petersburg Committee was properly reconstituted and work put in hand.

My position as a Frenchman in Petersburg was extremely precarious. All Frenchmen, as from 4 August (new style), had been called up and were preparing to depart for Marseilles via the Black Sea. I went on working at Ericssons, banking on the fact that the French consulate would not have the wit to call up its nationals through the Russian police and that my address was, I supposed, unknown at the embassy or the consulate. However, moving from one firm to another as I had imagined doing was now risky, and I decided to stay until the expiry date of the visa in my passport and the obligatory issue of a fixed residence permit by the city governor's office, and then leave Russia. That date was in September.

Party work at Ericssons was proceeding well. Arguments and discussion took place every day around my bench on all the problems of labour politics. One would very rarely meet patriotism in workers then, as the wave of social-chauvinism that began in intellectual circles had not yet rolled as far as the working masses. I got to know all the most active workers in the district. Comrades at the Ericsson works who directed the local party work would come to consult with me before conducting any campaign. Workers at Ericssons who did party work and work for the hospital fund included comrades Kayurov, Nazarov, Grigoriev and Sladkov. I quickly acquired the nickname of the "Bolshevik Frenchman", and with it the deep dislike of the Mensheviks, especially the intellectuals who worked in the hospital fund. After Vandervelde's famous welcome, several of them who had known me from Paris made some treacherous hints at Ericssons regarding my true homeland. But worker comrades quickly put these customers in their place and stated through their representatives in the hospital fund that if there was any unpleasantness towards the Frenchman then the whisperers would be branded provocateurs.

As the acts of war developed, so the work of the patriots intensified. The chauvinism of the bourgeoisie and its lackeys in the newspapers reached frenzy point, and pogroms occurred. Black Hundred thugs added the "Yid" to the German, and national hatred was systematically fostered. Only the workers' circles did not succumb to this. I could observe this not only in the Vyborg district but elsewhere.

I even had a clash with a Black Hundredite outside the Neva Gate, and the workers' sympathy was wholly on my side. I was heading for my own people's place on the Steklyanny and settled down on top of a Neva steam tram. The overcrowding of trams that has since become usual was then already beginning. There were many passengers, mainly workers. The conversation was about the war. One clever gent, who looked like a police clerk, started a speech about arresting Germans and expressed a desire for "Yids" to be arrested too, as in his opinion they were all spies. I could not take any more and asked why exactly he wanted to arrest the Jews, when they were Russian citizens? He swore about the Jews and replied that it was obvious I was a Yid, otherwise I would not start defending them. Seeing that I had before me an inveterate Black Hundredite, I decided to punish him. I brought my passport out and showed it to him and the people nearby. Then I let him have a proletarian box on the ears and sat down. The whole car was on my side The Black Hundredite leapt at me, but was escorted from the upper deck by the passengers themselves. At that point we were approaching a stop and the anti-semite rushed off to get the help of a policeman, asking about the bye-laws on offences against the person. The policeman kindly requested me to alight, but the working-class passengers would not let me go and explained to the policeman that the complainant ought himself to be sent to the police station. The latter, now reinforced by the policeman, summoned up the courage to start a slanging match with the workers. But the policeman had decided not to go against the passengers and a foreigner; the conductor, hearing the complainant swearing, refused to back him up but gave the bell a tug and the tram moved off. I got off at the next junction; the hooligan was sitting in the corner, pretty quietly now. Two workers got off with me and accompanied me for about two hundred yards and then went back.

But there was no such mood in the city centre. The patriotic hooligans would enjoy immunity and beat up passers-by who did not remove their hats when they met a demonstration singing "God save the Tsar". I remember how once, travelling along the Liteiny from the Nevsky Prospekt, we met a mob of caretakers, secondary-school pupils, students, petty bureaucrats and all sorts of riff-raff singing "God save the Tsar". As soon as the strains were heard, everyone in the car promptly, and for different motives, removed their headgear. I alone remained in my bowler hat, much to the indignation of the woman next to me, who struck up a rhythmic chant of "hats off, hats off". I read my newspaper without paying any attention, but the patriotic lady took her complaint to the passengers: "Gentlemen, he's not taking his hat off." Everyone fell silent. The car braked and sliced into a straggling crowd of demonstrators. My neighbour leapt to the doorway and exclaimed, "Shame on you," in a tone of injured patriotism, evidently inviting the demonstrators to have a go at me. Tearing myself away from my newspaper, I asked her, *"Mais pourquoi ça?"* The effect was remarkable. The good lady clasped my hand and exclaimed loudly: "So you're a Frenchman," and started to chatter away about her French acquaintances. I solemnly responded to her fraternization with the French with, *"Fichez-moi la paix,"* and made her sit down again. She kept trying to smooth over her tactlessness and excuse herself to the now excited people around her, but could not take it and got off at the very first stop.

The end of September arrived, and with it the end of my rebellious and happy-go-lucky way of life as a foreigner in my own country. Never in my life had I enjoyed so much freedom in my homeland nor even the respect of the caretakers as I did in those six months as a French citizen of Petersburg. But those six months flew past like a sunny May day, leaving happy memories of working-class struggle, solidarity and readiness for sacrifice. I have never wanted to think that it would again be necessary to go wandering "across frontiers", adjust to new conditions and tear myself away from the day-to-day struggle of the Russian proletariat, but my proletarian friends raised the question of international communication and contacts with our Central Committee abroad. All these tasks could be accomplished best by myself, so comrades proposed that I take the job and not apply for a Russian passport but make use of my privileges as an alien to make a trip abroad.

The Petersburg Committee along with the Duma faction decided to make me their representative abroad. Our organizations had very little money, so I could only be assigned twenty-five rubles. By now I had managed to earn enough for the journey and a month's living abroad, and also to leave some for my ageing mother. The Duma faction gave me several specific assignments and a reply to Vandervelde's telegram that was to be printed in no. 33 of *Sotsial-Demokrat*. This ran as follows:

A reply to Emile Vandervelde
Dear comrade,
Now we have become familiar with your telegram from the Russian papers we consider it necessary for our part to make the following statement:
    The great conflict that has brought the chief civilized nations into collision cannot leave Russian social democracy indifferent. This war

deeply affects the interests of the world democratic movement, on the one hand, placing the French republic and the British and Belgian democracies under the blows of semi-feudal German militarism and, on the other, leading to the growth of the political influence and retrenchment of the Romanov monarchy.

While fully bearing in mind the anti-democratic nature of Prussian hegemony and Prussian militarism, we Russian social democrats cannot forget also that no less dangerous enemy of the working class and democracy, namely, Russian absolutism.

In the sphere of domestic policy it remains as before the exponent of ruthless oppression and limitless exploitation. And even now when it might have seemed that the war required it to act with greater caution, it remains true to form and continues a policy of suppressing all democracy, all oppressed nationalities and the working class in particular.

At the present time all socialist newspapers have been closed down, workers' organizations dissolved and arrests and exiles without trial continue. If the war ends with the total victory of the Russian government and the democratic movement does not regain its position, this government will after the war continue its anti-popular policy both at home and abroad where it will become the centre and bulwark of international reaction. The Russian proletariat cannot, therefore, under any conditions, march hand in hand with our government nor conclude any truce with it, however temporary, nor afford it any support. There can be no question here of some loyalty. On the contrary we consider it our most pressing task to wage the most irreconcilable struggle against it, standing firm on our old demands so unanimously advanced and supported by the Russian working class in the revolutionary days of 1905 and again meeting such wide acceptance in the mass political movement of the Russian working class over the past two years. During the war into which millions of peasants and proletarians have been dragged, our immediate task can be nothing but one of resisting the disasters produced by the war by extending and strenuously developing the class organizations of the proletariat and the broad layers of the democratic movement and making use of the war crisis to prepare the people's awareness, so as to assist the quickest possible realization of the tasks of 1905 by the masses of the people. Thus our most immediate slogan remains the convening of the Constituent Assembly.

And we are doing this precisely in the interests of the democracy whose support you invite from Russian social democracy in your telegram. Russian social democracy forms by no means the least significant detachment in the ranks of the world-wide democratic movement, and by fighting for its interests we are thereby defending the interests of the latter, extending its base and strengthening its forces.

Besides, we do not think that this struggle of ours runs at cross-purposes with the interests of the European democracy so dear to us all. We are convinced on the contrary that it is just the existence of absolutism in Russia that has given the chief support to reactionary militarism in Europe and made Germany the hegemon of Europe and a dangerous enemy of European democracy.

In addition we cannot close our eyes to the future of European socialism and democracy. After the war an era of the further construction of European democracy will inevitably ensue. And then the Russian government emerging from a victorious war with redoubled strength and prestige would form one of the most solid obstacles and threats to this democratic movement.

That is why all-round exploitation of its difficult position by ourselves in the interest of Russian liberty forms our direct duty and will in the final count prove beneficial at the same time to the cause of democracy, which is as dear to us as to all members of the International. The true interests of European and world democracy can be guaranteed not by Russian tsarism but only by the growth and strengthening of the democratic movement in Russia.

Thus, from every point of view, history sets us the task of continued struggle against the régime ruling in Russia and for immediate revolutionary slogans. Only in this way will we render a true service to the Russian working class, world democracy and the International, whose role must, in our deep conviction, inevitably grow in the near future with the balancing of accounts of this terrible war, as this war will without doubt open the eyes of backward layers of labouring masses and force them to seek salvation from the horrors of militarism and capitalism only through the realization of our common socialist ideal.

Central Committee of the RSDLP.

Towards evening on one of the last days of September 1914 I got safely over the Finnish border. I had decided to stop off on the way at Mustamiaki to see comrade Kamenev. A little Finnish coachman whisked me off to the settlement where the comrades lived and waited there to take me back. Comrade Kamenev had already received the theses on the attitude to the war from our party's Central Committee and expressed a measure of disagreement with them. I met Yordansky there too, who had already turned patriotic, and comrade Steklov, who had been through a lot in Germany yet none the less was in tune with Yordansky, although at times for opposite reasons. In his opinion, by the war France was paying the price for her alliance with Russia. He saw in Germany's economic might the inevitability of her victory over her opponents. Beyond such propositions he would not go for the time being.

2
Scandinavia and England

THE JOURNEY to Tornio was pure relaxation. Early autumn is so beautiful among the lakes and forests, the gentle hills and plains. I got to the frontier just before dawn. On the instructions of the gendarme I crossed to the far side of the Tornio-ioki river, stayed the night there, leaving my things at the gendarme's guard-post, and in the morning when passage over the border was permitted, accompanied by the good wishes and kind assistance of the gendarmes, walked across the long wooden bridge to the Swedish frontier settlement of Haparanda. At that time the railway had been laid only as far as Karunki, some thirty kilometres north of Haparanda. With the launching of hostilities in the west all contact with abroad began to be made across this border. In the towns along both sides of the frontier hotels had already appeared, but communications between Haparanda and Karunki were maintained by an enterprising motorist. The region was on a war footing, and assiduous agitation was being conducted in favour of Sweden's entry into the war against Russia. The attitude towards myself, as a "Frenchman", was trusting, but Russians were somewhat feared and suspected of being spies. Waiting for the train at the border, I spent several hours in the hotel chatting to some Swedish officers. They were engaged in strengthening their frontier against an expected Russian invasion. All the officers were ecstatic about the victories of the German forces. They were quite carried away by German tactics, weaponry and the general organization of their army. They had an extremely vague notion of Russia but had no doubts about the future defeat of her army.

The route from Karunki to Stockholm lay first through impassable, unpopulated marshland and forests and between mountains and ravines. Many troops were in the area, hastily building barracks. At Boden, a fortified region of northern Sweden, surveillance of passing foreigners had been mounted and they were not allowed to travel outside the town. Not far from the town there were mines. Along the line we passed many special wagons loaded with ore. It was all heading for Luleå, a Swedish port on the Gulf of Bothnia where it was loaded on to German vessels and sent to the blast furnaces. The industrial and underground workers in this district backed the left wing of the Swedish party, the "young socialists". In many towns they had their own social-democratic newspapers and buildings which accommodated social clubs, canteens and workers' organizations.

At Stockholm I was met by the emigrants I had known from Berlin, such as Kollontai and others. The large colony of Russian Mensheviks from Berlin had moved to Stockholm. They included Y. Larin (M. Lurie), the Levin brothers, Uritsky, Seydler and others. There were a few emigrants from Russia, but they were mainly soldiers and sailors from the Finland garrison who had fled following the celebrated Sveaborg rising of 1906. In Stockholm there was a common organization of Menshevik and Bolshevik social democrats, which had been joined by all the Russians who had moved out of the belligerent countries.

Among the Mensheviks the position of international socialism had been adopted by Kollontai, Uritsky and the printer N. Gordon (a Bundist). The emigrant workers were all on the side of the minority of Swedish social democracy and consequently joined the Stockholm group of Bolshevik social democrats. Immediately upon arrival in Sweden I set about carrying out my assignments. I established contact with the foreign section of the Central Committee, sent the reply to Vandervelde's telegram on to the central organ, *Sotsial-Demokrat*, and wrote to Lenin and Zinoviev, briefing them on the state of affairs in Russia. I wrote up several reports which were included in our *Sotsial-Demokrat* and other newspapers abroad. I received information and directives for forwarding to Russia from the Central Committee. Parts of my letter to the Central Committee were published in the central organ in the form of reports on a number of issues.

> St Petersburg.
> The war caught us in a period of struggle. Mobilization was announced when proletarian blood had still not been washed off the streets. We greeted the declaration of war with secret hopes for the mighty power of German social democracy, from which we awaited the initiative for an active struggle agqnst the war. The Russian press and refugees most kindly kept us informed on the course of the "negotiations" and the conduct of the Germans. Each report was more horrifying than the one before. It was unbelievable that the German social democrats could fall so low as to march hand in hand with Kaiserism . . . even if in the name of the "struggle against Russian tsarism". Such support the Russian revolution neither sought nor wished for. Throughout the city, and throughout Russia too, the news was spread about that Wilhelm was counting chiefly upon a Russian revolution. The behaviour of the Germans, or rather their betrayal of the international solidarity of workers, and the decision of the Stüttgart Congress and also the whole situation deprived us of the possibility of coming out actively against the war during the first week of mobilization.
> Democracy reacted to the question of the war differently from the

proletariat. The views of democracy were fairly accurately expressed by the Trudovik group. And this viewpoint was shared by certain "Marxist" intellectuals too. We, Petersburg workers, are all the while trying, and, despite the difficult conditions, succeeding in maintaining an internationalist standpoint. A nationalist approach to the question cannot find sympathy in our circles. We can think of one thing only: the necessity of a "government of the proletariat" and an authoritative voice against the war which might be able to break through the thick skull of German reformism.

Arrests are taking place over the struggle against the war. About a month ago a proclamation was put out with an appeal for an armed struggle against the war. Afterwards, eighty people were arrested. Some were accused of composing it. They are all in custody.

Sotsial-Demokrat no 33, 1/11/14.

10 October.
The liquidationist intelligentsia have been strongly infected by jingo patriotic tendencies. Many of them did not wish to hear of any war. But at the very point when we were terrorized by the military machine they were the first to "adjust" to the demands of the hour and hold collections for benevolent societies jointly with the factory managements. But this was unsuccessful with workers. We on the Vyborg bank opposed this with a demand for state support for the families of those who had left for the war. We decided moreover to organize collections in aid of "war victims" having in mind aid for the families of comrades who had gone off to the war and aid for unemployed and convicts. But all this could be done only where we were able to take matters into our own hands and not surrender our resources to the "societies". At certain works (Neva Mechanical, Neva Stearin, Obukhov and Semenov) there were percentage deductions. These are run by the management and workers. Beyond the Neva Gate money is going to the local orphanage which is a great shame. Thanks to the activity of our worker comrades the liquidationists are not having any success. Even bellicose-minded liquidationists quickly soften their tone when they run into their workers. The "liberation of the Slavs" is meeting very little success with workers. Many wish in secret for the victory of the French, British and Belgians but would be content with their own country's defeat. It must be noted that the confused situation which is being thus further confused by all and sundry has had a very serious effect upon workers. Accounts and tales about German atrocities even if qualified are given a certain credit by workers as there used to be German foremen and engineers and others in many firms who enjoyed the reputation of boors. Chauvinism cannot be sensed in working-class circles and will not, I think, take root in spite of the "work" of the venal press. In the provinces the mood is less clearly defined but there is much grief and poverty. The war is tolerated but unpopular.

Sotsial-Demokrat no 35, 12/12/14.

11 October

I think you received my letters after the Petersburg barricades with the detailed description of the state of affairs. I shall not dwell on the individual peripeteia of that struggle which cost us some 1,000 arrests.

A few days or perhaps a week prior to the declaration of war all the guardsmen and other forces returned from their camps to Petersburg. We thought at first that this was for the "maintenance of order" but then we sensed the spectre of an approaching war. The majority of factories and plants were closed. The syndicate of industrialists had decided to punish us with a "nice little lock-out" until about 22 to 25 July. But the advent of mobilization prompted the government to demand that manufacturers reopen their plants to placate the workers and this was done from 16 and 17 July. Many workers were on the verge of dispersing to their homes on the outskirts and only learned of the start back some time later. Mobilization was announced on the night of Saturday 19th with the call to report to local police stations at 6 o'clock next morning. When we arrived at the factories we could see that at least forty per cent of the male workforce was absent. Without changing they went out into the streets of the Vyborg bank singing revolutionary songs and shouting: "Down with the war!" All the Bolshoi Sampsonievski Prospekt was overflowing with people who had left their work. There was the weeping of women and the wail of lamentation at the assembly points. Sometimes the voices of individual women shouted through their tears "Down!" but most just wept. . . .

The war had caught us organized workers unawares. On the very first day of mobilization a proclamation was hastily written and hectographed which said that the culprit for the war was the predatory politics of capitalism. It pointed out that the German, Austrian, French and British workers had always fought and are still fighting against the war into which Russian workers and peasants had been dragged by tsarism which had suffered a reverse in its Far Eastern adventure and wished to regain ground in the Near East. It pointed out that the Russian government was lying when it said it was marching to free the Slavs as, within its own country, it kept the people in complete slavery. The leaflet ended with an appeal for a struggle for the democratic republic and a declaration of war on the war. The leaflet was to have been printed but the equipment was seized.

During the first days after mobilization the centre of Petersburg was swamped with officially-inspired patriotic demonstrations against which we had to conduct a struggle by trying to turn them from "patriotic" to "red". This involved a few clashes. At a time when the city had taken on the look of a military camp we could have undertaken something bold but we had no decisions from the organization for that. We would not of course have been sure of success as we could have been isolated, for all means of communication had been placed under military control and there was no contact with the rest of the country. And when later a Petersburg Committee leaflet came out with a call to stock arms and fight actively we found ourselves greatly weakened for any sort of political action because of the departure of the reservists. We keenly felt the impact of the wartime terror in the shape of the "state of war". Reservists working in the metalworking industries have been released from military service in cases where they worked in enterprises fulfilling government contracts. That applied to nearly all Petersburg's metallurgical and engineering industry. But this sector of the Petersburg working class was still under military conscription and so was governed by military regulations. Once they "adjusted" to the state of war the mood became more buoyant and people started to think and work towards resurrecting their ailing organizations. The German social democrats' betrayal had at first a depressing effect upon the general mood. The fact was that although we had all been internationally-minded we did not have any opportunity to draw on any facts of the internationalism of workers in Austria and Germany in our propaganda. Their behaviour untied the hands of the diffident elements and the Russian opportunists and knocked the ground from under the feet of us Bolshevik workers.

The news of our Paris Bolsheviks going off in the army, the "cosy chats" by that old man of Geneva, Plekhanov, and the situation as a whole also casts quite a gloomy shadow across our heads.

The individual nationalists decided to "support" the government in the hope of obtaining perks or indulgences. The (bourgeois) Jews offered prayers for victory in the synagogues and in Petersburg marched with the Tsar's portrait; they joined up as volunteers and, in Odessa, fell upon the necks of the Pelicanovites. All this is utterly repulsive and false. As before, the Jews are harassed and there has been no "appeal" from the Tsar to them.

All is also patriotic among the Armenians while among Ukrainians there is discontent over the "liberation" of Galicia. The Young Turks' party had made a proposal to the Georgians to stay neutral in the event of Russia declaring war and promised autonomy for them and the Transcaucasian region in exchange but the Georgian social democrats declined to negotiate.

The Germans had offered Finland to Sweden and yet promised their services to the Finns if they took a stand against Russia. But the congress of Finnish social democracy resolved to win improvements in Finland's condition through joint efforts with the Russian revolutionary people and decided to fight against the sectional interests of a part of the Swedish bourgeoisie.

Sotsial-Demokrat no 35, 12/12/14.

I got in touch with the Swedish social democrats, who had at that time a single organizational apparatus despite the disagreements that were tearing it apart. I became acquainted with that marvellous comrade, Fredrik Ström, the party's secretary and a member of the Upper Chamber and the leader of the young social democrats. We talked in a mixture of German and French. In a brief space of time I also got to know other leaders of the "young men", as the left social democrats were called there: Zeth Höglund, the favourite of Swedish revolutionary social-democratic workers, the mayor of Stockholm, Carl Lindhagen, Karl Kilbom, the talented linguist Hans Scheld, and others. They were all very interested in the revolutionary movement in our country. My report that the majority of Russian social-democratic workers had taken an anti-militarist stance was greatly welcomed. They personally offered active participation in my work on communications with Russia.

The young Swedish social democrats were staunch anti-militarists. But their anti-militarist ideology contained a lot of bourgeois "pacifism". The ultimate slogan of Scandinavian left social democrats was "lay down the weapons", conscientious objection and other such Tolstoyisms. This stemmed partly from the situation of these extremely small countries, where (in Sweden in particular) the bourgeoisie were very militaristic. In that country especially, the army had clearly showed that it existed not so much to guard against invasion from the north as for domestic purposes.

With great curiosity I went to a meeting with Hjalmar Branting, the old leader of Scandinavian social democracy and an equally old opportunist of the Second International. I found him during a session of the party's Central Committee. Tall, grey, with a kind but firm expression on his face and bushy eyebrows over deep-set intelligent eyes, he made a formidable impression. My official proposal to publish our Duma faction's reply to Vandervelde's telegram and to send it to other countries was put to the Central Committee that same day and approved. I made a formal report to their Central Committee on the situation in our country and the attitudes to the war of the different social classes. From our exchange of opinions it was easy to discern Branting's own views on the recent events. Our negative attitude to the war and the rejection of any support whatsoever for the tsarist government's war machine was "appreciated" by Branting, but he did not wish to appreciate or share our criticism of the parties of Germany, Austria and France which had betrayed international decisions and the whole spirit of socialist teaching. He adopted the standpoint of "defence". He subordinated the theoretical approach towards wars in our time to questions of strategy. The one who was the first to fire, to cross a line called a frontier, was the offender and thus to blame for the war. Branting condemned the Germans for their conduct but at the same time he tried to "appreciate" their position, and readily accepted that the German social democrats were acting on the assumption of a threatened onslaught by tsarist forces. His position was a hopeless one, denying as it did any opportunity for the proletariat to act in concert yet providing the "diplomats" of socialism with "principles" for establishing the "culprit" of the war. In his own country, however, Branting waged an energetic struggle against the bourgeoisie's Germanophilia and efforts to drag Sweden into the war. But this struggle was not founded on a fight against chauvinism itself but on the desire to rebuff Germanophile chauvinism and replace it with Francophilia. Despite our differences and my sharp criticism of the opportunists, we parted friends, and Branting promised all kinds of assistance for my work for Russia.

The activity of the leaders of the Scandinavian socialist parties in the remaining "neutral" countries (Holland, Denmark, Norway and Sweden) amounted to diplomatic mediation between the "sparring brothers". They tried all ways of prevailing on their own governments to make official offers of peaceful mediation. However, the capitalists in the belligerent countries quickly let it be understood that they were in earnest until the utter rout of one or the other. Meanwhile, the neutral countries strove to exhibit their "neutrality" by avoiding upsetting either of the warring blocs. This common fear brought the small countries into a military and political alliance.

Our Revolutionary Work and Diplomacy by the Conciliators

Thanks to the large number of businessmen and emigrants liable to conscription returning to Russia, communications with Petersburg were pretty fair. At first I managed to have letters sent direct, via passengers on the steamers plying between Stockholm and the Finnish ports of Turku and Rauma, but with the extension of hostilities and the onset of winter these means could not be used. Likewise tighter measures were being taken at the frontiers and passengers were thoroughly searched. All this had to be taken into account and secure communication lines found.

In my attempts to organize transport I made the acquaintance of leading figures in the Swedish trade unions. Sweden's trade unions were organized on the model of the German and were akin to them in tactics. The trade-union movement was considerable and already had rich experience of combat. I got to know the chairman of their centre and some metalworkers, tanners and transport workers. The representative of the latter, Charles Lindley, a great admirer of the English transport workers' union, gave me great help in organizing links with Finland. He was acquainted with fishermen and seamen along the entire Gulf of Bothnia and I managed to confirm the possibility of arranging transport by smuggling across the gulf, which could be done on quite a large scale providing that there was money. I reported this to the Petersburg Committee and the Duma faction, but received the sad news that they were not in a position to give the necessary sum of some 300 to 500 rubles a month. It was hard enough for them to send out money for my keep, and, having once sent me 100 rubles, the comrades recommended that I arrange all my own expenses. I could not even begin to think of finding work, as those first months of war had caused great unemployment in Sweden and the plants were operating only a few days per week. No opportunity presented itself of finding resources in the local emigrant community, although there were a lot of speculative racketeers there. Our party's foreign-based Central Committee was too poor to allocate such a sum for this operation. In order to keep the work going I resorted to loans and sent back news only occasionally.

During the first days of November issue no. 33 of *Sotsial-Demokrat* came out, and we had to think about how to deliver it to Russia. For this I decided to make use of my cobbler acquaintances. In view of the searches at the border, people returning to Russia were refusing to carry anything compromising and we had to think about concealment. There were many methods: in trunks, book bindings, dresses, umbrellas, walking-sticks, footwear and so on. I fancied footwear. I gave my boots to a cobbler who had been specially recommended and worked in strict secrecy, and suggested that he cut hollows inside the heels and soles and fill them up with the thin issues of *Sotsial-Demokrat*. I broke them in so that they did not seem too newly mended. Into that first pair went a small number of copies which were sent by roundabout routes to Petrovsky in Petersburg. The cobbler comrade subsequently became so adept that he could tuck up to twenty copies away in each pair of shoes.

The appearance of our party's printed organ with its leading articles defining the position of revolutionary social democracy on the war, and the spread of news from Russia and the Duma faction's reply to Vandervelde's telegram, published in the Scandinavian press, stirred up all the forces hostile to the Russian revolution. There were in the emigrant circles of Stockholm at that time some inveterate enemies of our party such as Messrs liquidators Larin (M. Lurie), the Organizing Committee's representative and correspondent of *Russkie Vedomosti*, Levin (Dalin) and others. These men harboured a deep hatred towards me personally, even though I was not acquainted with them. All my reports on Russia and the news I had received direct from Petersburg were greeted by these people with an incomprehensible hostility. They, and Yuri Larin in particular, ran around the Swedish party comrades systematically undermining confidence in our party and our illegal organizations in Russia. But their endeavours were not crowned with success. The young social democrats soon realized with whom their interests lay and attached no importance to Larin's intrigues. I was to be frequently amazed at the opportunism of this sick man.*

---

*In 1917 Larin joined the Bolshevik Party and became one of its chief spokesmen on economic affairs. — Ed.

At the end of October 1914 the diehard opportunist, Troelstra, the leader of the Dutch social democrats, arrived in Stockholm. He had come with a special assignment doubtless entrusted to him by the German social democrats. This was to obtain agreement for the transfer of the International Socialist Bureau to Amsterdam, and also to clarify the vacillating sympathies of opportunist Scandinavian socialism about why the Germans had been right to "defend their fatherland".

Troelstra had conveyed via the Swedish party his desire to meet me as representative of the RSDLP. I agreed. The meeting was held in a hotel, and the OC representative, Larin, had been informed; he arrived accompanied by Dalin. Kollontai and others came too. I gave him information about Russia and handed him our "Manifesto" and the letter to Vandervelde. Troelstra asked me to convey to him, in letter form, the attitude of Petersburg workers to the war and also an explanation as to why Russian revolutionaries were treating the current war differently from the Russo-Japanese War. I have preserved the rough draft of this letter, which runs as follows:

Dear Comrades,
You ask me to write to you about what the Petersburg proletariat thinks about the German socialists' view of the question of the "struggle against tsarism". I must above all, dear comrades, state to you that the declaration of war caught us workers of Petersburg, Moscow, Riga, Baku and other industrial centres at a moment of active economic and political movement. A few days before there had been barricades in Petersburg. On mobilization day protesting masses of workers marched through the city with red banners as they escorted reservists to the assembly points. In those first days we Petersburg workers could not somehow believe in the possibility of war. We knew that on the other side of the frontier there were powerful cadres of organized workers who would neither permit nor allow themselves to be pushed into bloody clashes with each other. So how could anyone in the International doubt our readiness for self-sacrifice?

But sad news reached us. We saw the great German social democracy betraying socialism and international solidarity. Reports also reached us that the German General Staff was banking on winning its victory over the Russian forces with the aid of our revolution. We likewise knew that our former teachers (Kautsky and co.) had treacherously cloaked German imperialism in the toga of "liberator" of the Russian people. We knew too well the nature of this war to trust and enter into a deal with the bourgeois government of this or that country. Our government is also coming forward in the role of "liberator" of Slavdom while keeping its own multi-millioned people in ignorance and disenfranchised. But however dreadful the conditions of our life might be today with the complete absence of our press, our working class is, with the exception of certain individuals, as far from chauvinism as it is from trusting the

Tsar's government.

We are as deeply indignant at French "democracy's" exchange of kisses with Russian tsarism as we are gladdened by the fact that away in a country cut off by the seas there is a section of the party of the British socialists which, amid the universal debauchery, has not forgotten the ABC of socialism but is fighting with every means against the greedy passions of British imperialism. You are surprised that "Russian society" and Russian revolutionaries have modified their attitude to the war now being waged by tsarism, and especially incomprehensible to you is the contradiction between the attitude of "Russian society" to the war against Japan against which it protested to a man and its attitude today when it is apparently wholly reassured by and reconciled with tsarism in this sorry world drama.

Above all, dear comrade, I should tell you that the Russian socialists' attitude of principle to the war has remained one and the same but the situation in our country has changed substantially. Above all we have lived through a revolutionary period in which the counter-revolutionary and cowardly nature of Russian liberalism clearly exposed itself. The Russo-Japanese War met with a negative response from the Russian bourgeoisie because Manchuria and the other Far Eastern territories had no interest for capital because of their remoteness and small populations and therefore that war was looked upon as a dynastic enterprise, an adventure by the Tsar's camarilla which profiteered out of forests. The current war, though fought in the name of the liberty of Galicia, the French Republic and Belgian democracy, also has a dynastic interest for Russian tsarism but for the Russian landowners and capitalists it has an economic interest too. Tsarism is seeking salvation from approaching revolution in the idea of a "Greater Russia" while capitalism and landowner interests are seeking the passage through the Dardanelles and a revision of the trade agreement between Germany and Russia whose interests were sold off in 1904 by the diplomats of the Tsar to the benefit of German capitalism. It is only that which can really explain the "change" in so-called Russian society from which, however, the proletariat should be excluded.

The German socialists' surprise that we are not rejoicing over their recently announced alliance with their government for a "holy war on Russian tsarism" is nothing but a hypocritical cover for their own betrayal of the International and socialism from the eyes of the masses.

We have always been glad to accept a helping hand from comrades in toil and ideas in our arduous struggle against tsarism but we have never demanded nor expected assistance to the Russian revolution from the part of German feudalism and Wilhelm II, the Russian Tsar's reactionary counsellor and friend.

We do not renounce our struggle against Russian tsarism but in that struggle we are counting only upon our own forces.

We would ask the German social democrats not to send Wilhelm II with his 420-millimetre gun to our aid but to try to put this war material to use against their own feudal lords just as we hope to use ours against

Russian tsarism.

The Finns, our brothers in toil, have also given a negative reply to all the ploys of Germany's bellicose capitalism and take the same standpoint.

The revolutionary proletariat of Russia, along with all the oppressed nationalities, hope to emerge victorious without doing deals with any government whatsoever.

With comradely greetings,
A. Belenin

During our exchange of views it became clear that Troelstra was the prevalent type of social chauvinist, the Germanophile. He stressed the liberating role of German social democracy in relation to Russia. I refused to accept the liberating effect of 420-millimetre shells upon Russian workers and peasants. I recommended that these sophisticated appliances be set in action against their own landlords and bourgeoisie, for we had no need for such assistance. I asked him to convey the profound indignation of our workers, in Petersburg and elsewhere, at such a "liberating" provocation and also their greetings to Karl Liebknecht and the comrades standing by him.

Larin tried to prove that they, the Mensheviks, Trotskyites, Plekhanovites, Bundists and so on, were "quite the reverse" of the Bolsheviks. Here he told how a special committee had been formed in Warsaw made up of representatives of the Polish Socialist Party (left group), the Social Democracy of Poland and Lithuania (Warsaw opposition), and the Bund. The chief task of this organization was, in his words, "the struggle against Austrophile influences in Polish society". In actual fact this inter-party council had been organized for an entirely different end. Our Polish comrades were far removed from the Russophile chauvinism ascribed to them by Larin. Their position was akin to ours, and they fought against militarism without respite. Larin's own contribution could not have conformed better to the theory of "defence of the fatherland". As a counterweight to my hostile attitude to the Scheidemannite *Vorstand* (the Central Committee of German Social Democracy), he asked for greetings to be conveyed to the *Vorstand* on behalf of Chkheidze's Duma faction, along with assurances of their solidarity etc. Troelstra was unspeakably delighted at this and carefully noted it. The remaining Mensheviks were apparently a little aghast.

It was decided as a result of the meetings between the Scandinavian leaders and Troelstra to organize a congress of "socialists of the neutral countries" in December. The socialist 'parties of the "belligerent countries" received invitations to submit written reports. The American socialists also consented to participate in the congress, which was postponed until 17 January 1915 in order to have them present at the conference.

At the end of the autumn of 1914 certain Russian socialists began to be shadowed by the police. I was summoned to the police for a "pass", as it was explained to me. I had observed local security police posts near the flat. Gatherings at the People's House were similarly subject to surveillance. Reactionary newspapers, especially Germanophile ones and those published at the expense of the German Embassy, waged a campaign against Russian socialists, suspecting them of espionage and accusing them of plotting and so on. Comrade Kollontai, who had taken quite an active part in the work of the left social democrats and the women's organizations, was subjected to the sneers of a reactionary Stockholm paper and was honoured by a special denunciation to the police. This was followed by her arrest, trial, imprisonment and deportation to Denmark. I had to be extra careful not to lose my right of residence and freedom of movement within Sweden. Over Kollontai's case I had to seek the assistance of Branting. He seemed to be angry at this sacrifice to the Swedish police and kept repeating with visible dissatisfaction that she was to blame, for disregarding his advice not to get involved in Swedish political life. But the leftists reminded me that Kollontai's deportation did not go against Branting's own wishes. At that time I was discussing with him the possibility of moving the foreign section of the Central Committee to Stockholm. He had assured me that all Russian socialists who had not been accused of acts of terrorism could live freely in Sweden. The Kollontai incident did not square with this promise, but Branting added a new condition: newcomers "should not involve themselves in the local political struggle".

At the Swedish Social Democrats' Congress

On 23 November 1914 the congress of the Swedish party opened. I decided to deliver a message of greeting in which I could throw some light on the Russian revolutionary movement on the eve of the war and during it, and also set out the attitude of the organized proletariat to the war. I managed to do so in the following greeting:

> Respected comrades,
> I bring you greetings from the organized proletariat of Russia and its class organization, the RSDLP. I wish the Swedish social democratic party success in its work. At the present time of general decline when the bourgeoisie of nearly all Europe, both west and east, is, under the guise of "national self-defence", following a policy of armed conquest, we socialists must carry high our internatonalist revolutionary red banner and not allow ourselves to be overwhelmed by the waves of reformism which has put its theory of the "union of classes" into practice in the present criminal war.

We Russian, and in particular Petersburg, workers have followed with great joy your struggle against the current that wished to drag the Swedish people into the world war and we are highly delighted that all the efforts made in that direction by the commercial travellers of militarism have suffered an utter fiasco in your friendly country.

Allow me to say a few words about our own workers' movement which, starting in 1912, has experienced a period of upsurge and has distinguished itself by an unusual growth of the strike movement and especially the growth of the so-called mass political strikes. To illustrate my point I shall give you some figures concerning our struggle.

In 1911 the total number of strikers in our extensive country had reached 105,000 while one year later, in 1912, it had risen to 1,070,000 of which 855,000 were accounted for by political strikes. In 1913 the strike movement was equally widespread: in the course of that year, 1,185,000 employees took part in strikes of which 821,000 were due to political strikes; moreover the official statistics of the Factories Inspectorate are incomplete as they do not cover small-scale industry and state-owned enterprises.

The ferocity and persecution of the authorities and organized capital could not break the solidarity of the Russian working class. The current year serves as a graphic example. This year the workers' struggle sharpened to the extreme. All economic and trade-union conflicts turned quickly into a political movement on account of the government repression. Once again the working class proclaimed its readiness to fight for the republic, the Constituent Assembly and the eight-hour day.

In July the political struggle flared up with unusual vigour. The working class of Petersburg answered the government's bloody provocation with a general strike that in Petersburg alone involved over 250,000 workers. In many areas the city's streets were covered with barricades and workers' blood was shed. By now the movement had spread to the rest of the country and took in the Baltic provinces, Poland, the Caucasus, Moscow and the south.

But at the very point that our struggle had reached this stage the monster of war advanced upon us. The bourgeoisie sounded the alarm: its fatherland, the fatherland of money-bag, was in danger. Soldiers in grey greatcoats, the sons of peasants and workers, headed for the frontiers.

In the days of the mobilization Petersburg workers downed tools and noisily protested against the war. Workers escorted their mobilized workmates to the assembly points singing revolutionary songs and carrying red banners and streamers.

We conscious workers had not believed in the possibility of a world war. We had turned our hope-filled eyes towards the west and our organized brothers: the Germans, French and Austrians. We had expected to find support there and hear a mighty summons to struggle against the bourgeoisie's diabolical plot. But bitter reality brought us something else. The government press and bourgeois newspapers, and also fellow-countrymen fleeing from abroad, informed us of the betrayal committed by the leaders of the powerful German social democracy and later by many others who also looked on things "from the standpoint of national self-defence".

But our social-democratic party has not been consumed by the universal conflagration for it has not forgotten the true causes of today's war which the imperialist policies of the bourgeois governments of all countries have brought about. The Duma faction has given true expression to the organized proletariat by refusing to vote for the war budget and stressing its negative attitude to the war by leaving the chamber. Many local organizations have issued illegal leaflets on the war (Petersburg, Moscow, Riga, Warsaw, the Caucasus and so on).

Our party's Central Committee and its central organ, *Sotsial-Demokrat*, have entered a fight against international opportunism and call proletarian revolutionary elements in all countries to this struggle in the name of the common interests of the proletariat worldwide.

In conclusion I wish the congress of our fraternal party successful work. Long live the Swedish proletariat and its class party, social democracy! Long live the International!

For fear of police persecution and upon the advice of the young social democrats, I wrote this speech out and one of them, comrade Scheld, translated it and read it out to the congress. The message caused a stormy clash between the two tendencies, a speech by Branting and Höglund's protest. I quote here material on this from the congress minutes:

> *Branting* takes the floor on a question over which he considers it essential to take a decision. He had just familiarized himself with the text of a greeting, originating from one of the Russian parties, where it speaks of a betrayal by the German party. The speaker points out that it does not befit the congress to express condemnation directed at other parties and considers it necessary that a motion of regret be formally moved with regard to the paragraph inserted in the greetings.
>
> *Höglund* (Stockholm) considers it improper for the congress to adopt such a resolution, because within our own party there are also comrades who regard the Germans' behaviour as a betrayal. He moves that congress does not pass judgement but contents itself with entering Branting's statement in the minutes.
>
> *S. Vinberg* (Stockholm) considers that we should state merely that the judgement expressed remains the responsibility of the Russians.
>
> *Branting* repeats his demand and asserts that otherwise the misunderstanding will arise that delegates to congress are in sympathy with the aforementioned judgement.

The congress defeated Vinberg's motion and accepted Branting's by 54 votes to 50.

I was personally present at the congress and Branting considered it his duty to explain to me that his statement was necessitated by my direct raising of such an important question as the attitude towards the defence of the fatherland. I replied that was not just my own personal view, but the principled attitude of both our centre and the huge majority of Russia's organized workers. He and I had, in the main, established "chivalrous relations" though. Branting had given me his address and would do small favours. With his help, I managed to obtain a passport from the French consul which was valid for transit to France, and so on.

During the congress of Swedish social democracy we received the report of the arrest of our Duma faction in Petersburg. This event made a deep impression on the delegates to the congress. A resolution of protest was carried. A wave of protest at tsarist barbarity swept across all Scandinavia. I found I had a portrait of comrade Petrovsky on me and it went the rounds of many Scandinavian social-democratic newspapers.

The deputies' arrest greatly impeded our party's contact with and information from Russia. I had, prior to this, managed to arrange the forwarding of brief commentaries on the international situation, information on the state of affairs in Scandinavia and the anticipated conference of socialist parties of the neutral countries and to send on several letters from Lenin and also some literature (*Sotsial-Demokrat* nos 33 and 34). But news from Russia was very hard to come by.

In the middle of November the Menshevik's reply to Vandervelde's telegram was received in Stockholm. The document was received by Larin, the OC's representative, and was kept in strict secrecy, but I still managed to get hold of the actual original with amendments added in Larin's hand. I quote it here in full:

> To Minister Vandervelde of Belgium.
> Dear Comrade,
> Your telegram reached us allowed through by the war censorship. We greet the Belgian proletariat and yourself, its representative. We know that you, like all the international proletariat, have vigorously opposed the war when it was being prepared by the ruling classes of the great powers. But the war began against the will of the proletariat. In this war your cause is the just cause of self-defence against all those dangers threatening democratic liberties and the liberation struggle of the proletariat emanating from the aggressive policy of Prussian Junkerdom. Irrespective of the aims which the great-power participants in the war are setting themselves, the objective course of events places in question the very existence of that citadel of modern militarism, which also stamps down the liberation struggle of the German proletariat with a heavy heel, namely, Prussian Junkerdom. We are profoundly convinced that *along the road to its elimination* the socialists of the countries compelled to take part in this war will come together with German social democracy, the glorious vanguard of the international proletariat [and assist it in the task

of Germany's political and social reconstruction]. But, unfortunately, Russia's proletariat is not in the position that the proletariat of other countries at war with Prussian Junkerdom is in. It is faced with an incomparably more complex and contradictory task than its western comrades. The international situation is further complicated by the fact that in the present war against Prussian Junkerdom another reactionary force is taking part: the Russian government which, by reinforcing itself in the course of the war, may in certain conditions become the focus of all reactionary tendencies in world politics. This possible role for Russia in international relations is closely bound up with the nature of the régime that has undivided rule over us. But even at the present moment the proletariat of Russia is, as opposed to its western comrades, deprived of any chance of openly expressing its collective opinion and realizing its collective will: those few organizations that it had before the war have been closed down. The press has been wrecked. The prisons are overflowing. This prevents social democracy in Russia from taking up the position that the socialists of Belgium, France and Britain have taken and accepting responsibility for the actions of the Russian government both before the country and before international socialism by taking active part in the war. But, in spite of the presence of these factors and bearing in mind the international importance of the all-European conflict as well as the active part of socialists of the advanced countries in it that gives us grounds for hoping that it will be resolved to the benefit of international socialism, we declare to you that in our activity in Russia we are not opposing the war. We do, however, consider that it is necessary to draw your attention here and now to the need for preparing vigorous opposition to the great powers' policies of conquest being now planned and demanding in any annexation a preliminary plebiscite of the population of the territory to be annexed.

In the original, the passage in brackets has been crossed out by Larin and the words in italics written in. It was received in Stockholm on 15 November. Larin's Germanophile sentiments could not tolerate the point about "aid" to Germany in the work of political and social transformation. He personally believed that such "aid" was already being objectively carried out by Germany in relation to all the countries at war with her. This correction had been apparently accepted by the foreign organ of the Organizing Committee, as it had been published by the "Larinite" editorial board.

The fruits of the information gathering activity of the OC's representative, Larin, soon began to reveal themselves. Protests started coming in from Russia about the distortions of the truth permitted by one of the leaders of Scandinavian opportunism. Without realizing it, the latter found themselves in a tight spot. This was the case for Troelstra also, to whom Larin had reported in my presence: the Warsaw socialists sent him a disclaimer.

The Copenhagen Conference

The persecution of Russians, and the police shadowing of myself personally, prompted me to leave Sweden temporarily. There had been a few more deportations after the sensationalized case of Alexandra Kollontai. Branting and Ström also found my temporary absence from Stockholm highly expedient. There were no permanent properly established links with Russia. We had to use the good offices of passing emigrants, and also Finnish comrades, for transporting the precious funds. Various commercial and manufacturing firms were running contraband traffic in both goods and personnel. Heading some of these establishments were Russian engineers glorying in their former social democracy, but these gentlemen were afraid of losing their cosy niches and did not wish to lift so much as a finger in the business of aid for revolutionary work in Russia.

Russian social (and other) patriots constantly repeated their dirty suspicions about the "German" money with which our literature was supposedly produced and our transport organized. In the war period a considerable portion of this work was carried through with my direct participation. No monies were received from Russia. Because of the small size of the Russian colony in Stockholm there was nowhere to obtain funds from. We had to cut work to a minimum and resort to loans. The Central Committee of the Swedish Social-Democratic Party loaned me 400 kroner, several comrades managed to rustle up the same amount, dribs and drabs came in from our Central Committee abroad, and this formed all the income for 1914 and the spring of 1915. With these funds we managed to sound out possibilities for sending people over and forwarding literature but not for making full use of the routes themselves. This was a huge disappointment for the party workers. The lack of funds brought me to despair and drove me to prospect in various fields but it was not even possible to find a job, never mind funds for such an unprofitable enterprise as revolutionary work in Russia.

In December I crossed to Copenhagen. The low cost of living there was striking. This had attracted a large number of profiteers of all nationalities, emigrants from Russia, wives of German bourgeois who had come over to recuperate, and deserters. Quite a few Russians worked at Parvus's "Institute for the Study of the Social Consequences of the War". Some had got jobs at the Russian Red Cross Society dealing with prisoner-of-war welfare. Copenhagen was teeming with spies and reporters from all countries. It was from here that all worldly gossip, fabrications and *ballons d'essai* originated during the war.

The Danish Social-Democratic Party was preparing for the international congress. Our foreign centre, jointly with the Swiss and

Italian social-democratic parties, had declined to take part in the congress. I merely had to report this diplomatic concoction, brewed up by the Scandinavian opportunists.

In Denmark itself, a country of small peasants, socialism was devoid of even a trace of revolutionary spirit. The country was regarded as democratic even though it had a king, albeit one without "pretensions to power". Denmark's peninsular position gave its agriculture and livestock a favourable place in the market by affording cheap sea transport for exports to England and Germany. With the development of food shortages in the belligerent countries, the prices of these products rose to fabulous heights and Danish proprietors secured handsome returns.

On the eve of the war Danish workers and peasants were fighting for universal suffrage for women. At the elections the Social Democrats and the Radicals, who stood for giving women the vote, gained a majority in the Folketing. The Social-Democratic party received the largest number of seats in parliament and, in accordance with custom, ought to have formed the government, but they declined and the Radicals took the job. One of their tasks was to draft a new constitution, and the Social Democrats promised the liberals their "loyal support". However, the slight reactionary majority in the Senate took advantage of the war to halt any debate on a new constitution. So the liberal government, supported by the socialist majority in parliament, submitted to the reactionary will and ceased their reforming work.

The government's chief concern was to preserve peace, and in the interests of this the socialists made a "holy alliance" with their bourgeoisie. And of course they propped up the government by every means, voted for the war budget and so on. The trade unions were "happy" at the absence of conflict between labour and capital. This was not to be explained by a "happiness" reaching down into working-class quarters, for there was in no sense an improvement in living conditions. The war had produced colossal unemployment in this neutral country. Out of 120,400 organized workers, 13,900 were out of work. Aid for the unemployed was given by the unions and the state. Local authorities gave some assistance to unorganized workers directly, and subsidies to the unions.

The Danes claimed to observe their neutrality very strictly. The slightest expression of sympathy or anger over this or that act by the belligerents was equated with a violation of neutrality. This did not, however, prevent the capitalists from unloading their products on whoever, belligerent or not, would pay the highest price.

By the time I moved to Copenhagen, the Social Democrats' support for the Radicals had developed into close collaboration. The Danish

Social-Democratic Party was taking an active part in the cabinet. Stauning, the leader of Scandinavian social democracy, had joined the government. With him I had a totally unexpected experience, though one typical of the middle-class psychology of the Danish socialists. Stauning would invariably evade the questions I put to him and even avoid meeting me. This forced me to approach him "officially", by a letter on our party's headed paper. Now he could no longer back out and fixed a special meeting for me at the premises of the Central Committee. Here he stated to me that he was unable to express his opinion on the party's attitude to the war, as that would mean a violation of neutrality: he would only be able to proclaim it when the war had ended. However, as a pupil of German social democracy and, like many others, an admirer of its organizational and tactical methods, Stauning supported it on the question of the war. For him an "attitude" to the war was equivalent to expressing sympathy with one of the warring alliances, which was impermissible for an advocate of neutrality. He would discuss the International as an organ of action only after the war. The International was, in his opinion, a peacetime instrument. At the moment of the greatest crisis for the working class, the International Workers' League ceased activity and the "socialist leaders" contented themselves with fine hopes for the day to come after the crisis. Such specimens were no rarity in the socialist parties of every country.

I did obtain valuable information from citizen Stauning about the struggle over the International Socialist Bureau. The Germans were trying to use the Dutch to get the ISB into their own hands. But the socialists of the Entente held tightly on to the apparatus, not wishing to "hand it over" even to the "neutral" hands of the socialists of America.

The idea of an international congress enjoyed fairly wide currency. The first attempt was made by the Socialist Party of America. Stauning handed me a copy of a printed invitation with the seal of the "National Committee of the Socialist Party of America" and the following letter:

> Chicago, United States,
> 24 September 1914.
> I enclose with this letter an appeal for the convening of an extraordinary meeting of the International Socialist Congress devoted to the question of peace. This appeal comes from the National Executive Committee of the Socialist Party of America. It has been sent out because: (1) it maintains that an international assembly is absolutely essential in the current crisis; (2) it maintains that the International Bureau is unable to function because of the war in Belgium; (3) the United States is the only great nation not participating in the war;

This assembly should be held in Washington (USA), The Hague or Copenhagen.

Desirous of receiving your vote for one or other venue and receiving by telegram to our Bureau.

Should you choose Washington, the American Socialist Party will undertake to meet travelling and any other expenses on the basis of five delegates per country having twenty votes and the others *pro rata* with a minimum of two per country.

Fraternal greetings,
Walter Lanferseik,
Secretary to the EC.

The American socialists' wish to see an international conference in their country did not, however, meet with sympathy in the Scandinavian countries. The voyage to America would occupy too much time and would put the party leaders too far from contact with the situation in Europe. The majority of the neutrals therefore declined the invitation.

By 17 January 1915 the following representatives to the International Socialist Conference had arrived in Copenhagen: Branting and Ström from Sweden; Knudsen from Norway; Troelstra and another, an editor, whose name I have lost, from Holland; and Stauning from Denmark. Other countries refused to take part. The conference sessions took place behind closed doors. There were no deep differences between those assembled. Only two lines of "sympathies" clashed: the Germanophiles, Troelstra and Stauning, against Branting, the Francophile and Knudsen, the Anglophile. It was not hard to reach agreement with such differences.

At roughly the same time another conference was taking place in London, with the socialists of the Entente countries, France, Britain and Belgium and some representatives of Russia taking part. This conference attempted to find consolation in the International's past, recognized the struggle between the two imperialisms but took the imperialism which was "on the defensive" under their protection. German imperialism, having "assaulted" Belgium and France, had placed these socialists on the side of "their" capitalists. The best forces of the Second International were being directed to "the defence of the fatherland". The representatives of the Entente socialist parties had joined bourgeois cabinets and harnessed themselves to the chariot of war. (An exception was the Italian Socialist Party which, from the first days of the war, had taken up a resolute struggle against it and all who "recognized" this war.) The resolutions of the London conference were distributed by the governments of the Entente countries.

All the reactionaries, rogues and profiteers making fortunes out of human slaughter had gambled on the reputations and public activity of the leaders of the Second International, who had accepted the war on behalf of their governments. The socialists of the German coalition countries did not lag behind their "rival brothers" in inciting their peoples to the "defence" of the fatherland and the mutual destruction of the proletariat. Chauvinism celebrated a victory on all fronts. The capitalists could be proud of such socialists.

Social Chauvinists as Servants of the Bourgeoisie

After the Scandinavian socialist conference I headed once again for Stockholm. There I met some new arrivals from Russia who passed me some bits of information which I forwarded to our central organ, *Sotsial-Demokrat*. I set about reinforcing the working group of Bolsheviks in Stockholm and training several proletarians in the conspiratorial work of smuggling literature, etc. The Petersburgers had displayed no initiative in organizing communications. My activity in this direction ran into obstacles through lack of funds. Smuggling could be managed at great expense, but I had no money and not a hope of obtaining any. We had to improvise. This was far from satisfactory, especially when with some 500 rubles a month I could have showered our working-class organizations in Russia with literature and maintained a regular monthly contact with every corner of the country. But such a trifling sum could not be managed, so there matters rested.

In February a strange gentleman came to me in Stockholm who introduced himself as a former Bolshevik, Finn-Epotaevsky. Larin, whom he had dropped in to see, had informed him of my work. The Petersburgers had, in his words, "been frank" with him about me and he had come along to "persuade" me of the mistaken nature of our tactics. He was a fervent patriot, a contributor to Yordansky's *Sovremenny Mir*, believed in the inevitability of Russia's victory, etc. His persistence and boastfulness were limitless. I was very glad when he left. All his references to commissions received from various Petersburgers proved to be false. From later meetings with comrades, I established that they never passed any assignments to the Finn.

At the very start of my work in Stockholm I got to know many Finnish, Estonian and Zionist party workers who had been engaged in revolutionary work in Russia but who now in those bloody days maintained a rather odd orientation towards the German General Staff. One man named Keskula, who turned up from Switzerland with all the appearances of an Estonian social democrat, offered to supply funds, arms and everything necessary for revolutionary work in Russia. All this was offered in such ways and through such individuals that their origin might have seemed reliable. However, being always wary, I managed to establish that behind these figures lay a strategic manoeuvre by militarism. All such offers were always turned down by my comrades or myself. I firmly instructed the comrades I was leaving behind for the work of smuggling literature, the secretary of our Bolshevik group in Stockholm, Bogrovsky, and others, not to accept funds from anyone other than Swedish party organizations.

On this visit I managed to establish that the Russian political police had agents in Stockholm. Our organizations and certain individuals were placed under observation. There was evidence of mail being tampered with, and this suggested that the Swedish police, despite its national predisposition against Russia, was assisting the Okhrana. Branting had to be made aware of this, and he questioned the Minister of the Interior, but naturally received an assurance that the "official" police was not itself involved, although he could not vouch for private investigation bureaux. I was summoned to the local police station to register as an alien. This was a simple formality that in no way inhibited my residence in Sweden.

Having sorted things out with the group, I decided to move on to Christiania (Oslo) where there was less police intrigue and living was considerably cheaper, which was of great importance to me as my funds were coming to an end. I imagined that I might find a job in a Norwegian engineering works more quickly. I found Ibsen's land clad in its luxuriant winter attire. Wooded hills, sprinkled with snow, sparkled under the rays of the March sun. The lightly covered trees in the woods and forests looked like a kingdom of snowy columns studded with icicles gleaming in the sun. An endless, all-absorbing stillness spread everywhere. Christiania, the capital of Norway, hemmed in by hills and strewn out along the shore of an ice-free fjord, overflows into the plain and its outskirts ascend the hillsides. From one of those hills, Holmenkollen, an enchanting view of the city opens up at night-time. Millions of tiny electric lights twinkle like stars in the nocturnal distance, merging with the Milky Way, thinning out towards the foot of the mountains, disappearing into the expanse and blending into the stars of the night. It seemed as if that part of the night sky which is hidden from our eyes by the horizon might be visible from that mountain.

The Norwegian comrades received me with kindness. Of all the Central Committee only one, Videns, the editor of *Social-Demokraten*, the party's central organ, knew foreign languages. The Norwegian Social-Democratic Party was somewhat more left than its Scandinavian sisters. On the war the Central Committee held an internationalist position and upheld the neutrality of the country, but often wavered towards Anglophilia. The "young" social democrats were in solidarity with their Swedish counterparts. They too had their own organ, *Klassekampen*, which followed a line of revolutionary struggle against the war, but it too veered towards pacifism with its slogan of "lay down the weapons".

My search for work did not yield the desired results. Industry was in the grip of the war crisis and at the beginning of 1915 it was only just starting to recover. Ignorance of Norwegian was also a hindrance. I had to consider what to do next. The idea occurred to me of a trip to England for work. I had previously managed to obtain a "foreign" passport from the French consul in Stockholm and, not without some difficulty, I succeeded in getting the consent of our party's foreign centre. I obtained some money for the journey and all that was needed was the agreement of the British consul. My well-meaning manner and numerous testimonials from French factories swung him rapidly in my favour and, collecting the appropriate fee from me, he stamped a visa in my French passport. I also took with me my personal Russian passport of 1907, a red one, in case of need, and set out at the beginning of April.

To England

Communications with England during the war were maintained by steamer from Bergen to Newcastle, with the risk of touching off mines, encountering German submarines and warships and so on. But these hazards and difficulties only increased the price of passenger tickets and cargo rates, and provided additional profits for the shipping line.

The route to Bergen by rail is regarded as one of the most beautiful in northern Europe. The iron ribbon of the railway track twists through the mountains and gorges, passes along lakesides and deep precipices, dives into the ground and ascends into the realm of perpetual snows. Every year thousands of tourists come to pay tribute to these beauties of Norway.

The small but extremely lively port of Bergen shelters at the foot of the mountains on the shores of the Bergenfjord, an inlet of the Atlantic. Shipping movements were considerable in spite of the war but the whole life of the port, and especially sailings for foreign ports, lay under the strict control of the British.

Mail and passengers were transported in rather small, uncomfortable steamers with a displacement of under 2,000 tons. Passenger embarkation took place under supervision and a personal appearance before an official specially authorized by the British to check the passports was required, in addition to the visa in the passport. Here the interrogation and examination of the departing passenger was conducted, and if the latter appeared suspicious he would be refused access to the vessel. I safely passed this check.

The vessel's departure had been veiled in some secrecy. As we neared the English coast passengers were forbidden to go up on deck. The approaches to the Tyne had been mined and passengers sat in their cabins all the way up river to Newcastle. After forty hours' passage from Bergen, the steamer docked at the quay in Newcastle.

After a brief passport and luggage examination there was free exit to the city. I made for the railway station and, among the numerous stairways, entrance and exits, found a train to London; twenty minutes or so later the train set out smoothly on its journey, without any of that special commotion of noise and bells customary in our country. The coaches were first and third class only, built for comfort and designed for easy boarding and alighting. Every compartment had its own door opening directly on to the platform. The coaches glided along without noise or jolting. The tracks had been so aligned so that the danger of travelling at speed was reduced to nil. All the way there was cleanliness, comfort and an absence of excited crowds. In a few hours I arrived in London.

I had been in London several times before the war. I had worked at an aerodrome in Hendon and walked around out of work, and had closely studied the ancient, soot-covered capital of Great Britain. The war could not yet be sensed in the streets of London. Only at night-time did London not shine with lights as before: the street-lamps had been covered so that they only cast light downwards in a hardly noticeable patch. But large numbers of soldiers were in evidence everywhere.

I looked up an old friend, "Daddy" Harrison, Litvinov. Through his good offices I moved into the flat of an old exile and at once set about job-hunting. In the morning I would get a *Daily Chronicle*, where vacancies were advertised. I wrote off to my old job at Hendon. In response to one advert for turners I headed for a car plant at Wembley, a branch of the Italian firm of Fiat. There I met the Swiss manager who spoke French, several Italian fitters and one Englishman who spoke French. The offer of my skills was accepted and I started work the next day. After a test I got a bench as a first turner at a day-rate of one shilling an hour. For the first few days I travelled back to the flat in London, but that took two hours each day and my new workmates found a furnished room in the same area for only eighteen shillings a week with meals. The working hours came to fifty-two and a half a week, five days of nine and a half hours and five on Saturdays. Work was easy-going. The English workers worked well but without rushing, and they did not like to be chased. My relations with everyone were excellent from the very first days. All the workers learned that I was a revolutionary and an opponent of the war, and we often had simple arguments over the benches, sometimes with the participation of an interpreter. The men were mostly members of the Amalgamated Society of Engineers. Before the war it was very difficult for a foreigner to get into this union, for the leaders of the British trade unions were great nationalists and, although the unions had formally joined international trade-union organizations, their participation in congress decisions was highly platonic.

I asked the works union representative to admit me as a union member and presented my subscription cards from unions in other countries. The comrade went down to his branch at Chiswick and explained when he came back that my "knowledge of the trade and work practices" entitled me to join the union. He proposed that I turn up at a meeting the following Saturday for my final acceptance. The union rented several rooms in a local restaurant. About fifty comrades were in their seats waiting for the meeting to open. A few novices were awaiting the rites of acceptance. The meeting was declared open and the chairman announced the wish of the new comrades to join the union. The first candidate was myself. Our shop representative stated that I knew my job and the work rules well, and that I would observe the union ruling on the minimum wage. The chairman added that I had already been for many years a member of unions in France and Germany, but they had still to acquaint me with the obligations of a new member. All the new entrants gathered round the table and the chairman opened a small booklet to read out the "rules" on the obligations, duties and rights of union members. After this solemn ceremony the novices became fully-fledged members. This atmosphere of solemn initiation and secrecy was redolent of the good old days of "camaraderie", when apprentice craftsmen formed their clandestine associations against the master craftsmen.

Within the British proletariat, which was organized into socialist parties — namely the British Socialist Party and the Independent Labour Party — and into trade unions also, the war had given rise to the same attitudes and the same splits as in other countries. The Independent Labour Party's most popular leader, Keir Hardie, who was familiar to us in Russia as an "opportunist", proved to have been a vehement and a serious opponent of the British war party. He died at the beginning of the war gloriously as an anti-war fighter, and the loss was keenly felt by British workers. Another leader, known in Russia as Britain's "only marxist", the aristocrat Hyndman, had become an inveterate nationalist and chauvinist. Some Russian comrades who had had dealings with him back in the 1905–8 period referred to him as a two-faced politico. Comrade Martins, a social democrat and exiled engineer who was working in Britain, had information that Hyndman was a shareholder and director of a machine-gun and rifle manufacturers. Thus his "warlike" disposition was justified by some "warlike" income.

Widespread anti-war activity was carried out by the ILP. In addition to its parliamentary statements this party expended great energy outside parliament. At the very beginning it issued a "manifesto" on its attitude to the war in which it set out its pacifist anti-militarist stance, without being able to give so much as a clue to a practical way out of the new situation for workers.

The party's weekly paper *Labour Leader* carried constant pacifist slogans against the war. The party's publishers put out several dozen books, pamphlets and booklets against the war, in which the blame for the slaughter was placed on the British government. Especially valuable was the book *Secret Diplomacy*, which exposed a whole number of Anglo-French machinations against Germany. The bourgeois press slandered the ILP over this book, accusing them of selling themselves to the Germans and so on. The government seized the journal and pamphlets and ordered the printers not to handle them, but that did not stop the ILP from further work. They also organized public meetings. The police tried everything to break them up, mobilizing hooligans and planting agents to shout down the speakers and disrupt the meetings in other ways.

The activity of the British Socialist Party was less conspicuous. It did, however, issue quite a few leaflets calling for a struggle against patriotic chauvinism. Both parties searched for all sorts of ways to organize international contacts.

With the help of comrade Litvinov, one of the oldest exiles, I made the acquaintance of an MP, the independent socialist, Anderson. He familiarized me with the parliamentary struggle conducted by their party and their work as a whole. This comrade showed great interest in revolutionary work in Russia and asked me to write an article for them outlining the current situation in our country. English trade unionists, although in a considerable number of cases only their chiefs, took the side of the government on the question of the war. The Trades Union Congress had published a manifesto of lackeyish content beneath which were the signatures of several unions. A happy exception was the Amalgamated Society of Engineers. Among metalworkers there was no such "drunken" nationalism. But while working at the plant and mingling in the pub and the union I was greatly struck by the low level of political awareness of even the English metalworkers' organizers. When I came into the shop following May Day, when I had stayed away from work, several workmates came over to see whether I had been sick, as they had missed me at work. I explained that I did not go to work on May Day. Some of the youngsters were quite amazed and starting asking questions about the meaning of May Day. Yet these workers were living and working at the very centre of Britain's labour movement — London!

Among the Russians in London

The number of Russian exiles in London had grown considerably during the war. Many had come from Belgium. Pressure put on all Russians of call-up age by the French government had prompted many to leave France also. The exile community had fragmented into a number of party groupings, with their *siège* at the Karl Marx People's Club in Charlotte Street. The non-party Herzen Circle was also based there.

Our party organization required a report from me on the state of affairs in Russia. The gathering listened with great interest to my accounts of the Petersburgers' summer demonstrations and the first months of the war. I had to repeat the report several times at other meetings of national sections.

Living near London I was able to observe at first hand every day, from the newspapers and the mood of the inhabitants, the skill of the British bourgeoisie in manipulating society. By forming a land army the British bourgeoisie had successfully exploited its purported "unpreparedness" for the war. It was this same "unpreparedness" that had enabled Lloyd George to make capital out of the British government's "peaceful nature". The press sought to make use of raids by Zeppelins, aircraft and ships on Britain's coastline to inflame hatred for the Germans and in that they succeeded. The strike movement had weakened considerably, thanks to the policy of "alliance" carried out by the trade-union chiefs. This was also helped by the conciliatory attitude of both the government and manufacturers, who had prospered on large profits. But in the summer of 1915 I happened to be witness to a number of strikes (on the trams, etc.) and to take part myself in demands for pay increases. The employer agreed to raise the wages of all workers by the penny an hour demanded by the workers. I had, prior to this, managed to win a personal rise of a penny so that my daily wage was now one shilling and two pence an hour. Thanks to the low cost of living in England I was very soon able to bring some order back into my clothing and to re-equip myself with underwear, which had got pretty tatty during my illegal travels. I also started to give thought to procuring funds for my return to Russia and illegal work over there. I fulfilled a request from the Russian and English comrades to write an article on the situation in Russia. I received a request from America too. I made copies on a typewriter, giving one to the comrades for the English and sending one each to Norway,

Switzerland and America. The effect of the despatch was wholly unexpected. I was placed under observation as a spy, and a British secret police agent came to visit my landlady in order to get to know me a bit better.

One day when I came in from work, the landlady asked me to come downstairs to the sitting-room where a young man was waiting for me. The landlady furtively introduced us and then hastily shut the door and left us alone. Before me was an Englishman, a tall chap, intellectual-looking and smartly dressed. He began with apologies and frankly stated that he had received an assignment of a quite unusual nature from his superiors: to trail me and elucidate my character, because of some article I had written. He was most interested in this article, two copies of which had been intercepted by the military censorship on their way to Switzerland and Norway. The copy for America had got through. He had obtained only an excerpt from the article, and realized that it was directed against the tsar and the war. I confirmed that this was the case. I asked, is the British government undertaking the defence of the tsar? The sleuth winced and said that he did not think so, but in half-an-hour's conversation tried to inspire me with trust in the British government. I protested about the interception of my manuscripts, demanding their return or an official notification of the reason for their seizure. The sleuth replied that under the Defence of the Realm Act, the military censorship had the right to seize mail without any explanation. I applied to the Post Office for compensation for the undelivered manuscripts, but when I was back in Sweden I received notification from the Post Office that the manuscripts had been impounded.

In Wembley I got to know comrade I.K. Martins, who lived there under police surveillance as a "German". Comrade Martins had been born in Russia of German parentage, had taken part in the revolutionary movement and for this had been deported to Germany, where he had served two years as a soldier and then left for England. There he had worked on various inventions for the "combat tasks" of the Russian revolution. He had been working as a draughtsman in an engine works. In the summer of 1915 some of the firm's office-workers started a campaign against him as a "German" and the manager, to prove that he was not unpatriotic, agreed to sack him. Comrade Martins, with his wife and child, remained out of work, amidst the hostility of the middle-class patriots of the area. Only comrades from the Russian colony kept contact with him. Thanks to their trouble and his half-Russian extraction, comrade Martins managed to get himself out of Britain to New York.

In London I met the former party agitator and journalist, Stanislav Sokolov (Volsky). He was struggling to learn the lessons of the war, but was patriotically inclined. It was very sad to see a valuable organizer leaving the revolutionary path. I argued with him for a long while in order to try to shake off his social patriotism and went on a trip with him to Brighton.

There were many other organizers and journalists in London: Kerzhentsev, who was working somewhere "for defence"; Kapuskas with the Lithuanians; Berzin and Peters with the Letts; Chicherin, who had broken with the liquidators, and Petrov, who had become a Bolshevik in the British Socialist Party. Among the liquidators were Maisky and others.

In midsummer we had news that comrade Bukharin and his wife were on their way from Switzerland through France and Britain. On the day of his arrival in London, comrade Litvinov and I went to the station to meet him. I had not previously met Bukharin and did not know him by sight. Nor did Litvinov. However, we assumed that we would find them and meet somehow. The station was packed with soldiers leaving and their families seeing them off. Hundreds of passengers emerged from a train that had just pulled in. But none of them were "they", the "Russians". But then at last came a couple of vacant-looking Russians looking around in all directions. We decided that these must be the Bukharins. We went up and greeted them. The comrades were most surprised that we could distinguish them from among thousands of passengers, but the secret was simple: we could tell them by their wandering gazes, absent-minded expressions and the small bundles under their arms. We took them to our suburb of Wembley and lodged them with comrade Martins. Bukharin was travelling on the passport of a Jew, M.L. Dolgolevsky, and had as a result of this suffered a great deal of offence from French and English anti-Semites. I sent a number of assignments to Russia with N.M. Bukharina. The comrades underwent quite a few ordeals on the way but still reached Stockholm safely and N.M. reached Russia too.

The organizers of our party work in the London colony took seriously my search for funds for the return to Russia and to regularize illegal transport and communications. Comrade Litvinov found it possible to liquidate the circle and group assets and to allot about £50 from that to me for my work. In August I was ready to leave Britain, but this required certain formalities. My foreign passport was valid only for passage to Paris and was not good for the return. So I decided to use my old red 1907 passport, issued to me by the town elder of Murom. I put my photograph in it and went off to the Russian consulate. My "genuine" Russian physiognomy provoked no suspicions, and a stamp was placed in my passport for the exit from Britain to Russia. With this document it would now be easy to buy a ticket and get on the steamer. However, I only used this passport once, for the exit from Britain. Although the visa had been granted for through travel to Russia I did not use it, considering such a journey unwise.

I said goodbye to the comrades left behind who were envious of my journey, and set out on the pleasant route through the fields and towns to Newcastle. I was already at the quayside on the evening of the same day. Embarkation had not yet commenced; the passengers were waiting in the baggage shed. Among the travellers were many Russians, including some prisoners-of-war who had escaped from Germany through Holland. The British military control appeared to be checking the passengers' documents. I had to put myself out over the prisoners-of-war, as their consular escort had disappeared and they were getting upset not knowing the language. I got them sorted out. The British customs officers and emigration control examined the luggage and wallets of departing passengers without any hurry, swapping jokes. There was no talk about the war: the rising food prices were of greatest concern. Starting up a conversation in French with one of them who was closely acquainted with the industry of the area, the conditions of the workers and so on, I learnt that the night before there had been a Zeppelin raid not far off which had demolished several buildings in a village. My things were not examined, thanks to this conversation, and I got on to the steamer considerably sooner than the others.

The steamer quietly sailed at midnight. The passengers sat in their cabins. In the morning we were allowed to go up on deck, as by then we were far from Britain's shores. Everyone was living in fear of meeting a mine or a submarine. The crew explained to the passengers which cabins had to embark in which lifeboat in an emergency. Any dark object floating ahead of the vessel, any pole sticking out of the water or any puff of smoke on the skyline aroused anxiety. The steamer sailed slowly, not making more than nine or ten knots. The sea seemed to be populated by evil-doers watching over their victims from behind each wave-crest.

I got talking to the Russian soldiers who had escaped from captivity. They were all NCOs; they spoke with pride of the rigours of escape. In London some prince of the Romanov family had presented them with wrist-watches, but they were so bad that some of the "presents" were already broken. We chatted about the war. The travails they had undergone made them hostile to Germans. I began to interest them in the aims of the war. It was clear that people were already thinking about, and they said that Russia had gone in to support France. I gave them our literature to read and explained the true nature of the war. I did this unobtrusively and only in so far as the people interested wanted to talk. That removed any mistrust and we parted friends upon arrival in Norway, exchanging addresses as we said goodbye.

In Christiania I met Alexandra Kollontai, who was now actively assisting the Bolshevik party work: she was helping organize communications. In the Christiania district a "League of Russian Workers" had been formed, which was something like a political club. And what a funny thing: as soon as an organization of Russians is formed there at once begins the squabbling, the intrigues and other such "politics". I had a lot of trouble escaping the persistence of the intriguers and the idleness and stupidity of the different "parties" who wanted to involve me as a referee.

In Scandinavia

Communications with Russia had weakened and transport had come to a stop during my absence. But this time I considered that things could be remedied, as there was money. I decided to use the available funds to investigate all the routes that could serve for transport, and to send as much illegal literature as possible over the frontier, establishing several dumps near the Finnish-Swedish and Norwegian-Russian borders from where our party organizations in Russia could easily obtain all the necessary literature and through which they could transmit news, correspondence and reports back to our foreign centre and central organ.

I found out which routes had been used by our revolutionary organizations in the heyday of the underground from 1900 to 1905. Many of these routes lay in the war zones on the borders of Austria and Germany. Only Finland remained. The difficulties were enormous, as all the frontiers were closely guarded on either side. The summer routes from the north of Norway to Arkhangelsk seemed attractive. It was known that out on the remote shores of the Arctic Ocean the inhabitants along the border between Russia and Norway had good neighbourly relations among themselves, and Russian fishermen and small traders quite often passed in and out of Norwegian ports, coming down as far as Narvik and Trondheim. Russians in small flat-bottomed boats would put in at Vardø, a small town on an island off the north coast of Norway. Between the Murman coast (Kola and Alexandrovsk) and the Norwegian ports of Vardø, Kirkenes and Vadsø, there was a passenger and mail steamer service. Some Russian steamers maintained a regular service to Vardø. It was very tempting to make use of these routes for transport.

I left Christiania for Stockholm. There I found mountains of literature and also comrade Bukharin and the newly-arrived G. Pyatakov and E.B. Bosch. The party group had increased substantially. Comrades Bukharin and Pyatakov had got to know all the leaders of the Swedish left social democrats and were taking an active part in their work, though refraining from public appearances. They wrote articles for the periodical *Kommunist* and leaflets for Russia. I acquainted them with my plans for putting communications and literature on a sound footing and the preparations for my own journey. The comrades approved my proposals and offered their full assistance. They had moved from Switzerland to Stockholm solely because of the proximity to Russia, and to help in establishing revolutionary work there. I now felt a lot stronger knowing that once I had got back to Russia there would be people on the border who could deal with communications requirements.

I picked up the issues of *Sotsial-Demokrat* that had accumulated in Stockholm and sent them off to the Finnish frontier. Through my acquaintance with social democrats in the northern region of Sweden, and also the unions of seamen and river boatmen, I made many contacts in Luleå and Haparanda. Through Luleå, literature and people could be sent to Oulu by Finnish and Swedish fishermen. From Haparanda and its environs there were many routes into Finland. The most preferable and quickest would have been the ferry to Tornio and from there direct by rail to Petersburg. But this was the most difficult as it lay under the scrutiny of gendarmes, counter-intelligence, frontier patrols and customs guards. I nevertheless sought to make use of this route and strike up acquaintances. In Haparanda I was familiar with a social democrat, a small shopkeeper in the footwear trade, and he had many acquaintances among the Finns on the far side of the frontier. He had made contact with a Finnish social-democratic group in Tornio and found one worker comrade there: his name, translated, was "Voice in the Wilderness". I got to know several others but could not communicate as they spoke only Finnish and Swedish. Comrade "Voice in the Wilderness" took on the transport job and, through an interpreter, listened to my suggestions with enthusiasm. He was excited at the task of outwitting the gendarmes and servants of the tsar. He had already dreamed of organizing a special telephone link across the frontier and of setting up a special literature ferry across the Tornio-ioki in a hermetically-sealed container. You felt that this man would do the job with great zeal. I left all the literature with him at the shop-cum-flat, asking him to think it all over and prepare a route by mid-October. Having finished in this corner of the country, I set off through the extreme north of Sweden to Norway, to the shores of the Arctic Ocean and the island town of Vardø.

Just before my departure from Haparanda I met a familiar face. We got talking and I recalled that we had met before at the home of N.D.

Sokolov, who had introduced him to me as a Polish social democrat. His name was Kozlovsky, a barrister. He was travelling to Copenhagen and then back to Petersburg. I used him to tell the Petersburgers via N.D. Sokolov that I would be sending literature and that, for their part, they should apply themselves to its receipt. Kozlovsky was reluctant to talk about his own business, but it was obvious that his journey had nothing to do with the work of the Polish social democracy.

I travelled back to Boden and there changed to a train for Narvik. The railway northwards passes through forests and then desolate plains and as we drew closer to the Norwegian frontier it changed to hilly and then mountainous country. A considerable section of the line was electrified. Narvik is built on the mountainous shore of a fjord, and its inhabitants are engaged in fisheries and shipping. There was a social-democratic newspaper and a very strong party organization in the town. Often in the north of Norway socialists ended up controlling local authorities. From Narvik a long sea passage lay before me, first on a small steamer as far Lødingen but then I would have to pick up a steamer from Bergen to Kirkenes. It was the beginning of September and the north was looking autumnal. It kept raining. Ragged storm clouds often swept the sky and yet the voyage was most interesting in the powerful beauty of the north, along the fantastic twists of the fjords, now crushed by the mountains hanging over the water and now receding far back in gentle slopes behind broad pools of water. The small steamer, packed with passengers and cargo, also took the mail. Every so often it would put into a village landing stage to be greeted by the waiting crowds. At Lødingen I changed to a relatively large steamer and as we progressed northwards past Tromsø and Hammerfest, nature became more stark and off the North Cape took on a severe and majestic aspect. No longer was any forest or greenery in evidence. Black and grey cliffs looked down on all sides. A squally wind with light rain completed the picture. After several days' passage through the fjords and the Arctic Ocean the steamer docked at Vardø.

This small town is built on a little island of sand and stone and has some three thousand inhabitants occupied principally in fishing. There I found a social-democratic newspaper, *Finnmarken* (the name of this region of Norway). One of the party workers, Osman Norgaard, spoke Russian and showed me a dump of our literature left behind in 1906 and 1907. There were about ten thousand pamphlets: anthologies of revolutionary songs, pamphlets on the tax question, and the newspaper *Pomor* and other leaflets for the State Duma elections.

It was possible to send literature and people this way but the route was a long one: to Arkhangelsk or the Murman railway in summer but in winter to the latter only, or else by ski and reindeer over the polar wastes. Crossing the frontier here was easy; the difficulties started further on. The route might serve as a "reserve" in case of obstacles on the Finnish-Swedish border. Comrade Norgaard nevertheless took on the task of making contacts with the crews of Russian vessels. We sorted the literature out, but because many of the pamphlets were out-of-date we decided to leave them at Vardø with comrade Norgaard.

The majority of the working population of this town were socialists, and the fishermen's votes at elections were cast for the Social-Democratic Party. There was also a trade union, a library and a cinema. The town, as compared with Russian ones, was well equipped, and there was electric lighting and main water supply.

Each day in the hotel dining-room I would meet the Russian consul and the British consular representative. Every meeting would be accompanied by an acrimonious dispute about the war. Well, obviously, the official representatives thought as their governments wished them to and the Russian official was deeply shocked by my distrust of his government: my anti-patriotism quite likely provided him with the topic for a denunciation.

Having found out all that was necessary and made arrangements with comrade Norgaard, I set out on the return journey. In Stockholm I prepared for my journey to Russia, and wrote to the foreign section of the Central Committee, comrades Lenin, Zinoviev and Krupskaya. I mapped out a plan of work and a plan of communications and methods of transport. The three newcomers, Bukharin, Bosch and Pyatakov, undertook to maintain links over the routes established. To myself fell the major organizational task. Among my jobs was the formation of an all-Russian centre that could permanently direct the work there; I also had to regularize contacts with abroad and literature supply. Agreement was reached on all questions with Lenin, Zinoviev, Krupskaya, Bukharin, Bosch and Pyatakov. The long-awaited *Kommunist* nos 1–2 and thirteen issues of *Sotsial-Demokrat* had come out by the time I left and the delivery of this literature to Russia would give an enormous boost to the work.

An Illegal Journey

In the second half of October 1915 I said goodbye to my Stockholm friends and headed for Haparanda. I had sent several poods of literature there in advance. Swedish and Finnish comrades were waiting for me, they had succeeded in establishing communication with Helsinki and forwarding literature there from Kemi in parcels by rail using the railwaymen: it went directly to one of the stations on the line from Viipuri to Beloostrov (Terijoki, I believe). My blue-eyed comrade, "Voice in the Wilderness", was to send it over the frontier. To make things easier he had got on friendly terms with the frontier gendarmes. My comrades had devised a plan to get me across, and one evening we went to try it out.

Haparanda and Tornio are separated by the frontier, the river. A precarious wooden bridge some 350 sazhens long had been built across one arm of the Tornio river. In the middle of it was a toll-booth: the bridge was open from eight in the morning to eight at night.

A sentry stood at the Swedish end of the bridge while at the Russian end, some eighty paces away, there was a fence and a guard-post by a wicket gate; to the left were some Finnish farm buildings. My comrades' plan consisted in my crossing the bridge accompanied by "Voice in the Wilderness"; when we had passed over the water, we would use the darkness to jump off and run or hide under the bridge. The plan was risky and we decided to conduct a rehearsal. We set out on our way in the evening, a few minutes before the frontier closed. We had barely started to approach the Russian side when the gendarmes, hearing the creaking of our steps, made for the gate and scanned the bridge. There was nothing to do but turn back, as it would have been unwise to jump down before their very eyes. We tried this three times over, wasting three evenings without success. My friends were demoralized. They had not anticipated such vigilance from the Russian gendarmes, and started to seek new routes through the outlying areas.

I took a room at the Grand Hotel on the very top floor from whose window the bridge and part of the town of Tornio on the far bank were visible. Sitting many hours at the window I could study the tracks and the river-bank with its odd huts and buildings. I began to prepare a plan. It would be aided by the onset of winter weather, when the fields became covered with snow and the river with thin ice. Continuing snowfalls and frost would be necessary for its success. The latter was not long in coming but the snow stopped, the sky cleared and a huge moon commanded the scene, lighting the snow-sprinkled trees, fields and rooftops with silver.

The moonlight was a nuisance: but I could not wait any longer as there were secret police and spies from all countries in Haparanda. I acquainted comrade "Voice in the Wilderness" with my plan and proposed that he wait for me that evening from eight o'clock onwards beneath a red barn not far from the guard-post. The barn stood on high stones so that you could not only lie but even sit under it. The hand baggage and literature had all been ferried over to Tornio by the indefatigable "Voice in the Wilderness", and he had also arranged lodgings for me there.

I set out for the bridge just before eight, got past the Swedish sentry, who was looking aside indifferently, and approached the booth that stood in the middle of the bridge. The toll-collector was inside it. Under cover of the booth I got down under the bridge very quietly. The ice was very weak and I had to cling to the framework that supported the spans. The moon shone generously, and I had to seek shelter in the shadows of some high struts. I took a sharp look around and waited for the frontier to close. The occasional steps of a pedestrian sounded above me. At long last everything became quiet. A small red light was lit at the gate on the Russian side. This meant that the frontier had been closed. I attempted to move forward cautiously along the dark side. But the ice was still so weak that as soon as I let go of the framework it started to crack treacherously. I located a slightly smoother patch, pushed myself off from the strut with all my might, slid as if on skates to the next one and paused momentarily. My hearing grew sharper and my eyesight more acute. The Russian bank was nearby. The slightest unusual sound and my enterprise would be doomed. I could see a gendarme walking beyond the fence to put out the electric light at the hut entrance and then go in himself. There they were, the whole lot of them; sitting in the guard-post and now and again glancing out of the window at the moonlit surroundings. Another skate, and so on right to the bank. It was quiet in the village; only the dogs were barking on either side of the border. The moon rose high, completely removing all the shadows. The bridge began to curve down to the ground, so I could not walk but started crawling. Finally a hundred paces away were the gendarmes and further off to the left was the little red barn on its stone supports. Lying down, I tried to spot the enemies but failed, so I made a dash towards the old barn. There "Voice in the Wilderness" met me, joyfully shaking my hand and then taking me to the town. We cut through the back yards to the main street. All around it was deserted and frosty. We found the house where a comrade, a Finnish social democrat who worked in the tailoring trade, lived. The family was a big one but the house was orderly. We were welcomed most cordially, but the landlord and landlady did not speak Russian, so there was time for reflection.

The first step had been successful. What lay ahead? My "Voice in the Wilderness" was cheerful, and confident of a happy outcome. That same day he had been to Kemi. There too were comrades who were taking an active part in getting me through. They had a flat ready and had planned out my journey. By evening the next day I had been dressed in a worker's suit, my pockets crammed with apples, given a local passport and escorted by two comrades to the station. My erstwhile hosts wished me every success. We crossed the river by ferry, and at the station we found a mixed train going as far as Oulu. A gendarme examined the passport, and the train set out slowly on its way. Three or four hours later we were in Kemi. There we were met, but caution led one of them to take me by roundabout routes to my resting place. Soldiers were stationed in the town, and there were secret agents and counter-intelligence at the station. We found our way to the flat and there I was given a separate room. The hosts were very sorry not to know foreign languages because then they could have chatted to me. The attitude of them all was touching and comradely.

From Kemi to Oulu the journey was the responsibility of an organizer of local social-democratic work. The courageous, frank nature of this comrade won me over. Here I no longer had any doubts but felt sure that I would arrive safely. The following day we were on our way. Without travelling right into Oulu, where there was a gendarme check, we jumped off and walked some six versts along forest paths and the main road into the city. We crossed a bridge over a torrent and reached the offices of the Oulu social-democratic daily paper. In the editorial room I was welcomed by the organ's chief editor, the deputy for this constituency, and others. I was offered a room by comrade Uskila, the deputy editor. That same evening we went out in a small comradely company to a restaurant and took a private room, where my aides for the journey and my Oulu friends drank a toast to my happy journey and I made a brief report on the state of affairs abroad and the different viewpoints on the war. The comrades were in agreement with me on everything, but warned that the parliamentary majority and the majority of the Central Committee members of Finnish social democracy tended towards opportunism, while the petty-bourgeois and intellectual circles were infected with Germanophilia.

Many thousands of Finns and Swedes had gone to Germany to fight on the eastern frontiers for the "liberation" of Finland. The Social Democratic Party had to exert efforts to counter Germanophilia and so-called "activism", i.e. co-operation with the German General Staff against Russia. The situation was complicated by the increase in reactionary pressure from the Russian government. Several weeks before my arrival there were arrests and raids throughout Finland, mainly in connection with the activists, who had set up a fairly stable organization. They had special escape routes for German prisoners-of-war and an espionage network in the Russian army. The Finnish activists received large stocks of arms and supplies for their members, conducting agitation for an armed assault on Russian barracks, fortifications, dumps, etc. This agitation, however, met opposition from the social democrats and did not find advocates in the mass of workers or among the *torppari*, and instances of armed attacks were isolated.

From Oulu to Helsinki two people undertook to escort me: my

travelling companion from Kemi, comrade Adam Ljakonen, and comrade Uskila.

While they were preparing the journey and sorting out the formalities, I spent two marvellous days among kind warm-hearted comrades, looked round the city and tried to adjust myself to future illegal life in Russia. I came to an arrangement with the people in Oulu about transport of literature and the ferrying of people and information. They agreed to help. Everything was at last ready and we set off. At the station they pointed out by an agreed sign all the Russian spies and plain-clothes gendarmes. My physiognomy did not arouse curiosity, and I got into the carriage unnoticed by anyone. Comrade Uskila spoke German, so we could communicate with each other. The three of us occupied a compartment and we reached Helsinki in every comfort and without any special alarms.

The comrades stopped at a hotel but lodged me at the People's House, the building of the Central Committee of the Finnish Social Democratic Party, in a room belonging to the Swedish section of Finnish social democracy. Here I made the acquaintance of several members of the Central Committee and also some trade unionists. I looked up the deputy, Persinen, whom I had got to know in Berlin, and comrade Rovio, a Finnish metalworker who was very familiar with Petersburg party workers. With his assistance I found a Russian worker who for some money surrendered his passport, which would be necessary for me to cross through Beloostrov, and I also got to know the city and its party organization.

My constant companion and guardian throughout Helsinki was comrade Wiik, a social-democratic deputy in the Sejm, the editor of a Swedish-language social-democratic newspaper and keeper of the party archives. With him I went round all the Helsinki co-operatives, the huge dairies and bakeries whose equipment was the last word in technology. The People's House was the pride of the Helsinki organizations and in fact would have done credit to any West European capital. The workers' movement in Finland was clamped down in a military vice. Troops were deployed throughout the country, though it was chiefly sailors who were posted in Helsinki. Revolutionary work among them was conducted wholly by Russian organizations, for ignorance of the language and fear of provocations prevented the Finnish social democrats from carrying out propaganda among Russian soldiers.

It was odd to see a city with such working-class amenities only a few hours' travelling time from the capital of the tsarist bashi-bazouks. Reaction's hatred for this little country, doggedly defending its independence from the tsarist authorities, was quite understandable. However, as the situation developed, it became harder for Finland to maintain its freedom and the fate of that country was tied inevitably to the revolutionary movement in our country. The revolutionary social democrats of Finland were already attempting to approach their policy from this angle, but things did not yet go beyond the services rendered in transport and ferrying people over the frontier.

Before my departure I made arrangements with comrade Wiik for the despatch of literature and exchanged codes and addresses.

3

Petersburg

I SPENT the journey from Helsinki to Petersburg in the company of naval officers and military personnel. I got safely through the gendarme post at Beloostrov and a gloomy morning greeted me in Petersburg with a light autumn rain. The sleuths and spies who met passengers at the Finland station did not yet know me, and my appearance in no way bothered them.

The existence of relatives in Petersburg spared me the need to go immediately round the illegal rendezvous. I turned up as an unexpected guest at my own people's place in the working-class district beyond the Neva Gate. I at once received a lot of information about what militant workers in Petersburg were doing and thinking.

I decided to spend the first week or two, that is, until I fell into the spies' net, with my sisters, who lived in the Steklyanny district. I sought out everyone whom I knew or merely remembered from party work, but they were mostly people who had already left it.

On the information of the Petersburg Committee I found the bourgeois apartment of the "young gentleman" (Starck) and that same evening met S. Narvsky (Bagdatiev) and V. Schmidt at his place. They acquainted me with the state of affairs on the Petersburg Committee. All party workers were at that time under the impression that a victory had been won over the social chauvinists on the question of elections to the War Industries Committee. I, in turn, acquainted them with my assignment and also with the state of affairs abroad. Party workers had come together sufficiently in Petersburg by this time for work to be carried out in all districts, but especially well in the Vyborg district. A strong party organization had been formed in that district which was run exclusively by the workers themselves.

It was very difficult to convene a plenum of the Petersburg Committee, so I made my report in sections and to each group of party workers separately. Comrades were very glad at my arrival and for news of West European workers. The Central Committee's proposal to organize a Bureau of the Central Committee was approved by all with the exception of Starck and "Miron" (Chernomazov). "Miron" indulged in some demagogy at the expense of the foreign members while Starck had his own proposal, to make the Petersburg Committee into the Central Committee Bureau. His argument was that by now the Petersburg Committee was the effective centre of our work in Russia. This view was not shared by the majority of members of the Petersburg Committee, nor by the leading party workers. Dual membership of the Petersburg Committee and the Central Committee Bureau would anyway be inconvenient and risky.

On questions of tactics and strategy we were completely unanimous. The principal activity of the Petersburg Committee would be to lead economic conflicts, political demonstrations and, anywhere and everywhere, the struggle against social chauvinism and the liquidators, its errand-boys in working-class circles. And everywhere our comrades emerged triumphant, having behind them the enormous majority of workers. The most notable work of this period was without doubt the election campaign for the War Industries Committees, which took place in September 1915. Unfortunately, I have found nothing on this in the archive of the Petersburg Committee for that period. I have however managed to compile a relatively complete picture of that work.

I had arrived in Petersburg about three weeks after the fiasco of the Guchkov-Gvozdev scheme to bring workers into the War Industries Committees. The campaign had been legally prepared by the bourgeoisie and defensist socialist circles for more than a month. Our organizations also took a wide part in that work but, because of their anti-defensist, revolutionary internationalist position, they could only operate illegally. They had to work under very difficult conditions; but the Petersburg Committee emerged from this struggle against the defensists' bloc with the bourgeoisie for influence in the Petersburg proletariat with honour and glory.

The Central War Industries Committee arose in 1915 as a result of the campaign for the "militarization of industry". It had existed until August merely as an administrative department of the Council of Congresses of Representatives of Commerce and Industry, the all-Russian organization of lockers-out. The basic objective of the Central War Industries Committee was to procure orders for the army and share them out among factory owners. They were thus aiming to remove "unfair" competition between industrialists, winning orders by backstage methods and speculating on different ministers and greater and lesser princes and their prostitutes in sharing out the juicy revenue. Of course, help for the army and a firm wish to ensure all necessary supplies also formed part of their plans. A congress of representatives of local and regional War Industries Committees was held from 25 to 27 July 1915 at which statutes were drafted. On 27 August these statutes were approved by the State Duma, received the tsar's assent and became law in the form of the "War Industries Committees Act". Only later were the words "of the Council of

Congresses of Representatives of Commerce and Industry" removed. A place on these committees had by law been allocated to a workers' delegation.

Practical-minded industrialists were concerned no less than the government with the struggle against the mounting revolutionary movement but hoped, by harnessing workers to the chariot of militarism not from fear but conscience, to isolate them from the "Bolshevik and defeatist virus".

The awakening of working-class revolutionary activity, in the Petersburg area especially, where until recently over a half of the output of war material was concentrated, greatly perturbed bourgeois circles. The more percipient "captains of industry" found Okhrana and police intervention in the workers' movement to be most damaging, as it exacerbated relations between capital and labour, and it regarded such intervention as one of the causes of the political protests that disrupted the normal reproduction of profit in the factories. The red spectre evoked no idle fear among the Minins and Pozharskys of our day, who were distinguished from the Nizhni-Novgorod merchants of old only by the fact that they brought no offerings to the "altar of the fatherland" but on the contrary contrived to grab a large slice of the contracts, all in the name of the homeland and its defence. But industrialists who had no faith in the ability of the military dictatorship to solve the labour problems, devised a scheme for latching workers on to their own business, involving them in the cause of the war, thereby making the whole workers' movement prey to their own fortunes.

In its invitation for workers' representatives to stand in the elections, the Central War Industries Committee defined their function as follows: "Workers' representatives will, by taking part in the work of the Central War Industries Committees, assist in the great and sacred task of aiding our army. They will co-operate in the most thorough investigation of the conditions necessary for raising the productivity of factory labour and aid more effective work towards the defence of country." The "defence of the fatherland" required exactly as much of workers as was necessary for employers to secure the greatest profits.

The bourgeois defenders of the fatherland waged their campaign in Petersburg first, hoping, by conducting it successfully there, to force all the Russian proletariat to follow, laying down all means of class self-defence in the face of organized capital. In their campaign the employers in the War Industries Committees found loyal allies among those "socialists" who had accepted the war. The latter exploited their proximity to the working masses and placed all their authority at the service of the bourgeoisie's imperialist interests. The bourgeois ideologists of "Great Russia", from Struve to Guchkov and Ryabushinsky, never managed to "condition" workers in even small numbers, so bad were they at concealing their true interests. The talents of the Potresovs, Maslovs, Plekhanovs and other lesser fry were necessary for that role — they knew best how to administer nationalist poison to working-class people. The whole fund of marxist phraseology was put into action: here you had the interests of economic development, there freedom from German "domination", and there the interests of "democracy" and the "internationalism" of defence. A new form of solidarity — the patriotic, mutual extermination of proletarians!

However, all attempts to create a "class peace" were unsuccessful, as Russian workers were disinclined to become the cattle that the capitalists and the tsarist régime had condemned them to be. The Association of Factory and Plant Owners remained as reactionary in its labour policy as ever, even if it had a protective "defensist" coating. In its struggle against workers' discontent it relied as of old upon the police and the Okhrana. We heard, in the press, at conferences and even from "opposition" representatives of patriotic capital, about "petitioning" for the repeal (with, of course, the reservation "for the duration of the war") of all the restrictions prescribed by the factories acts concerning the employment of female and adolescent labour, and also "suspension, for the duration of the war, of the restrictions in force on the length of the working days and overtime". The coal-owning sharks of the Donets Basin and the patriotic iron and steel employers of the south were dreaming of one thing alone: abolishing holidays, increasing the number of compulsory working days to 360 per year and demanding as much cheap manpower as possible, such as Chinese and prisoners-of-war. You had to have a thoroughly defensist psychology to preach class peace under such conditions!

War Industry Socialists

IN ORDER to realize his desires Guchkov approached the workers' group of the Insurance Council and several major hospital funds for support. This approach was received by the workers' representatives at the beginning of August. The members of the Insurance Council's workers' group told Guchkov that they had been empowered by the workers only on matters of insurance and could not enter into any discussion of questions connected with the elections to the War Industries Committees. The insurance people suggested that he approach the working men and women in the factories and plants directly. The hospital funds answered him in the same vein. So the industrialists were unable to make use of the workers' insurance bodies for their chauvinist ends.

After this a special patriotic proclamation befitting the occasion was issued by the Central War Industries Committee, together with election rules. Both items were displayed in the factories and were also handed out as leaflets. The Petersburg Committee decided to utilize this campaign to unfurl the revolutionary internationalist banner of social democracy. This campaign, for the first time during the war, openly and legally laid before workers questions of the domestic and international policy of tsarism. And workers did not fail to make broad use of the opportunity. Party organizations used every tactic to prolong the campaign. Meetings were arranged in the plants at which two world-views met — internationalism, which knew of only one fatherland for the working class, the socialist system — and the other, conciliatory defensism, proposing a "fatherland" for workers even in the conditions of tsarism. The appalling situation within the country tied the hands of the patriotic socialists, so they tried to link their policy to the revolutionary tasks standing before all Russian workers at that time.

The bourgeoisie of all shades and the legal "democratic press" agitated for workers to participate in the War Industries Committees and tried everything to inflame chauvinist passions. The social patriots, or the "War Industry Socialists" as they were then called, did not lag behind the bourgeois chauvinists. They put all their reserves of "marxism" into action to prove that the "defence of the fatherland" principle, dressed up in the guise of the War Industries Committees, did not diverge from the idea of workers' internationalism. The social-patriotic newspaper *Rabochee Utro* ("Workers' Morning"), taking into account the revolutionary mood of Petersburg workers, played upon their "militant mood" and invited workers "even if the bourgeois would not let them in [in reality the bourgeoisie were beckoning them most enthusiastically] to unlock the doors with their horny hands".

Chkheidze's Duma faction, which had been rendered impotent by the internal split — Chkhenkeli's and Khaustov's open patriotism — vacillated on the question of participation in the War Industries Committees. N.S. Chkheidze, who regarded himself as more left than the rest, still stood for workers' representatives' participation. In a personal meeting he proved to me at great length that although he stood for joining he was in no way in favour of working as part of that organization, but for organizing workers and anti-government forces. The social patriots would quote his "pro-participation" position, dropping all the qualifications. Thus the Menshevik Duma faction was also guilty of hoodwinking the workers over the elections.

Numerous resolutions and mandates adopted at huge meetings in the plants indicated the scale of the pre-election work of the

Petersburg Committee. At the giant Putilov works a special mandate was adopted; but at the majority of the others resolutions like the following one at the New Lessner works were adopted:

> We, workers at the New Lessner works, having discussed the question of participation in the War Industries Committees and the election of deputies to works committees, have resolved: the present world war has been hatched and is being waged exclusively in the interests of bourgeois-capitalist society. The proletariat has no interest in the current war. It will bring it nothing but millions of comrades fallen in the field, millions of cripples and destitute. Simultaneously with the declaration of war on the Central Empires, the commanding classes of Russia have declared a ruthless war upon the whole labouring class, the proletariat. They have strangled the workers' trade unions and destroyed the workers' press. They have vilified and despatched the proletariat's representatives to the State Duma to do hard labour. And now, after thirteen months of war, after innumerable defeats, and convinced of the impossibility of beating the external enemy without flattening the country, they are now making a bid to lure the working class over to their side, and the workers who only yesterday were being shot down are being called to the defence of the "fatherland". Our reply can be one only: the proletariat will fight for the emancipation and liberation of the labouring masses of the population, whatever nationality they belong to. We reject any activity connected with support for the international bloodbath, or support for the commanding classes who have crushed and oppressed the labouring population for centuries on end. We recognize that only the complete destruction of the capitalist police-autocratic régime will be able to bring the country out of the situation that has come about. We demand the immediate convening of an All-Russian Constituent Assembly elected on the basis of universal, direct, equal and secret suffrage. We demand the immediate restoration of all the proletariat's trade unions and cultural and educational organizations; we demand freedom of the press, freedoms of assembly and association. We regard the broad organization of the working class in trade union, cultural and educational, and strictly class political organizations to be the most pressing urgent task of the hour. The police-autocratic régime is pushing the country towards a whole series of catastrophes: having clapped our best comrades into heavy convicts' shackles, it still holds them to this day behind locked prison gates, in exile or hard labour — these, the fighters for our better future. We demand the immediate release of all those arrested, exiled and sentenced for political activity.

Very little material is preserved from the first delegates' meeting. The most detailed description of the events of 27 September 1915 was made at my request by comrade Sergei Narvsky (Bagdatiev), who was sent to the delegates' meeting by the Petersburg Committee with the mandate of the Putilov worker, Kudryashev. This letter was sent by me to the central organ, *Sotsial-Demokrat*, and was printed in no. 30.

I shall use it as a historical document and take from it the extracts that are of interest to us.

On the main point, that is, the attitude towards the war, the majority of workers accepted our point of view. But with the mental confusion at present reigning in the workers' movement, it is no wonder that in the broadly correct resolutions and mandates adopted in the majority of plants extraneous points crept in, consciously or unconsciously taken from the ideology of the other camp (liquidationism). In particular various "conciliators" and "unifiers" sinned in this direction. The latter's organization almost evaded making a clear decision whether or not to enter the War Industries Committees. They wanted to call a workers' congress and decide the question there. By contriving to unite opposing elements, they gave in at their very first serious political test. At the delegates' meeting they split up according to their sympathies: being either for us or for the liquidator-Narodnik bloc. . . . 198 delegates were present at the meeting (in all there should have been about 220). We had managed to hold preliminary meetings for only a part (about sixty) of our delegates, the core of whom was the delegation from one very large works. At these preliminary meetings a proposed plan of action was presented for the party and its supporters at the delegates' meeting; but the necessity was pointed out here that from the viewpoint of the Petersburg Committee, speakers presented before the meeting had to be able to put the internationalists' point of view on the current war and the consequent non-participation of workers in the War Industries Committees boldly and distinctly without superfluous rhetoric. To put these intentions into practice it would be more convenient to send to the meeting as speakers individuals who had not been elected in the plants. The delegates' names and addresses were registered officially and therefore the public appearance of the delegates themselves with anti-war and revolutionary speeches might give the authorities and the public prosecutor opportunities that speeches by "unknown individuals" would not give them and this was a major consideration. There were two such individuals at the meeting, i.e. by no means sufficient for it to be said that their voice could decide the question. The majority was ours even without them. They were able to abstain from voting but the malevolent and treacherous gossip issuing from the liquidators at the meeting about the presence of outsiders and their threats to announce this openly to the meeting, forced the "appointed" comrades to cast their vote too; but when the ballot papers had been counted up our majority was a clear one even without their votes. It should be remembered that the second vote was by the list of delegates' names; besides, we could not have known what was awaiting us once we had gone out of the doors of the meeting. All this was perfectly well known and understood by the liquidators and their representatives on the platform. But having suffered a reverse and being left in a minority, not only among the social democrats but even in their bloc with Narodniks and non-party delegates, these fraudulent proclaimers of "unity" conducted a not only divisive but treacherous policy. . . . On our side there were two speakers who each spoke twice. The reporter from the Petersburg Committee at the meeting was "Vladimir" (V. Zalezhsky). On the other side, under the guise of different "tendencies", more than a dozen noisy emotive speeches were delivered. Our speakers took the Petersburg Committee mandate as their basis and elaborated upon it. Starting out from this mandate they also proposed a form of "declaration" to the War Industries Committee on their refusal to join it. The declaration had been drafted in advance and distributed by the Petersburg Committee. At first we got 95 votes at the voting by name, but when some of the comrades had already left, thinking that the question was settled and the meeting would thereupon end as it was now very late (1 o'clock), we got 90 votes against (the liquidator-Narodnik-non-party bloc) 81 votes. At the beginning of the session the liquidators had been sure of their majority. The choice of Gvozdev and not "Kudryashev" as chairman was a false omen. Kudryashev did not appear as chairman, first because several unifier internationalist votes had been cast for Gvozdev before "Kudryashev" had arrived at the meeting and so it "would be awkward" for them, as they said, to vote for someone else in the run-off; secondly, at the start of the meeting when the line of struggle was still unclear, many people did not attach importance to the question of the composition of the platform. Be that as it may, the liquidators, once having suffered defeat, completely lost their heads. Not daring to check the votes themselves, they raised a rumpus and started to leave. They demanded that Gvozdev leave the chair as their representative on the platform but he refused, stating that the voting had been checked in every way and was quite proper and that he could see no grounds for leaving the meeting. We still had to move our mandate, to which we had wanted to append to the declaration, to the vote. The delegates from Sestroretsk and the Izhor works said that they had to go as the last train was leaving soon. The atmosphere of the meeting had by then reached its peak. They had been in session since twelve noon with nothing to eat. (The War Industries Committee had treated us to tea, or rather, hot water, without even any sugar. . . .)

Much was made in the social-patriotic resolution of what we had already heard from their speakers. A few workers had been arrested at several plants. At the election of delegates the liquidators' bloc had put on their list these arrested workers, who had not yet been dismissed from the plant. The mass voted for that list in the hope thereby of getting their workmates released. In the middle of the debate at the delegates' meetings, the liquidators proposed to discuss this matter. For their part, they proposed to approach the Central War Industries Committee with a proposal that it mediate for the release of those arrested. A section of our people, thinking of continuing the meeting the following day, considered backing the motion and adjourning the meeting until the arrested were released. It was clear to us that this meant breaking off the meeting and finally dispersing without having passed a principled resolution covering the war and the War Industries Committees. A conflict with the authorities over such a purely police issue had no international significance and deprived the campaign of the importance that we attached to it. Comrade "Kudryashev" spoke therefore against the proposal to adjourn the meeting with a demand for the release of the arrested. In the event of the arrest of any of the delegates the proletariat would try to utilize all means of struggle open to it. It demanded moreover the release of those already arrested. Comrade "Kudryashev"'s motion was carried. The internationalists who had vacillated on that question realized the danger of adjourning the meeting.

A Repeat Election Campaign

The refusal of Petersburg workers to accept the slogan of "defence" and collaboration with the Guchkovs and Ryabushinskys threw all the patriots into great confusion. The Menshevik defensists were the first to recover, and tried to demonstrate the "uninternationalness" of the "boycottists' " position. The bourgeois press supported them and lent its pages to the ideas of the social-chauvinists. The defensists, learning from their unsuccessful experience in Petersburg, wished to regain ground in Moscow and managed things more cunningly there. The elections were planned in a hushed-up way, without pre-election meetings or any kind of agitation. The Okhrana helped the social patriots by arresting hundreds of Bolshevik internationalists. Thus Moscow industrialists obtained a docile majority of backward workers from the textile and other factories, but a considerable portion of Moscow metalworkers refused, in spite of the deception and threats, to take part in the elections to the War Industries Committees. But here the liquidators did not baulk at a split. After Moscow they reared their heads again in Petersburg.

Soon after, Gvozdev's letter denouncing the "irregularity" of the elections appeared. The majority of the industrialists at first regarded fresh elections with scepticism. They knew the Petersburg proletariat. Still, Guchkov managed to overcome his colleagues' scepticism and force them to accommodate Gvozdev. The hopes of the lockers-out from the "Council of Congresses" to split Petersburg workers had been dashed, so they decided to "assist" Gvozdev. Rumours had been going round Petersburg about backstage negotiations between the Gvozdev lot and Guchkov long before any public statements. It was known to us that Gvozdev had been a private guest at Guchkov's cabinet, but their preparatory "electoral pact" had been kept secret. In the week following 20 November a notice appeared in the newspapers announcing elections for the Central War Industries Committee on 22 November. Guchkov personally petitioned the City Governor to hold a meeting of electors, but the latter resolved not to give permission without first consulting the minister Khvostov. He found no obstacles to further elections. News of the election preparations appeared in the press a couple of days beforehand. From this it could be understood that Guchkov and Gvozdev wanted to catch their Bolshevik opponents off-guard. The Petersburg Committee succeeded with great difficulty in organizing a meeting of some of the electors and discussing a prepared resolution on the second elections, and this was adopted on 21 November. The story went around working-class circles that in view of the shortage of time and for greater "authenticity", Gvozdev would himself distribute the election notices from a motor car belonging to the War Industries Committee. However much the Guchkovites rushed things, the meeting on the 22nd could not be held — there was not a single hall free that day. So despite the wishes of the liquidators, the workers had a whole week in front of them. During that time the internationalist electors proved unable to assemble in large numbers as they were persistently trailed. The Okhrana tried to ensure the "freedom" of the Gvozdev company. Searches of several comrades were carried out. No less than five electors were detained in that period. For the rest of the week workers at several plants where the "liquidator-narodnik" bloc had prevailed, as at Eiwas, organized meetings and stripped their electors of their mandate to take part in the second elections. The Petersburg Committee conducted a struggle against Gvozdevism throughout the various districts.

Organized industrialists wholly supported Gvozdev and co. and even protected them from attacks by the police, although all the documents on the elections had been already passed to the Okhrana. It was important and desirable for the bourgeoisie to divide the workers, in order to deprive them of their power to resist the increasing exploitation, and also to convert all those who went along with defensists into wires conducting bourgeois politics into the mass of workers. The Petersburg Committee took good account of this and firmly disassociated itself from the re-run elections to the War Industries Committee.

The "Petersburg Initiative Group" took the work of the Gvozdevites under its wing, issuing a special appeal in defence of the Gvozdevites where they spouted indignation at the Bolsheviks for using an "illegal printing-press" in the struggle against themselves. The appeal did not hesitate to lie, stating that their friends had not joined the committees "for defence".

The counter-revolutionary and anti-proletarian physiognomy of the workers' group in the Central War Industries Committee was soon to exhibit itself in practice. The defensists tried to use their position as "workers' representatives" to fight the developing strike movement. They drafted proposals for conciliation chambers, interfered as mediators and tried in every way to minimize the number of disputes. Through their supporters they advised workers to address petitions to them, organized questionnaires and so on. During disputes they displayed unusual zeal, but their diplomatic efforts had no success. Labour diplomats proved as powerless as any others. Class struggle developed according to its own laws, conflicts took their course and resolved themselves according to the balance of forces.

A *Secret Meeting of Industrialists*

From every corner of Russia I received information on the strike movement which the military censorship banned from legal newspapers. These reports were, of course, very sketchy, but I could already piece together a general picture of the relentless growth of the movement from the spring of 1915 onwards. In that year the Petersburg area marched ahead as before followed by the Moscow and Ivanovo-Voznesensk areas. The movement began to shift from economic demands to political struggle and, in July and August, overflowed into a series of political strikes. Petersburg was the centre of political activity. Our party's Petersburg Committee served effectively as the leading organ for the provinces.

The government of Nicholas II was greatly perturbed by the growth of the revolutionary movement and worked out means of fighting it. Arrests, banishments and the despatch of the insubordinate to penal battalions at the front were practised wholesale. But alongside this it strove also to bring "pressure" to bear on the factory-owners too. Thus in the autumn of 1915 a secret conference between their representatives and the Okhrana was arranged. I received the following report on it, which is almost verbatim:

> A conference took place in Petersburg at the end of October at the army headquarters under the chairmanship of General Prince Tumanov.
> *Tumanov* (in the chair): Gentlemen, I have gathered you here to find out what you are doing for your employees with regard to improving their conditions. At the present time criminal propaganda is being carried out among workers and a certain disquiet can be observed among them. It is necessary to counteract this to some extent. . . . Of course the most effective way is to eliminate the possibility of discontent arising from the shortage of goods. At present it is really hard to obtain goods in the shops and everything is dear. To get at the root of this discontent it is essential to make it easier for workers to obtain basic necessities by setting up a number of retail shops. In addition, it would be desirable to establish canteens for the workers, which would give them the chance of obtaining a good quality lunch at a reasonable price. With this in mind, would you

be so kind as to report what you are doing in the plants.
A representative from the Neva Shipyards: Some 5,000 work in the yards and there is a canteen and a store. The former is used by about 1,000 and the latter by 4,500.
Thornton: 3,000 work here and so there is a shop and a canteen which are used by some 2,000. The average wage for labourers is 90 kopeks for women and 1.30 rubles for men.
Lessner: 9,200 people work here. A retail shop is currently being organized for employees at Lessners, Eiwas, Nobels, Phoenix and other plants for about 22,000 altogether. All the management is unreservedly in the hands of our boards: in accordance with the rules of statutes, anyone can have as many votes as shares he has purchased in the firm. Shares are at ten rubles. Anyone who has paid the initial fee can obtain goods. As regards sitting on the board and the commissions you can rest assured on this, your Excellency. Only those who have purchased a full share can be elected to the board and that is pretty difficult for workers. The Association of Factory and Plant Owners is at present forming a large organization bringing together all plant-owners who wish to join. The purpose of the organization is to form a chain of co-operatives as a counterweight to the workers' co-operatives. Working capital has been raised by five- or six-ruble contributions from each worker employed in the undertaking. Each worker shall in addition contribute ten kopeks to cover the work of administering the co-operative. This money is only a loan and, when the need has passed, it will be refunded to the plants that contributed it. By this method it will be possible to set up more viable shops than purely workers' organizations can.
Prince Tumanov: How quiet is your place? Did you have a clean-out after the strike?
Lessner: Indeed we did, your Excellency! Seven were arrested and we can say that the workers are now even content "We can work in peace now," they keep saying. One hardened agitator was among those arrested. Just imagine, it had been quite impossible to find him! He was working in the plant under a foreign name, he would take two caps with him and acted out a comedy of disguises and remained elusive for quite a time. He had been taken on under a foreign name. And ex-Duma member Ozol was arrested at his house.
Prince Tumanov: 1,300 rubles in German and American money was found at Ozol's. Apparently he had only just arrived from abroad.
Atlas: 750 work here. There are no organized facilities.
Metal Works: 7,000 work here. There is a canteen for 350; everything's quiet.
Baranovsky: 2,300 working here. There is nothing to report.
Voronin, Lutsch and Cheshire: This firm is a combine of seven factories with 5,500 workers all told. The average wage for a labourer is 1.90 rubles.
Siemens-Schuckert: The works produces military and naval equipment. 800 are employed; a fully-equipped canteen exists, but the workers are not using it as yet. At the present moment the workers themselves are

organizing the canteen with the assistance of the management; they are also organizing a retail shop.

Parviainen: 5,500 working here. There are no shops or canteens. Average wage for labourers is 1.60 rubles.

Prince Tumanov: How are you managing after the strike? Have you cleared out the dubious elements?

Parviainen: Indeed so. 160 have been dismissed and five of the most hardened arrested. It's quiet now and everyone's working.

Prince Tumanov: Are there any due for call-up among those dismissed?

Parviainen: Yes. We immediately reported them to the military governor, so they have probably been rounded up by now.

Prince Tumanov: And how, gentlemen, do you arrange it so that dismissed workers can't get into someone else's works? Are there concrete safeguards that they remain outside the gates?

Voronin, Lutsch and Cheshire: We have blacklists kept by the Association of Factory and Plant Owners. Information about all workers, but chiefly all those dismissed for unreliability, must immediately be paused to the Association of Factory and Plant Owners who will, in turn, circularize all factories and plants which are members of the association, to the effect that the aforesaid workers should not be taken on at the plant. A dismissed worker may start at any plant or factory but the management is obliged to dismiss him within three days without reason being given. In this way we are able to rid ourselves of undesirable elements simply and conveniently.

Wagon Works: 2,500 employed. There is a canteen for 500.

Prince Tumanov: How are you managing after the strike? Many dismissed and arrested?

Wagon Works: No one has been dismissed.

Prince Tumanov: How can that be? You had a strike so you could have cleared out the undesirable elements but you didn't take advantage of the occasion? You're surely not waiting for another strike?

Wagon Works: We are to blame, your Excellency. At our works, the workers stand so closely together that we are afraid to dismiss anyone for fear of serious repercussions. The workers have stated bluntly: "If anyone is victimized for this strike we shall not go to work." And we knew that they would stand by their promise. We handed a list of the fourteen most dangerous ones to the Okhrana with a request to have them arrested on the quiet, but the Okhrana have not yet done anything.

Prince Tumanov (to the gendarme acting as secretary): Note that down and make the arrests.

Siemens-Schuckert (Dynamo Works): 1,800 are employed here and there is a shop and a canteen.

Skorokhod: 3,000 work here and there is a shop. We also, your Excellency, have sent a list of those whose arrest we would greatly appreciate to the Okhrana but no one has yet been arrested.

Prince Tumanov (to the gendarme-cum-secretary): Note it and have them arrested! Tell them up there to make immediate arrests when they are requested.

Putilov: 24,000 working here. There is a shop and a canteen for 2,800. The management of the shop is concentrated entirely in our hands, as we joined it as members and have been elected to the board.

Prince Tumanov: What was afoot at your works yesterday?

Putilov: Permit me, your Excellency, to report on that in complete confidence. . . . (It subsequently emerged that on that day, unknown persons not from among the workers in the factory had organized a meeting and sought to provoke action by the workers.)

Prince Tumanov: And what else are you doing for your workers? Are you contributing anything to the consumer association?

Putilov: Nothing.

Prince Tumanov: Why nothing? You have such colossal revenue — you should allocate some of it to the workers.

Putilov: How can we, your Excellency? We are squarely in debt and we can hardly make ends meet.

Cable Works: 1,300 are working here. There is nothing to report.

Mechanical and Boiler Works: 850 working here. There is a shop with the usual rules.

One of the representatives states: Your Excellency has been good enough to suggest that canteens be organized for workers. This is indisputably important and useful in fighting criminal organizations, but it does pose a certain risk. For workers can use the canteens for clandestine meetings and gatherings. Besides, any undesirable conversations and so forth are possible over lunch. It is essential to give serious thought to how we can avoid this danger. It is very awkward to install foremen in the canteen as overseers.

Prince Tumanov: Can't you somehow shorten the lunch break so that workers have only just enough time to get their dinner down? That would exclude the risk of conversations.

Factory-Owners: Not at all. Many workers with families go home to dinner and they wouldn't have enough time. The workers would not as a whole agree to that.

One of the gendarmes: Then fit them up with gramophones. Have them turned up loud so that no one can hear a word. In for a penny, in for a pound: then everything'll be all right.

Prince Tumanov: Exactly! And what's more, we could fit the factories out with paintings on patriotic subjects. Everything will then be nice and peaceful. Gentlemen, I am most grateful for the reports you have made and may I apologize for tearing you away from your normal work in the plants; it has been necessary owing to highly important considerations. You are earning enormous revenues and to ensure that the work continues it is vital you give a little to the workers. Let me say, in closing, that I am always at your service. Do turn to me in case of any need and I shall do everything in my power. Until we meet again.

The Ninth of January

In December, the Petersburg comrades began to prepare for public activity on the traditional day of 9 January. The Petersburg Committee put forward a plan for a one-day strike and demonstrations under the slogans: "a constituent assembly", "an eight-hour day" and "a democratic republic" for discussion in the various city districts. On the demonstrations the attitude to the war would be expressed by the slogans "Down with the war" and "Long live the revolution". The districts adopted the Petersburg Committee's proposed plan and began to prepare. It was decided to hold the demonstrations in the morning when the workers came out of factories after meetings had finished. After the pattern of July 1914, workers were to link up with neighbouring factories and head en masse for the city centre. The Petersburg Committee issued a special leaflet "To the soldiers" and "9 January".

Our workers in the plants had to wage a struggle against the Mensheviks and Gvozdevites over 9 January. They were all against strikes and demonstrations. They justified their attitude in various ways: the chauvinists, like Gvozdev and Breido, were against them because they "would harm the cause of defence" and would be at variance with the view of the bourgeoisie on the Central War Industries Committee; others, who were smarter, with a mysterious air warned workers against public activity on 9 January as they "foresaw" a more important struggle ahead for which they appealed for "energy to be preserved". Of course both these positions received the most heartfelt response from works managements and the police. The left SRs issued a proclamation "On 9 January" in which they called for a strike. The Socialist-Revolutionary patriots went along with the defensist Mensheviks.

The strike and demonstration passed off with a high level of enthusiasm and organization. The Vyborg district marched at the head, with over 40,000 strikers; behind them came the Moscow, Narva and other districts. Once past the Neva Gate, the workers waited for the police to come and "pick them up". Many small establishments and printshops went on strike. According to information from employers' sources there were in all some 100,000 workers on strike. Demonstrations took place in the outskirts only, as the police would not allow them in the centre. Many demonstrators were arrested. The managements of certain establishments applied a number of repressive measures to individual groups of workers. During the demonstrations workers met soldiers; a friendly exchange of greetings would then take place. At the sight of the red banner (as, for example, along the Vyborg Chaussée) the soldiers took off their caps and shouted "Hurrah!" The mass that had been stirred to action by the strike and demonstrations was a long time in calming down. On the evening of the following day, a vast column of working women and men and soldiers paraded along the Bolshoi Sampsonievsky Prospekt for several hours on end. Revolutionary songs were sung, speeches made and "Down with the war!" shouted in unison. All the while, the police kept themselves to the sidelines. The fact that a good third of the crowd were soldiers restrained the police: not only did they not try to disperse it, they did not even make verbal threats.

On 19 January a strike of maintenance men in the city tram depots in Petersburg began. The movement had been well prepared and from the start involved all four depots: Moscow depot, with 700 workers; Vasiliev Island depot, with 500 workers; Petersburg depot, with 400 workers; and Rozhdestvensky depot, 300–400 workers, making about 2,000 workers all told. Leading the strike were members of our party's Petersburg organization. The demands were broken down as follows: a pay rise for those on 50 rubles a month of 50 per cent, those on 60 rubles, 40 per cent and those on 70 rubles, 30 per cent; an increase in the cost of living supplement; complete abolition of fines; free travel on city railways twice a day; bonus payments at Christmas and Easter at the rate of one month's pay; severance pay at the rate of one month's pay for each year of service; daily-paid to have equal rights with monthly-paid; payment for leave not taken; overtime pay for both monthly and daily paid at one and a half times the day rate; lodgings to be found or a rent allowance to be paid; issue of pay-books; cost of living supplement to be paid twice monthly; establishment of a training school for senior employees; no elected representatives to be victimized for petitioning.

In spite of the ban on newspaper reporting of the strike, it soon became known to everyone in the city. The strike was followed with feelings of unconcealed sympathy. The disruption to transport was blamed wholly upon the city fathers, who would not make concessions and were trying to pay the maintenance men 1.50 rubles a day, on which it was impossible to exist in Petersburg. On 23 January, the strike was joined by more than 150 workers at the central power station, and after them, all the sub-stations with some 80 men came out. For many hours the trams did not run. The military authorities despatched 50 soldiers to each depot and to the power station. 40 men were exiled and some taken before the military governor and returned to their workplace under escort of soldiers as "conscript workers". The city Duma appointed a commission of inquiry to examine the dispute.

Of the vehicles put into service on 25 January, 79 were still unrepaired, and during the 26th another 99 vehicles were taken off. On the 27th, the city Duma accepted the workers' demands and the strike was called off. The Petersburg Committee had directed the strike and issued a leaflet for the occasion. The action had passed off in a mood of solidarity. There were only four strikebreakers at the power station.

Linked directly to the success of the strike by the central power station workers was the celebrated industrial action at the huge Putilov plants. The electricians in the Putilov shops, whose wages did not exceed between 2 and 2.50 rubles a day, presented demands to the management for higher wages. But the directors of the works, as stooges of an alliance of French and Russian capitalists, brusquely turned down the workers' just demands. At the beginning of February the electricians stopped work and were supported by the remainder of the workforce. Nearly 15,000, most of the day shift, joined the strike. Nor did the night shift fall behind, and the next day the works was closed down by order of the Okhrana General Tumanov. Conscripts were summoned to the military governor. This was the start of events that were to attract the attention of all Russia and form the subject of discussion in the State Duma.

Almost simultaneously, a sectional dispute in the Petersburg Metalworks was, thanks to General Tumanov, turned into a general one: the works was closed on 8 February. In March the movement had acquired vast dimensions and was accompanied by mass exile and arrests.

The protracted nature of the war, with all its incalculable calamitous consequences which fell mainly upon the shoulders of the urban and rural democratic movement, brought about a clearer awareness that became known in Russia as a "change of mood" about the war. The patriotic hysteria of the war's first days had been dissipated by the savage blows of reality. The democrats' self-deception and "illusions of liberation" in that predatory war had been dashed by the ruthless policy of government repression within the country. Russian industrialists had given such a twist to the idea of a struggle against "German militarism", "German dominance" and so forth that even the philistines sobered up. The dislocation of all spheres of economic life struck at the poorest layers with the unprecedentedly high cost of living, and schooled the philistines to connect small causes with large effects.

More than once the mood of wide masses of people reached rebellious anger. The events in Moscow in the previous May, with inhuman attacks on Jews and Germans, had been provoked by the authorities to defuse the atmosphere of public discontent following the reverses in the Carpathians.

The revolutionary mood at the beginning of autumn had been dispersed by appeals for calm and by arrests. But both merely intensified the spontaneous growth of mass discontent. It passed from the rear out to the front and, reinforced by the grievances of trench life, rebounded into the villages and towns. The boys in the barracks notwithstanding the tough wartime discipline, were openly restive and indignant. The discontent of the soldiers — peasants and workers dressed in grey greatcoats — sprang above all from the barbaric regulations that held sway in the tsar's army. The soldiers, who lacked any rights, were objects of ridicule for the young masters dressed in officers' uniforms. The fighters for the "liberation of western democracy" were kicked in the teeth, and flogged just as in the era of Nicholas I; a host of penal measures were employed against them, including firing squads, all in the name of "discipline".

The treatment of soldiers by officers and by the police provoked the crowd to mob rule. In the previous autumn, a bloodbath along such lines had occurred between police and Muscovites. There were many dead and injured.

The commandant of Petersburg, together with the General Staff of the Northern Army, were waging a constant "war" on the soldiers by prohibiting them from using trams. Numerous "rulings" were issued restricting tram travel by soldiers, requiring them to pay for their ride or preventing them from going inside the car, allowing them to stay only on the end platforms. All these orders were deeply resented by the mass of soldiers, who systematically refused to obey them. Finally, just before Christmas, the military governor issued a disposition totally banning tram travel for lower ranks. Squads of as many as six soldiers were stationed by each tram stop. In addition, special detachments of city constables went out on the hunt for soldier passengers. In the evenings, armed patrols roamed the city removing detainees to the commandant's headquarters. The soldiers showed utter contempts for the "orders", leaped aboard moving trams, avoided the guard-posts at the stops in any way they could, and quite frequently put up open resistance. The public always supported the soldiers and as a result quite a few cases of "obstructing the police in the course of their duty" arose. The scale of the insubordination can be judged by the number of those arrested for riding on trams on the first day of the Christmas holiday: according to accounts by soldiers, their number exceeded a thousand. The following day, it was even higher. With such stubborn disobedience, they did not dare punish any greater numbers. The mood in the barracks was aroused. Soldiers said openly that they would repay the military authorities on 9 January together with the workers. Realizing the impact that the order had had on the soldiers, the governor hastened to revoke it on the eve of 9 January.

How far the mood of the broad masses of Petersburgers had moved from the jingo-patriotism of the beginning of the war can be gauged by the fact that the patriots proved unable to celebrate the victory over the Turks and the capture of Erzurum with demonstrations, although attempts were made. The organizers were forced to confine themselves to fireworks and the obligatory military parades.

The philistines' scepticism and distrust of the government at times went as far as "defeatism". Quite often opinions could be overheard on the tram about "our customs" with the conclusion: "They'll know all about our customs when the Germans arrive." But this still only showed itself indirectly; there was not yet visible in this discontent any sign of a transition from criticism to independent political activity.

The Situation of the Workers and Party Work

The strike struggle, especially by the advanced workers of Petersburg, produced an unlikely number of interpretations and at times even contradictory arguments among Russian "society". Rumours grew like a heap of dirty spring snow, became intertwined with specific facts and were laid before open and closed sittings of our statesmen, who took alarm at the stormy conflicts between capital and labour which would not be constrained even by "defence of the country". The workers' irreconcilable mood and their stubborn refusal to submit to the idea of "defence of the fatherland" or to bear the brunt of intensified exploitation in its name without a murmur, found its accurate reflection in the patriotic profits of the industry of the fatherland. But particularly displeasing to the Russian bourgeoisie was the anti-patriotic nature of the workers' movement, which served to demonstrate the total collapse of the influence of liberalism upon the working class. Its hostility to internationalism reached a point of frantic hatred for Bolshevik social democrats, the representatives of international socialism in Russia. The bourgeois press would not "recognize" any socialists other than the Gvozdevites. The so-called "progressive" papers, *Den, Rech* and *Sovremennoe Slovo*, were reduced to spreading falsehoods, as over the first elections to the War Industries Committees or during the elections for the Insurance Council, where workers' representatives spoke up for the "internationalist" social democrats: the papers tried to present the incidents as an accident "Suddenly" the elections had turned out to be on a factional basis, the other side had "unexpectedly" won, etc.

All the ideological defenders of capital who denied class struggle (especially in wartime, as these gentlemen had "no doubt" about the patriotism of the worker) went to great pains to locate the causes of conflict outside social relations, namely in "foreign influence", payoffs, provocation, etc. They sought to attribute the discontent of workers in the early days to the influence of "defeatist ideas". Under the leadership of the social chauvinists, patriotic society anathematized the "Leninites", and the Okhrana rushed to uncover the required quantity of "defeatist" leaders, hoping thereby to kill off opposition to the war and exploitation. But the movement did not stop.

To counter the rising discontent of the workers, rumours about "German money" were put about. The venal newspapers financed by police stations and the Okhrana spread reports about German bribes to strikers. But although the reports came from *Zemshchina, Russkoe Znamya* and other sinks of police iniquity that were apparently very well-informed about "bribery" through their own closeness to ruling circles in Germany, such rumours had no success, although the General Staff used them in its war on the strike movement.

Left and liberal circles of society found another cause for the growth of the strike movement: provocation. They linked such provocation, that creature of the Russian autocrat, directly to "intrigues" by Wilhelm II. Stories that the Okhrana was in the service of German imperialism circulated in Russia from the start of the war. There were cases of Okhrana agents being discovered engaged in espionage for Germany. The case of the colonel of the gendarmerie, Myasoedov, only went to justify such rumours and lend them greater credibility.

As a result of the government's police and censorship measures, an atmosphere of mystery developed around the workers' movement that encouraged rumour. The bitter struggle by government agents against the political opponents of tsarism who did not subscribe to the "defence of the country" drove philistine opinion to the facile explanation that all power in Russia — the court, the ministers, generals and civil servants — were all Germans. The campaign by the authorities against legal public organizations, and their simultaneous patronage of every type of extortion, only convinced the wider public of the correctness of its opinion and the government's lies were turned against itself.

The causes of the strike movement ran, of course, far deeper than those invented by popular chatter. The war had not eliminated class struggle but, on the contrary, having intensified the exploitation of the working class, had given rise to more acute forms of it. The strike struggles of the working class in Russia could not be viewed in isolation from the general bourgeois democratic movement. The break-up of feudal practices in the course of the war created an extremely onerous situation for the working sector of the country. The bourgeoisie attempted to exploit the new situation to increase its wealth and consolidate its political influence. Behind the ballyhoo about the "alliance of classes and peoples" the bourgeoisie had concluded a forward contract with tsarism at the expense of the economic and political interests of the masses of people. Under the guise of "defence of the country" this deal was foisted on to the backs of the democratic movement and the working class by the renegades from democracy: Kerensky, Maslov, Rubanovich, Potresov and their ilk. This deal brought the bourgeoisie immediate benefits in the form of "participation in aid of our gallant army", through the intermediary of every conceivable public organization. "Aid" brought in million-ruble orders while the objects of the war, if achieved, held out promises of all sorts of other "empires" for Guchkov and Ryabushinsky. But for the moment they set themselves up in motor vehicles and munitions. Industry worked flat out, the capitalists took advantage of the dislocation of transport to profiteer, and the whole entrepreneurial wolf-pack enjoyed such affluence as they never even dreamt of in peacetime.

The employers' wartime labour policy did not differ in principle from its peacetime one. The policy of Franco-Belgian-German-British-pure-Russian organized capital on the labour question was simple: a ruthless struggle against any demands, rapacious exploitation, lock-outs and police reprisals. When the guns started to boom in the west, this cosmopolitan capital donned a "pure Russian" guise and, stocking itself up with profitable orders, rushed to the aid of the "fatherland". The managements of even known "German" firms opened up hospitals and donated kopeks and supported every kind of patronage for the patriotic absorption of the workers. Wartime was giving cosmopolitan capital resources for the coercion of workers such as it could not have dreamt of in peacetime.

The factories, now overloaded with military orders, had an interest in raising production by extending the working day. Thirst for high profits led them to exploit women and children and to import cheap Chinese and Korean labour. The government acceded to all the employers' requests over this matter and repealed the statutes that safeguarded the health of workers. The contradictions between labour and capital sharpened and led rapidly to disputes. The workers had but one tool of struggle — the strike. Employers resorted to spying, provocation and lock-outs. The police, the Okhrana and the General Staff were at the service of the employers too.

Influenced by the previous summer's strike movement, and out of concern for "normal working" in all enterprises, Petersburg's organized employers made representations to the Council of Ministers for the "militarization of all workers". Petersburg capitalists thus hoped to kill any spirit of protest among the workers and eradicate strikes by means of discipline and martial justice. The organization of plants on the pattern of barracks, bestowing on the management stooges of capital "officer" powers with an arsenal of punishments and rewards, was the ideal of this "cosmopolitan" capital. The Council of

Ministers wholly accepted the views of capital, prepared a bill and passed it at the spring session of the State Duma. But the strike movement of February and March said plainly that workers would not reconcile themselves to such a statute and it was left in abeyance.

Influenced by the rising discontent among the working masses, the General Staff started to "interest itself" in the movement. Militarism extended its powers further and further towards the rear, directing all its "rear units" into the working class, which would not forget its own war-cry, "Workers of the world, unite".

The strengthening of reaction during wartime had an adverse effect on the building of organizations in Russia's workers' movement. In the final years before the war, the working class was striving to reinforce itself with illegal and legal bodies. Of the latter, the strongest was the workers' press. It was the first to fall and, following it, all the other ones were destroyed or disarmed.

The incipient, though very small, influx of intellectuals into the workers' movement, which marked the last years before the war, was again cut off. This element, alien to the working class, succumbed to social reaction and once again (as after the 1905 revolution) began to drift away. Many of them were mobilized, but more than a few voluntarily joined some office of imperialism. Almost everywhere workers' organizations found themselves without intellectuals, but this did not paralyse their activity as in the previous period of pre-war reaction. The workers' organizations had thrown up their own purely proletarian leaders. The whole movement towards organization was forced to "dig in" behind an illegal wall of clandestine workers' associations.

As in peacetime, the organizational basis of the illegal associations was the plant, workshop or factory. Factory organizations were grouped together into city districts, districts into city organizations, committees and so on. Apart from our party's standing organizations, some plants that had groups from other illegal organizations foreign to us (socialist-revolutionaries, "unifiers", anarchist-communists etc.) held occasional meetings of individual groups on matters of local importance, mainly during disputes.

The central point of the ideological work of the illegal cells of our party, scattered around all the industrial centres of Russia, was the attitude to the war, the struggle against chauvinism and "patriotic" exploitation. The work of our organizations during the war period has yet to find its historian. Its scale can be judged by the strike waves that never ceased to shake the rotting shell of the tsarist monarchy. Evidence of the active work of the workers' organizations during wartime is provided by the exiling of thousands of organized workers, arrests, and the posting of strikers to front-line positions.

Our organized comrades opposed the zoological nationalism of the Purishkeviches and the chauvinist sophistry of Plekhanov with the international interests of the proletariat and the power of the socialist, revolutionary ideal. They opposed the ideas of defence of the country and alliance with the bourgeoisie (Gvozdevism) with agitation for the revolutionary overthrow of tsarist power and irreconcilable class struggle against the capitalist predators, the real culprits of the mass slaughter.

The demand for illegal socialist literature was so great that the poor illegal technology could not meet it. Private initiative came to its aid. Every sort of manuscript, hectographed or retyped copy of individual proclamations, articles from illegal publications abroad, etc., circulated among workers. A typewritten copy of Lenin and Zinoviev's pamphlet "The War and Socialism" was passed from hand to hand around Moscow. *Sotsial-Demokrat* and *Kommunist* were such luxuries that 50 kopeks or a ruble would be paid for one reading. There were demands for hundreds of copies of *Kommunist*; and workers would readily put aside three rubles of pay for a copy. Besides this, declarations of an internationalist tendency by various groups of party workers circulated throughout Russia. Picture postcards of our Duma deputies exiled to Siberia were sold out in two months in Petersburg alone — a quantity of about five thousand prints.

Membership of local organizations in the south, the Volga region, the central region and Petersburg was swelled by social-democratic elements from the evacuated areas of Poland and the Baltic lands. Thus in Petersburg two national groups, the Estonians and the Latvians, were affiliated to the Petersburg Committee with the status of city districts. There was also quite a large number of Polish workers evacuated deep into the country; there were even workers from Warsaw factories in Petersburg. The Poles, however, kept separate and did not join the local organizations.

Of the legal workers' organizations the insurance bodies remained everywhere. In one or two places in the centre, Moscow, Tula and the south, several trade unions and associations still survived, but their activity was greatly hampered. Later on co-operatives grew up which party elements had also penetrated. The same struggle of the two currents was conducted on insurance matters in the hospital funds: between the liquidators, painted in a national-patriotic hue, and the Pravda-ists, remaining true to the old red internationalist banner. The elections to the Insurance Council on 21 January 1916 bore a markedly anti-Gvozdevite, anti-liquidationist character. The Petersburg Committee's proclamation to workers over the Insurance Council elections appealed for a struggle against the "Guchkov boys".

The Pravda-ist list was voted for in full. Thirty-nine representatives were elected on the basis of the seventy votes cast for the list. The number of liquidationist, Narodnik and non-party votes was in all twenty-six, who together elected two alternate representatives.

Following the scandalous Gvozdevite business, the elections provided a clear indicator of the strength of the two currents and a true witness to the internationalism of the politically conscious representatives of Russian workers.

Many months had passed since gunfire and the crackle of machine-guns drowned the voice of international workers' solidarity. Over the course of many years, lies, treachery and nationalist poison had driven nations and their working masses against each other. The governing classes had tried to exploit cunning theories of the "defence of the country", the "protection of culture" against the idealism of the working masses who had been reared on revolutionary socialist propaganda. In the bloody affairs of the bourgeoisie and monarchies of the belligerent countries a faithful ally was international opportunism, which, behind the intoxication of war, sought to put its hoary old theory of class peace into practice. The allies of the bourgeoisie's imperialist appetites, the social patriots, discovered in each of the belligerent countries "peculiarities" of a local nature, and each tried to justify his position by the "interests of the working class". German opportunists from Scheidemann to Kautsky were fighting "Russian autocracy", the French were "defending the republic", the British were "liberating Belgium", while the Russians "would not obstruct" hangmen generals from waging war to "liberate western democracy". This was how the job of diverting the thoughts and actions of democrats and the working class from their own situation and the struggle for their class objectives, was carried out.

Each country and each coalition of warring capitalist forces was quite happy to speculate on a "revolution" in a rival country. Even the Russian Imperial General Staff gladly allowed through and even dramatized stories about the revolutionary movement in the Central Powers. The bourgeois press kept Russia fully informed on the revolutionary discontent of the Austro-German peoples. These reports were lapped up by the Russian worker but he took them in quite a different sense from the bourgeoisie. For while the latter were seeking a strategic buttress from the enemy's hard-pressed internal situation and called on the masses for "just a bit more patience" and "one more push", the working class drew its own, opposite, conclusions. For the Russian worker and socialist would find strength in the final victory of class solidarity over the narrow, pernicious, "supra-class" nationalism and this awakening of revolutionary moods. A movement in this direction, which had been dormant at the start of the war, was growing daily in the fight against the bloody designs of capital and tsarism.

The long months of carnage and the deteriorating state of democracy showed that the democratic movement could expect nothing from the war. Thinking workers in our country had never linked their fate and aims with a victory over "those Germans", just as in the former revolutionary years they retained trust in their own forces and in awakening the urban and rural poor for the final toppling of a tsarism that had graced itself with the "liberationist" lie of the war. Russia's proletariat, although weighed down with military and police shackles, was preparing, alongside those workers throughout the world who had remained loyal to the International, for a great worldwide struggle for the class interests of the exploited and for socialism.

Organizational Plan

I was not able to enjoy my freedom from being shadowed for very long. Within two weeks of my arrival I came under observation as I travelled to and from the rendezvous of the Petersburg Committee and meetings with individual comrades in working-class districts. At first this observation did not bother me too much; but then, as time went on, the sleuths became more brazen. However, I always found a lodging-place for the night away from the gaze of spies. I soon adapted to the illegal conditions and the constant moving around. Life in the underground had, over those last ten years, changed only in respect of its participants. Instead of the student youth and intellectuals of 1903–5, only workers were in evidence in the war years. Likewise, the secret meeting-places in flats and lodging-houses were all in working-class districts and in workers' flats. Intellectuals were a rare exception.

Of the old party intelligentsia there remained very few who had maintained their ties with the workers. An exception was A.M. Gorky. As before, workers would crowd into his house, bringing with them all the problems that confronted them.

I too dropped in on Aleksei Maksimovich many times. He took an internationalist position and followed the development of illegal work with the closest attention, rendering us various services. Around him throbbed the many-faceted life in which the most diverse elements of the Petersburg intelligentsia took part. Aleksei Maksimovich was himself keen on the idea of organizing radical-democratic groups.

At his flat you could obtain the very latest political news of the parliamentary and extra-parliamentary life of our bourgeois opposition. It was by its nature a unique central point. On politics and tactics Aleksei Maksimovich was not qualified to speak and working-class people went to him simply to have a heart-to-heart with him, to pour out their anxieties. This procession of workers was well known to the Okhrana, and spies were permanently on duty around the building.

I was extremely interested in the life and structure of our illegal party organizations. In their "pure" form I had known them well between 1902 and 1907 but later, when I returned from abroad in 1914, I found them already considerably diluted and softened up by legality. There was a legal press; unions and novelties like the insurance bodies etc. had appeared, which had been non-existent in the previous period. The war had wiped out all these liberties at a stroke, and prompted workers to start building totally illegal organizations.

Close familiarity convinced me that the essence of the organizations would remain as before. Similarity of conditions determined their identical nature. Just as earlier, the factory circles were the basic party cells, electing a factory delegation which formed part of the district conference which in turn elected the "district committee", while a conference of the latter committees elected the Petersburg Committee in line with the appropriate district representation. However, because of the clandestine conditions it was sometimes difficult to call a conference, and the Petersburg Committee accepted direct delegates from the district committees as members.

Attached to the district committees and the Petersburg Committee various colleges were set up: the college of propagandists and agitators; the literary college; and the organizers' college. The organizer was the guiding spirit. The scale and depth of the revolutionary work would depend upon his degree of activity. And the Petersburg Committee paid a great deal of attention to that college. Even special hectographed guidelines on the organizers' college and its functions were issued which ran as follows:

> The organizers' college has representatives of the delegations of all the local organizations: those elected by individual groups and those co-opted. The organizers' college is a subsidiary organization of the Petersburg Committee and, at the same time, a school for training new organizers. As a subsidiary organization of Petersburg Committee, the organizers' college sets its aims as follows: (1) the expansion and strengthening of organizations in the localities; (2) the resurrection of organizations that have temporarily ceased activity or have lost contact with the district bodies; (3) the organization of new groups; (4) supply of literature to party organizations.
>
> These tasks shall be carried out in the following manner:
> (1) Each organizer shall assist the district representative (the leading organizer) in finding flats for classes and meetings of his group, in notifying both group members and speakers of the dates and venues. He

shall also check on the implementation of decisions of the Petersburg Committee, the proper contribution of members' dues and demand punctual presentation of his report and so on.

(2) Wherever the activity of any group begins to drop off or ceases altogether as a result of collapse, provocations, lack of propagandists, accommodation etc., the organizer is obliged to elucidate the reasons that have produced a halt in the group's activity.

(3) In organizing new groups the organizer must attempt to contact old comrades in the firm being organized; to use for this purpose contacts and acquaintances of other group members; to exert every effort to deliver the relevant literature there; and finally, where possible, to obtain employment in the given firm.

(4) Every organizer must promptly prepare for a literature store and promptly supply it to the groups. After distributing it, he must collect reports on the effect of the distributed literature upon the workers.

(5) The organizer must keep all addresses and all contacts at his own house in the obligatory code and, also, with a comrade who does not take an active part in party life and who, in the event of the organizer being imprisoned, must immediately pass all details of contacts to the organizers' college. As an education class, the organizers' college shall arrange meetings not less than twice a month for discussing problems connected with the current situation, inasmuch as current events may serve as material for agitation (May Day, 4 April, Women's Day, days of strikes, the growth of the trade-union movement and so on and so forth).

Discussion-group work during wartime proceeded fairly well in both Petersburg and Moscow. Those wishing to study socialist science were everywhere more numerous than the organization could cater for. From everyone wishing to learn, usually those comrades were chosen who could at once work on their own upon completing their discussion-group studies. The extension of discussion-group work to basic socialist education classes for all willing students was not within our means. The discussion groups were but an educational method of training party workers for the mass movement. The most intensive discussion-group work took place in autumn and winter. In the summer mass meetings were held where not only the political struggle but also the situation in the factories was discussed, questions of strike action decided, etc. When strikes flared up as at Lessners in the spring of 1915, the boldest and most influential workers would gather mass meetings and lead the movement illegally.

It is difficult to enumerate all the problems which were discussed here and at workers' meetings. I recall questions about the war, the United States of Europe, the high prices and the Second and Third Internationals. No question suggested by the life of the factory or city, or of interest to the whole country, would pass the workers by. They would discuss them during worktime as well. Factory cells and circles were generally composed of people who knew each other well. A question would therefore be presented for discussion and, if a decision required, settled wholly during working hours. The work of the factory circles of the "good old days" of intellectual discussion-group activity was sharply distinct from this later period. The old circles used to educate workers about the "theory of the workers' movement", but the circles of the later period were organizations for the actual practice of the workers' struggle.

Gathering the Party's Forces

Through my personal acquaintances who remained from 1914, I made contact with several groups of workers. Meetings were arranged where the international situation, attitude to the war, the tasks of workers in Russia and other such questions were discussed. Although chauvinism had had a difficult time, it had made some headway. Even old Bolshevik workers had succumbed to it. So my friends from the Eiwas works held a small meeting at comrade N. Nazarov's, where M. Kalinin, "Kirill" (Orlov) and others whose names I do not remember were present.

The old party worker, M. Kalinin stood openly for the "rout" of the Germans and agreed with the Gvozdevites over participation in "defence". His position did not find support among other workers; but the slogan "defeat of the tsarist monarchy" did cause stories to circulate. It had to be interpreted historically and examined in conjunction with our attitude to the policies of tsarism, in order to rid it of any cause for speculation by enemies of our party and agents of the German General Staff.

I met among the Ericsson workers a group of comrades headed by Kayurov which was conducting work at that factory. The war had brought many new enterprises to life in the Vyborg district and had drawn in a mass of women. Revolutionary social-democratic work was carried out among them too. In the same Vyborg district I met an unusual workers' circle of "Nizhni-Novgorod-Sormovans", D. Pavlov, A. Kuklina, Kayurova, Alexandrova and others working independently. This circle brought together former party workers who had taken an internationalist positon but had not linked up with the Petersburg Committee through fear of provocation. It took a lot of effort to turn it towards active work in the district. In this regard a major role was played by M.G. Pavlova who criticized the "Sormovans" quite sharply and aptly for their "tears" over A.M. Gorky and their love of words. In the end the comrades got down to work in earnest and subsequently through their experience made a huge contribution to the organization of the party.

On various occasions I went to workers' meetings at Lessners and Nobels. Small groups of six to eight would gather. At meetings of organized comrades and also from members of the Petersburg Committee I was to hear much dissatisfaction about the conduct of our Duma faction (they were by now in exile) at their trial. Comrades condemned Kamenev especially severely. The deputies who were suffering for anti-militarist work were popular with the masses. I managed to obtain a postcard with a photograph of our "quintet" in prison. I arranged for it to be reproduced (the photograph had been found on the Steklyanny, at comrade I.I. Kovalenko's), and shortly afterwards were able to produce illegally a few thousand postcards which were quickly sold out and brought income to the organization.

It was as hard to convene the Petersburg Committee as it was easy to get workers together. All my requests for a plenum of the Petersburg Committee proved abortive. I would nearly always, before his arrest, meet Bagdatiev, and later Starck and more rarely "Vladimir". I would be notified of the plenum at a venue for me to arrange only a couple of hours beforehand, although it was stipulated that twelve or twenty-four hours' notice of a meeting should be given. Sometimes for some reason the agreed venue was not used and I was sought everywhere. All this was done with the object of setting me against the Petersburg Committee, to which the "Mironites" had declared in my absence that I wished to have no dealings with them. On behalf of the Petersburg Committee Bagdatiev and Starck presented me with demands that I place the means of communications with the provinces and abroad in their hands in case I was arrested. But I found out from other members of the Petersburg Committee that they had not even discussed this. I sensed that Miron Chernomazov was operating through them, and exceedingly skilfully at that, and I categorically refused but indicated the contacts and intermediaries with whose aid they could find out everything in event of my misadventure. This was not at all to the liking of Starck and the others who stood for the Central Committee Bureau being picked from the Petersburg Committee itself. They therefore continued to weave their intrigues within the Petersburg Committee.

After familiarizing myself with the work of the Petersburg Committee I proceeded to seek out activists for the formation of the all-Russian centre that would be able to direct social-democratic work in Russia.

With the consent of the Central Committee's foreign group it had been decided to form, in either Petersburg or Moscow, a bureau of the Central Committee of the RSDLP, and I had been given the names of a few party workers.

It was desirable to bring into this bureau only workers, old party activists and Pravda-ists. Of the individuals indicated by the centre's foreign group, none proved to be in Petersburg or, if they were, no longer shared our viewpoint. It would have been quite easy to assign this work to the Petersburg Committee, which had been the ideological centre from the very first day of the war; but organizationally it had contact with only a few of the major industrial centres and no opportunity to work there. However, out of elementary caution and also through fear that the work of the Central Committee Bureau would become known to Miron Chernomazov, I decided not to link the all-Russian work to the apparatus of the Petersburg Committee. I soon found people able to maintain the work of the Central Committee Bureau. In the selection of these people great help was rendered by student youth and also Maria I. Ulyanova and A.I. Elizarova. We were quickly able to form a group which specialized in importing literature from Finland and storing it. Lack of funds hindered expansion. There were no returns from the areas, no factories were organized (financially) and even collections among workers for the Petersburg Committee were very badly run. I often had recourse to the financial aid of A.M. Gorky for our work.

K.M. Shvedchikov came to be both in charge of transport matters and to manage the storage of literature, and was also treasurer. Only very much later did we succeed in attracting a good underground organizer, comrade Vadim (Viktor Tikhomirnov), who undertook some of the work previously borne by K.M. Shvedchikov.

Having got the machinery of the Central Committee Bureau into operation, I nominated comrades who would be able to direct illegal work. They had to be selected most carefully, as the available circle was limited in the extreme. Many social-democratic workers from the pre-war period were in exile, prison or in the trenches.

Agreement was reached with individual activists of the Petersburg Committee about the composition of the Central Committee Bureau: comrades Ignat Fokin ("Petr"), Zalezhsky ("Vladimir") and active workers from the insurance group. The insurance organizers put forward S. Medvedev but they could not indicate where he lived and so the chairman of the insurance group, G.I. Osipov, was appointed as his deputy. Comrades Petr and Vladimir joined by right of co-optation from the Petersburg Committee. K.M. Shvedchikov joined as the leading organizer of the storage and distribution of literature and also as treasurer.

The supply of literature was put in hand: by the end of 1915 fifteen issues of *Sotsial-Demokrat* had been received in Petersburg with several hundred copies of each, and a small quantity of *Kommunist* no. 1–2. Of course this was inadequate to satisfy even the minimal requirements of Petersburg alone, never mind the rest of Russia.

There was therefore a great deal of animosity and complaints about the distribution which K.M. Shvedchikov was in charge of. We were unable to set up transport or reprinting arrangements through lack of funds.

Once I had set up the work of the Central Committee Bureau and also transport from abroad, I decided to travel round to several points in central Russia and take a look at our party work on the spot. I reached Moscow at the end of December. I had not been in that city for over eight years, since I was doing time in the Butyrki and other parts. It had changed little.

I had arranged to meet Petr Germogenovich Smidovich. I took refuge at his place but moved to a neighbouring flat at night. Both he and his wife, Sofya Nikolaevna, were doing party work and lived under the Okhrana's most intense observation. On this visit I came to meet I.I. Skvortsev (Stepanov). I also met there comrade Milyutin, who had taken on work in the middle Volga region, and comrade A. Saveliev, who had arrived from the front. A small meeting was arranged at Doctor Obukh's with comrade "Makar" (V.P. Nogin), M.S. Olminsky, Yakovleva, P.G. Smidovich and several other Muscovites. The proposal to create an all-Russian Bureau of the Central Committee was welcomed wholeheartedly. I acquainted the comrades with the state of affairs abroad, in the party and work in Petersburg.

I learned a great deal from them about the state of party work and the workers' movement in the same region. The patriotic and chauvinist agitation from the start of the war in all the bourgeois press had in May brought about pogroms against Germans and German businesses. Moscow workers had readily succumbed to patriotic provocations and held a protest strike against the "German take-over". The level of awareness of Moscow was considerably lower than that of the Petersburgers.

Moscow was becoming the centre for all sorts of legal conferences: of co-operatives, war industries committees, for the struggle against high prices and so on, in which workers also took part; sometimes resolutions in an internationalist spirit were carried, as for instance at the conference for the struggle against high prices.

Our party's work went on in all the districts of Moscow. All attempts to centralize this work by forming a single party committee for all Moscow were, however, unsuccessful. As soon as our comrades began to turn their work in this direction, convene a conference and appoint a "Moscow Committee", arrests followed and any practical activity was smashed. This pointed to the existence of provocateurs, and some people were actually suspected, but they could not be unmasked through lack of firm evidence.

In the Moscow industrial region July and August 1915 passed off stormily. The movement started over the struggle against high prices and to demand fixed price rates, but it ended in workers being shot. Meetings and rallies took place everywhere. In Moscow the movement coincided with the dissolution of the State Duma and this gave rise to thinking that the Muscovite proletariat supported the progressive bloc.

The Moscow region was richer than that of Petersburg in intellectual workers and writers. But thanks to the absence of a centralized party these forces were used very badly and irregularly.

In Moscow I received warnings from comrade Olminsky and other collaborators of Petersburg *Pravda* about Chernomazov, but again without concrete evidence. Nevertheless I decided that upon my return to Petersburg I would bring this to the notice of the Executive Commission of the Petersburg Committee and press for the expulsion of "Miron".

The Muscovites were pleased with the literature, and read it as voraciously as the Petersburgers. People put their names down to read *Kommunist*, which even brought in some income.

Having obtained reports about the work, established contacts and, most important, come to an agreement about the basic line of work, I moved on to Murom on the Kazan railway. I did not risk getting off at my native town but travelled on to Navashino and, taking great precautions, found my way from there on horseback to Doshchatoe where my old mother lived.

The Doshchatoe works was a branch of the Vyxun plants, in the back of beyond — it existed far and away from any politics. Women and old men worked without a murmur, submissively bending their backs for paupers' wages whatever the length of the working day. My family were all Old Believers and lived only for their faith and their own households. When persecution of Old Believers with their chapels, books and icons, ceased, the number of adherents began to drop. "Suffering for the faith" was now difficult. The wealthier types had now adapted to the establishment and there was no longer that earlier psychology of struggle by forbearance, suffering, prayer and fast so familiar to me in my childhood. The young people had given up prayer and you no longer heard the dreary chant of "the prophets have prophesied for one thousand years", etc.

I felt I was in a distant, incomprehensible world. Only childhood recollections linked me with the mud-caked machinery, the huge clear pond and the enigmatic, endlessly stirring forest; and the stern, archaic icons recalled the ardent love of God, the desire to be His preacher and to suffer for that love and the old holy book. The attitude towards me was very good, as one hunted down by the tsarist government. Among the old folk it was felt that their finest hours of struggle "for the faith" against the priests and the local authorities made their youth akin to mine.

After stopping there several days, I went back to Navashino and from there via Arzamas to Nizhni-Novgorod and Sormovo. Here I expected to find old party workers from 1902–1905, but I had also picked up some contacts in Moscow. Even in that year the railways suffered from overcrowding. At junctions crowds of passengers and soldiers spent whole days and nights, and there was a crush on disembarkation that could scarcely be controlled by the gendarmes and railway police. The conversation of the men and women travelling, mainly Russian country folk and mobilized soldiers, revolved around the universal sorrow, the war.

I arrived in Nizhni early in the morning. I left my bags at the left luggage office and set out in search of comrades. At once the neglect of the streets, with a lot of unswept snow, struck me: this was an effect of the war. The huge mills that ground "wheat-flour" for all of central Russia stood lifeless. New plants were going up and rumbling to produce only munitions and other equipment. It was still only January 1916 but the shortage of grain could already be felt: hoarders were beginning to profiteer.

I quickly found the contacts. One was working in an office, and comrade Saveliev was employed in the statistical section of the zemstvo administration. The organization in Nizhni was weak. All the work was chiefly carried out in Kanavino, where there used to be large old plants and factories which had been evacuated. There was a "workers' club". I got to know several Kanavinans at comrade Levit's, a small master carpenter. Leading the Kanavino work was comrade Kozin, who kept in contact with the Sormovans. Work was put in hand but at once we encountered and had to fight a battle against the social patriots. From the Nizhni-Novgorodians I obtained an address in Sormovo.

On one of the days over the New Year holiday I headed for Sormovo by the railway that connects the industrial zone and the village and reaches out as far as noisy, sprawling Kanavino. I had worked in Sormovo in 1900 in a rolling mill. The plant then belonged to the Benardak brothers. A decade and a half later the settlement and the plant had grown considerably, demolishing many residential quarters along the "ditch" (Kanava) and spreading towards the old wooden railway station. From outward appearance it was evident that business was doing fine.

An unpardonable mix-up occurred, The Nizhni-Novgorodians had given me the wrong password, which delayed our meeting till the next day when the Sormovans had checked back with Nizhni. A brake had been placed upon work in Sormovo by arrests. On the very day of my visit mass searches and arrests were taking place. The party workers were young and had little experience. No one was left from the old tested workers. We held a small meeting where I made a report to the comrades on the state of affairs in the party, work in Petersburg and Moscow and the situation in other countries. The Sormovans for their part informed me that work was getting under way: circles had been organized and meetings arranged. They suffered from a lack of leaders, especially when they had to speak out against the local defensists who had planted themselves in the hospital fund. The newly arrived folk from the countryside who worked there in large numbers in wartime fell under their influence. There was a great need for literature and the comrades were glad of what I had sent.

In Sormovo I looked up one of the old social-democratic workers with whom I had worked in 1900. I found him with his family in his own little house and now grown old. M. Gromov, an energetic comrade, had gone through much in his time. He had often been driven out of his factory for social-democratic work, imprisoned and exiled. His privations had whitened his head but had also made him a wholehearted "sympathizer" with the young, fresh forces.

Another comrade, Grigorii Kozin, lived in Nizhni in the celebrated Pechori. I had spent a year and a half in jail with him back in 1904 but had never met him since. The old activist had been ground down by life: family worries, unemployment and hunger. A talented propagandist and a good organizer, he had completely dropped out, tormenting himself with regrets and seeing the only solution in an influx of fresh forces. These were quick to come. The red banner of the workers' movement passed out of the weakening hands of the old men to a younger and more energetic generation of workers.

Arrests in Nizhni intensified. The Kanavino workers' club was wrecked in a raid by gendarmes. It was proposed that I disappear as there was not a sufficiently "clean" lodging for me. Having collected a few reports and addresses and agreed upon passwords, I set off for Petersburg.

Insurance Work and the Chernomazov Business

Standing somewhat removed from the Petersburg Committee was the workers' insurance group headed by chairman G.I. Osipov, contributors to the magazine *Voprosy Strakhovaniya* ("Questions of Insurance"), and the hospital fund organizers; A.N. Vinokurov, Gnevich, N.I. Podvoisky, K.S. Eremeev, N.I. Milyutin, K.M. Sundukov, K.M. Shvedchikov, A.I. Elizarova and others. The anomalous situation between the insurance organizers and the workers' insurance group on the one hand and the Petersburg Committee on the other soon developed into open conflict. The Petersburg Committee formed its "own" group of insurance organizers from the hospital fund secretaries. The guiding spirit behind this new organization was the secretary of the hospital fund at Lessners, Miron, alias Chernomazov. He was popular and did enjoy support among certain workers in the Vyborg district. The Petersburg Committee trusted him; L. Starck, S. Bagdatiev, V. Schmidt and others stood squarely behind him. Collaborators on our former *Pravda* of 1914, older insurance organizers and all the comrades who knew him closely harboured a unanimous distrust for Chernomazov. The divorce of the insurance comrades from the Petersburg Committee was an outcome of this distrust and disagreement with his demagogic activities. All the old insurance workers declared that they were unable to work with him.

From the first days of my arrival I landed myself in the quarrel. I soon managed to establish that Miron was a suspicious individual. From then on I wholly took the side of the old insurance organizers. They insisted that I take measures against Miron; but it was very hard to institute anything as there was no documentary evidence against him apart from my personal conviction of the man's dishonesty.

The struggle against Miron's influence in the organization dragged on, as I was the only illegal party worker to conduct a struggle against him and his followers on the Petersburg Committee.

All my doubts about Chernomazov, which I had expressed to the Executive Commission of the Petersburg Committee, had aroused protests and demands for proof. A rather ambiguous role in this matter was played by V. Schmidt who would support all my suspicions about Chernomazov in private meetings with myself but would support him in Petersburg Committee meetings or behind my back.

Alongside our party's usual colleges and district associations there were also attached to the Petersburg Committee various non-territorial groups, sometimes with craft names such as "The Marxist Building Workers" or "The Petersburg Railway Organization of the RSDLP". These groups also issued leaflets and carried out party work in their own spheres.

An attempt was made with my personal participation to organize the teachers, without big results. The teachers had become petty-bourgeoisified and did not respond to calls to revolutionary work. Among students in higher education work proceeded with success: serious organizations were formed which helped in the working-class districts. As before, young people were revolutionary-minded.

After the election campaign and without doubt as a direct result of our success at the electors' meeting for the War Industries Committees, the Okhrana exhibited an unusual zeal in trailing and hounding Bolsheviks. Arrests took place throughout the city and in the working-class districts in particular. Special attention was paid to the hospital funds. There were frequently swoops on the Putilov hospital fund. There were certain pointers to Chernomazov's involvement in these arrests. However, all evidence was of a "suggestive" nature. Some rumours came from the prison, but in no more definite form. Chernomazov's scheming against *Voprosy Strakhovaniya* and his desire to sow discord between myself and the Petersburg Committee convinced me that this "Miron" was highly suspect. His urge to worm his way in everywhere, to know everything and be the representative for everything, convinced me that the Petersburg Committee was dealing with a provocateur. Starck kept up a friendship with him: they jointly organized a publishing house called "Volna", at a time when "Priboi" and "Prosveshchenie" had still not been wound up.

Starck would behave in an amazingly frivolous and suspicious fashion. Above all he broke an elementary requirement of underground work: he tried to work for the illegal Petersburg Committee as well as in the publishing house, on *Voprosy Strakhovaniya* etc., ignoring the most elementary precautions. He dragged sleuths behind him to all the rendezvous known to him. Because of this he too fell under our suspicion.

At my very first meeting with members of the Petersburg Committee I reported the Muscovites' suspicions about Miron; K.M. Shvedchikov, who dealt with despatches and literature storage, made a protest about Starck. Starck systematically had broken K.M.'s ban on visiting him or sending people to him who were known to be under observation by agents. The Executive Commission decided to bring it to the attention of the Petersburg Committee. I demanded to be invited to this session of the Committee.

At the beginning of January 1916 I made the acquaintance of the former deputy to the Third State Duma, Shurkanov, who was working at the Eiwas factory. There were always rendezvous and meetings of party workers at Shurkanov's. Comrade "Yurii" (Lutovinov) would invariably stay with him when working in Petersburg. Sometimes there were searches, and often surveillance. However, the house's convenient situation allowed comrades to look in despite the risk, and use his services. Once, on my way to meet Orlov I met Aleksei Gorin (alias Volkov, Vorobiev etc.) there; in an odd fashion he warned me against using Shurkanov's flat, saying it was "a beacon for the Okhrana" promising to give more details later.

But Aleksei Gorin did not manage to give me the information about

Shurkanov's flat. Soon afterwards there was a large-scale round-up of eleven old party workers who had gathered on Aleksei Gorin's initiative to celebrate the New Year at one of the restaurants on the Petersburg bank. The gathering was held against my advice and personal refusal to take part in a social get-together. Through their frivolousness these comrades seemed to be meeting their arrest halfway.

You could observe an all-round decline in the old precepts of conspiratorial work. There were occasions when on meeting comrades in the streets of Petersburg, I noticed agents behind them; I would warn them, and give advice on how to shake them off. I personally had developed an incredible sensitivity to being tailed. But despite the caution with which I would visit comrades, I could not avoid it. There were so many jobs to be done and I had to visit so many people that it was hard to elude observation. I sensed instinctively not only sleuths following me but also people watching me at particular points such as tram stops and the bridges and alleys of the Vyborg district, so I never led them to the flat where I was going. I had to resort to all sorts of ruses: using back yards, slipping down other people's stairways and yards, etc. By now I had my own rules: don't spend two nights in a row in one flat; don't walk along one road more than once; keep changing your hat and coat. Knowledge of Petersburg's working-class districts helped me greatly. But it was difficult to exist for a long time in such conditions. Lodging each day among new people and in new conditions became terribly wearing. When I had grown tired of stumping round other people's flats, I would head for my sisters' on the Steklyanny. I could still relax better there, where the Okhrana could find me if ordered to, than elsewhere. Fortunately my sisters lived not far apart from each other. When going for a "rest" for a day or two, I would take great precautions: I would choose routes where it was easy to check whether there was any observation. When going to the home of one brother-in-law, I.P. Tyuterev, I would use my sisters, nephews and nieces to mount counter-observation on the agents. I would visit one house by day and move to another for the night, and would come out only in the evening. I knew many of the sleuths by their faces and dress. A particularly convenient flat was I.I. Kovalenko's photographic studio by the Skorbyashchii Church on the Steklyanny. The building did not have a doorkeeper, the door was not bolted, and many callers came to the studio, while the tram stop and the proximity of the church meant I could lose myself in the crowd when I went out.

I had a nice lodging and resting place at D.A. Pavlov's. Here I could take a rest and arrange meetings with any of the comrades and also learn about the state of affairs in the whole district. I could go to that flat at any hour of the night. In a tight spot at night-time, if I was overwhelmed by agents, I would find refuge at N.I. Nazarov's, an Eiwas worker who lived on the Grazhdanka behind the Polytechnical Institute. Often sleuths would pursue me relentlessly, trailing at my heels till late at night. Then like a hounded beast I would make for a safe refuge, Nikolai Ivanovich's place. The way there lay through an orchard where my followers did not dare encroach.

Chernomazov and Co's Provocative Activity

A.M. Gorky gave me great assistance with my work. At his place I could glean news from the world of the rulers and also about the work and thoughts of the democratic intelligentsia, whom Aleksei Maksimovich was trying to draw into revolutionary anti-tsarist work, and I could sometimes hold meetings with these individuals. I came to know Ivan Pavlovich Ladyzhnikov through whom, to avoid the spies, Aleksei Maksimovich passed me information, documents and sometimes money. I often took shelter at I.P.'s flat. At Gorky's I got to know the internationalist Sukhanov. Through meetings here I managed to bring back many workers and valuable party organizers who had dropped out of revolutionary work. I also received from him extremely valuable and extensive material on the pogroms and harassment of Jews during the war, which I succeeded in forwarding abroad in full. I was often at N.D. Sokolov's. Although not in agreement with our position, he did render valuable services to my work. He gave me information about the legal world, and comrades would go straight to him over legal matters. Here I also had encounters with Chkheidze, Kerensky and others. Chkheidze spoke about his solidarity with Zimmerwald, protested against Larin's machinations and declared that he had no common ground with the "Organization Committee". His attitude towards the Gvozdevites and the War Industries Committees was that one should "use the legal opportunities". He did not approve of the methods of Gvozdev and co.

Occasionally I would pop round for the night to see some of my countrymen at the home of Anatolii Nikolai Ryabinin, a Murom man, a geologist and Pravda-ist. The war had knocked him off his Pravda-ist rails, and his horizons were limited to the strategic perspectives of an allied victory over the Germans: a formerly good comrade had become a typical patriotic intellectual. And he was not alone. There were many who had left socialism for patriotism and worked in all types of organizations at the front and the rear.

During this period of illegal residence I came into contact with many extremely interesting Bolshevik workers. From some you could obtain reports on work in their city districts. I managed to send much of their literature abroad. One Eiwas worker, "Yurii" (Lutovinov), who lived at ex-deputy Shurkanov's, gave me enormous help in the struggle against Miron Chernomazov and also sorted out contacts in the south. Comrade Yurii was delegate to the Central Committee Bureau for the south of Russia, chiefly the Donets Basin, where he started to organize and was several times arrested.

Miron Chernomazov and Starck, becoming aware of the firm measures I was taking to clean up the Petersburg organization, went over to the offensive. They called together their "Little" Petersburg Committee and carried a motion against the editorial board of *Voprosy Strakhovaniya*.

From start to finish this resolution was false and had been pushed through an incomplete meeting of the Petersburg Committee by the Mironites. It bore the imprint of the Chernomazovian "special insurance policy", with which no one from the insurance group or the Pravda-ists were in agreement. All the "Bolshevik insurance activists" to which the resolution refers were young, inexperienced students who frequently changed, secretaries of hospital funds and Miron's own henchmen. The latter were dreaming of bringing *Voprosy Strakhovaniya* under his complete control and entrenching himself there. However, he received a rebuttal, and the old editorial board's resolution of 19 January in reply refuted all the Mironites' "factual" points.

With the support of many comrades I called together the Executive Commission of the Petersburg Committee where the far from regular conduct of Starck and certain others was brought to light and they were subjected to censure. I pressed for Miron and Starck to be removed from the Petersburg Committee. Fresh arrests quickly followed which devastated the ranks of Petersburg Committee workers. "Sergei" (Bagdatiev) was arrested first, followed by "Vladimir" (Zalezhsky) and others. The work went to new people and relationships changed markedly for the better.

With the approach of spring the usual growth of revolutionary feeling could be felt. The tsarist government strove to solve the labour question by instituting councils of elders in accordance with the act of 1903. Our organizations were against this, and however much it was praised by the Gvozdevites, this government ruse did not succeed. The Petersburg Committee took advantage of this act for agitation and, in one or two places, to organize workers. The resolution on this question by workers at New Lessner is typical and reflects that attitude of the revolutionary masses to the government's scheming. This resolution was apparently adopted not long before the strike at that works in March. I quote it from a copy in my possession:

> This general meeting of workers at the New Lessner works, having discussed the management's proposal to organize an institute of elders on the basis of the act of 1903, declares that this act was created by a base

servant of tsarism, minister Plehve, exclusively to oppose the rising revolutionary movement of the working class in those years.

The author of this policemen's act had the intention of forming a permanent cell among the workers through which it would be able to fish out the most active organizers.

The act had the aim of paralysing the revolutionary initiative of the masses and replacing it by a legal and amicable community with the enemies of the proletariat, capital and its accomplice, the government.

The working class has understood this with its sound instinct as the foul fraud of the policemen's lawyers and throws out the deal offered with a firm protest.

So now it is that thirteen years later when the working class is again gathering its strength to settle accounts with a government that has ruined it, this same act has crawled out on to the stage.

The working class will not allow itself to be duped this time either.

While decisively rejecting the management's proposal, we at the same time protest against the supposed friends of the workers who are trying to justify this campaign against the working class in the pages of the bourgeois press and from the tribune of the State Duma.

We demand trade unions and freedom for other class organizations of the proletariat, the restoration of the workers' press and recognition of the works commissions elected on broad democratic principles.

The works commissions of which the resolution speaks existed semi-legally in many major enterprises and were composed of representatives from the sections and workshops. All matters relating to the internal régime of the shops were subject to the purview of these commissions. The function of representation fell to them in any conflict between workers and management.

February passed and I had been in Russia exactly four months. Work was growing harder each day. I could go out only at dusk, meeting representatives of the organization and comrades of the Bureau of the Central Committee under cover of night. I had by now spent many nights beneath the open sky, eluding agents in back gardens, orchards and other people's back yards. Often I would only reach a resting-place by daybreak, by which time I was frozen stiff and tired out. All the comrades from the Bureau of the Central Committee and the Petersburg Committee workers were insisting on my speedy return abroad. I had collected a wealth of material and documents and set about organizing my departure. I found a transit passport through Beloostrov. For my departure I used the flat of M.G. Pavlova on Serdobolsky Street and I selected Lanskaya station to alight at and a train going just as far as Terijoki. My things travelled with comrade M.I. Stetskevich, to be on the safe side. Having waited about three hours as Terijoki I bought a ticket for Helsinki where, having passed through a tight formation of gendarmes and agents, I arrived early in the morning.

4

Scandinavia and America

IN HELSINKI I found my old friends, comrades Wiik and Rovio. They were overjoyed at my safe return and displayed great interest in the work and state of affairs in Russia. The Central Committee of Finnish Social Democracy decided to hear a report, which I made with Rovio as interpreter. My conclusions on the inevitability of revolution in Russia in the near future greatly encouraged the Finnish comrades, who were under pressure from tsarist reaction.

There was no point in settling down for long in Helsinki: it was dangerous, as agents were very active. My friend Uskila was expected from Oulu, and he was to accompany me there. I did not have long to wait. Two days later, having said goodbye to my Finnish friends and agreed plans for further work on setting up communications and despatch of literature, I set out for Finland's northern borders.

We got off at Kempele station and travelled on to Oulu by horse. Our caution proved not to be misplaced. My Finnish comrades had learnt through their contacts that I had been noted, and that an Okhrana man had arrived in Oulu from Petersburg. I decided to travel by horse direct to the Swedish frontier. Comrade Uskila found me a man who knew the route well. But he had no horse. At that time a horse cost 200–300 Finnish marks. My guide was most pleased about my decision to acquire one and had the idea of making a bit out of it by selling it for 700–800 marks on the Swedish side. So I had unintentionally succeeded in giving my escort an interest in the success of the trip. We decided to leave Oulu at night.

One February evening we headed into the polar north in a little peasant's sledge. A snowstorm overtook us, but the horse proved to be very hardy and though getting bogged down in deep snowdrifts, we reached a farmstead where we spent the rest of the night. And then wonderfully mild weather set in. The rest of the journey, which took eight days, was pure relaxation and pleasure. We travelled mostly during the evenings, nights and mornings and rested during the afternoons with poor Finnish crofters. The latter lived remarkably poorly and engaged in woodcutting and related trades, being ruthlessly exploited by the landowners.

The north was blossoming in its majesty and beauty. Finding our way along disused roads, we ended up in a magical realm of virgin snows. Our little pony and sledge were hidden beneath the arched forest trackway, illuminated by the miraculous patterns of the Northern Lights. The snow-white paws of boughs overwhelmed by the blizzard bent down over us. As we went deeper into the far north the high forest disappeared; it gave way to dwarf birch woods and mossy swamps.

Peasants, and sometimes even Russian soldiers, would run across us along the way, but everything about us was so ordinary that nothing caught their eye. Now and again my driver pointed out distant fires of Finnish villages with his whip-handle. We travelled far to the east of Kemi. From Tornio, the frontier town, only dogs could be heard. My escort decided to head northwards twenty or thirty versts beyond Karunki to where he had a peasant acquaintance, whose farmstead stood not far from the Swedish border. We arrived there in the morning. We were received gladly and given a separate, tidy room. To my questions about crossing the frontier the landlord and landlady, who spoke only Finnish and Swedish, replied in sign language that it was possible. The driver too was content, as the demand for horses was great. Upon selling it he was supposed to refund me part of my expenses and pay my escorts over the border and also for the lodging, but he started complaining about the difficulties of the market for horses and so forth. The "economic" psychology of the muzhik overtook the renowned Finnish honour.

At dusk next day we set out. There were three of us: one carrying the trunk and the other with his hands free. We had to go on skis. Only as a child had I been familiar with the art of skating and sledging, but never on skis. In all forms of sliding, however, the main thing is to know how to keep your balance, and I put on the skis without a moment's thought. A steep slope down to the plain started a couple of hundred paces farther on. I did not escape without a fall. The Finns moved lightly and swiftly but I in my heavy city overcoat found it hard going. I could scarcely keep up with them and was so engrossed that I did not notice the frontier markings. We admired the lighted gendarme post when already on the Swedish side. We walked into a small Swedish village and decided to drink some coffee to celebrate the safe crossing, as is the custom there. We found a well-meaning old peasant who had at one time lived in America and knew some English. He agreed to put us up and we got talking. I found out from both him and my escorts that all along the border from Tornio to Karunki there was contraband in goods, horses etc. In addition, German prisoners-of-war escaping from Russia would pass through. The border area as a whole had despite its apparent emptiness become quite busy. All my interlocutors were hostile towards the rulers of Russia and were evidently rendering all sorts of assistance to Finnish and Swedish activists.

Having settled up with our kind landlord and also with the guides, instructing them to obtain extra for escorting me from my driver, I went to the railway station. The train took me to Haparanda. There I found my cobbler collaborator and learnt from him about the misadventures of my good comrade "Voice in the Wilderness" and the reason for the halt in despatches. It turned out that in January "Voice in the Wilderness" had fallen into the hands of customs guards while ferrying literature over by night, and was handed over to the police. He had arrived one evening at the literature dump in Haparanda. Taking out about two poods of pamphlets and newspapers, he threw a white sheet over his shoulders and moved off through the snow to Tornio. On the way he noticed a customs guard on horseback and lay down flat in the snow with the parcels, covering himself with the sheet. The camouflage succeeded splendidly: the guard did not notice him, but the horse evidently took fright at the sheet rippling in the wind and shied. The guard then started to shoot towards the spot. "Voice in the Wilderness" had to declare himself. The guard sent him with all his goods to the lock-up at Tornio. The comrade lay there about two days and then, taking advantage of the guard's negligence, escaped at night straight to Swedish Haparanda barefoot and in his underwear. The alarm was raised, agents and gendarmes rushed out, but it was already too late. To avoid becoming the victim of any treachery by the Swedish frontier police, "Voice in the Wilderness" travelled off to work deep inside Sweden, in the mines. There were mass searches in Tornio but our comrades managed to evade capture.

The route had to be rebuilt from scratch. This fortunately proved feasible. Some twenty versts off Tornio in the Gulf of Bothnia is the little island of Seskarö where lived comrade Löteberg, whom I knew through the chairman of the Swedish Transport Workers' Union. From there it was possible to ski over the ice to Kemi, where comrades took on this hazardous job. Despatches were once again moving and I set off for Stockholm. There comrades Bukharin, Pyatakov and others were awaiting me. The documents and my reports on the state of affairs in Russia formed the topic of lengthy discussions. I sent off my reports to our central organ, *Sotsial-Demokrat*. My communications on the state of affairs in Russia went round a considerable proportion of the socialist press in Scandinavia. Branting was most interested and surprised that Russian workers were displaying so little concern for the fate of their fatherland and their allies' fatherlands; but he did not conceal his admiration for their heroism and tried to interpret our attitude to the war as a result of the barbaric policy of tsarism.

Among the Party Exiles

During my stay in Russia major disagreements had developed among our foreign group of party workers. The former *Kommunist* editorial board had fallen apart over the national question. As always in conditions of exile, these disagreements sowed such hostility that by the time of my arrival relations between our comrades in Switzerland (V.I. Lenin, G. Zinoviev and others) on the one hand and those living in Sweden (comrades N.I. Bukharin, G. Pyatakov and others) were extremely strained. Contacts with and work for Russia were the first to suffer, and these for me counted above all else. I had imagined that you could keep your own opinion on this or that point of our programme and fight for its adoption, but I could not see the need for animosity and least of all for damaging the workers' cause itself with such animosity. This phenomenon is, however, endemic in our intelligentsia, which is so doctrinaire in defence of its "principles" that it will even abandon the work in hand.

I found myself getting drawn into these disputes as a sort of buffer, attempting to reconcile the parties in order to prevent the publication of collections of articles for Russia being delayed simply because of the differences that had arisen. For a good two months I pursued a "conciliator" line but was compelled to abandon it as the parties started to exhibit pettiness. *Kommunist* was replaced by *Sbornik Sotsiala-Demokrata*.

In the Stockholm group working on the despatch of literature to Russia, one worker, Bogrovsky, proved unworthy of the trust placed in him and had come into contact with a suspicious group of Estonians and in particular one Keskula, receiving money from him "for party purposes", giving him receipts on the headed paper of the Central Committee of the RSDLP that I had left him and using my stamp of representative of the Central Committee of the RSDLP in French. This was discovered accidentally by Bukharin. Bogrovsky was expelled from the party and the Swedish comrades were informed about him. Bukharin conducted investigations and stumbled upon the trail of an organization of provocateurs which was aiming to ensnare Russian revolutionaries and Swedish young socialists. Keskula proved to be an agent of the German General Staff. Also an agent was his friend who was in charge of one of the sections of the Russian Insurance Society in Stockholm. Apparently the investigation by Bukharin and Pyatakov so perturbed the Swedish police that the arrest and deportation of Bukharin (who was living on the passport of Moshe Dolgolevsky) and Pyatakov followed almost immediately. These were justified by our comrades' "participation" in the congress of the Swedish socialist youth. Actually they attended the congress only as visitors. I was there too, but the police did not find out about me.

Police terror in Sweden had reached a remarkable level. Russians were being deported upon the slightest suspicion, and I stopped in Christiania as a precaution. From Christiania I got in touch with Branting over the arrest of my comrades, making at the same time some enquiries about the firmness of Sweden's neutrality.

These arrests caused panic not only among Russian exiles but also among Swedish young socialists. Proceedings for "high treason" were instituted against Höglund and others. Searches were made of many leading figures and the newspaper *Stormklockan*. The police assiduously sought out the contacts between young socialists and Russian revolutionaries. This led to us destroying part of our literature, but some was confiscated. The secret service of the German General Staff represented us Russian revolutionaries, the opponents of war, as agents of the Russian General Staff. The opportunist socialists likewise looked upon us with malice for our work among the young social democrats. But to the government we were all dangerous, and they tried all ways to get rid of us. Following Bukharin yet another of our people, the printer and Bundist, Gordon, was deported. Many of us were placed under surveillance and mail subjected to inspection.

Soon afterwards the whole Stockholm group, comrades Bukharin, Pyatakov and Kollontai, moved to Christiania. At first the police got worried, but after the intervention of Norwegian social democracy they left us all in peace. Here too comrades took a cautious part in the literature of the youth movement, but despair prevailed in the Russian work. The letters from the editorial board of the central organ became more and more shattering, and dreams of embarking on publications with the participation of Bukharin and Pyatakov had to be abandoned.

Relations with the Norwegian social democrats were as before good, but it was hard to expect any assistance from them for Russian work. All these Scandinavian socialists were, notwithstanding their verbal internationalism, little interested in other countries. They would listen eagerly to the unusual things about the lives of Russian revolutionaries and conspicuously publish sensational reports from Russia and that was it. Beyond that their help did not go.

In Norway, at Christiania, I met an internationalist Socialist-Revolutionary, Pierre Orage (Aleksandrovich), who had come via Murmansk from the Siberian taiga. Abroad he established contact with Chernov and other leftists. He arranged the supply of literature against the war, which at his request and for information I sent off to Russia together with our own. In the summer of 1916 comrade Aleksandrovich used my contacts to get to Russia.

A Trip to America

The material about the conditions of Jews in Russia during the war which I had brought from Petersburg greatly interested Stockholm Jews and they offered to purchase it, but I did not want to sell it as I was afraid that it would fall into the hands of agents of the German General Staff for their own strategic ends. So I demanded that the Jews donate money for a publishing house which I proposed to create with my comrades, but they prevaricated as they wanted to acquire the material outright.

Money for transport had dried up; our foreign centre was itself poor and I was counting principally upon my own resources. Not wanting to abandon work in Russia or to vegetate in the inactivity of exile, I decided to take the material on the Jews to America and hand it over to one of the Jewish socialist societies.

After lengthy correspondence with the Central Committee's foreign group, I obtained their consent and a small sum of money for the trip. At the end of June I set out on the Norwegian vessel *Kristianiafjörd*. I had a third-class berth in a stuffy cabin below decks, but secret documents were looked after by a comrade in the engine-room. I had no legal passport so I decided to get by with my membership card of the British trade union, the Amalgamated Society of Engineers, and an old French passport. The difficult part of the passage was the British blockade and military control.

It was a good time for the voyage. The sea from Christiania to Bergen, a passage of about twenty-four hours, was calm and the weather sunny. The steamship rounded the beautiful southern part of mountainous Norway. Here and there you could see snowy peaks in the distance and on the rocky shores fishing settlements with all the conquests of technology: telephones, postal service and electricity supply.

Among the passengers were many businessmen. There were also Russian officials and technicians travelling to America in connection with war contracts and ladies of all nations off to see the husbands who were profiteering from the war. This clientele was luxuriously established in the first- and second-class cabins. The third class had a few hundred passengers going out to "try their fortune", various nationalities, chiefly Scandinavians. There were some Russian Jews fleeing from London and conscription, and the wives of some Russians who had settled in the "New World". It was a happy trip: a band would often be playing on deck, and young people quickly got to know each other and danced gaily.

There was a twenty-four-hour call at Bergen and then the ship headed down the fjord into the Atlantic. There was an obligatory call at a northern British port, Kirkwall. Tugs armed with high-velocity guns came out to meet us. They acted as escorts through the minefields and brought the ship into a natural harbour on whose shores spread the small but ancient town. Many vessels large and small, flying the flags of all the Scandinavian states, lay in the bay. Many had been lying there for months, suffering all sorts of ordeals from the rapacious British. All this was cloaked in the interests of the war.

Fortunately for us the inspection of the ship did not last long. We third-classers were not bothered at all and after about twelve hours' moorage we sailed on.

As we sailed northwards the ocean became more menacing. A cold wind blew, and sunny days gave way to bad weather. Only off the shores of America did we again feel the summer. Once within sight of the lighthouses and pilot boats on the New York roads the passengers milled on to the now warm decks, waiting to see the shores of that legendary land.

We took on a pilot and later, upon entering the harbour, there was a stop for a superficial medical examination right there on deck. They looked at our eyes and hands. We entered the harbour before sunset and the ship docked. They let the first- and second-class passengers off without any special checks. But the third class were left to the next day. Ahead of them was a trip to the "Island of Tears" for the interrogation and examination of poor emigrants. It was hard luck on the sick and people with no property, acquaintances or relatives in the country. They would not be allowed in that "land of the free", and at best would be quickly sent back; there were cases of a month's forced detention.

Our big ten-thousand-ton ship seemed tiny among the gigantic installations of the port of New York. The heat was unbearable. It was impossible to remain in the cabins even at night, and the passengers went up on deck. By sunset the harbour was like an oven breathing fire.

In the morning after breakfast disembarkation of third-class passengers commenced. Tickets were given up and we went down to a quayside shed where scruffy bags were set out ready for the customs officers. After the examination, embarkation on a small steamer and a trip to the "Island of Tears". The half-hour voyage through the harbour among the steel and stone monsters had an oppressive effect. Finally we disembarked and passed one by one through the medical examination. The suspect ones were singled out and the healthy ones allowed on without delay. We found ourselves in a huge hall set about with benches for visitors and desks for the officials. Questioning: Where're you from? Where're you going? Have you funds? My trade as a turner proved sufficient. This was adequate grounds for immediate entry and I was given a permit. I walked along a long grilled corridor, reminiscent of a menagerie. On the other side of the grilles were the public, apparently awaiting their families and friends. Again on to a steamer, but now to the very centre of New York. I reached my friends' flat on the overhead railway.

The Russian colony in the city was enormous. Two daily papers were published (including a social-democratic one in Russian) and several other papers in Yiddish and other languages. In New York periodicals and magazines were published in all the languages of the world. I made the acquaintance of the colony and its representatives. All the Russian socialists were grouped around the newspaper *Novy Mir*. The leader of this group was Dr Ingerman, a Menshevik. He was also in charge of *Novy Mir* itself although the former Bolshevik, N. Nakoryakov, living under the name of Ellert, was the editor. Among the paper's permanent staff were Volodarsky, Lisovsky, Voskov, Zorin, Melnichansky and Menson, who was in charge of the technical side and acted as compositor. The printshop had two type-setting machines in slum premises. The paper was quite poor materially.

I made several reports on the situation in Russia and Europe and on the attitude to the war, which provoked major arguments among the *Novy Mir* socialists. Ingerman defended the European opportunists, but this defence did not encounter sympathy among workers' exile groups. A small group of Bolsheviks headed by comrade Minkin-Menson was formed and, relying on vacillating exiles like Volodarsky, Melnichansky, Zorin and others, campaigned for the removal of Ingerman and his friends from the leadership of the newspaper and the group. But the other side was not asleep and waged a struggle in the American style, introducing personal and sensational issues, hysteria and abuse.

Victory nevertheless went to our bloc; but it could not be carried through to the end as the Bolsheviks had insufficient competent party and newspaper workers.

With regard to my own business, I learnt that I had not chosen altogether the most propitious time to arrive. All the rich Jewish community had gone off for the summer to their country homes or were touring America. However, without losing hope, I established contacts. I was introduced to the editor of a Jewish socialist paper *Vorwärts* who agreed to use some of the material, but he was an ardent Germanophile and I was most reluctant to pass the material to him. I also met some Jewish scholars who undertook to find a publisher. My condition was: pass the material to any Jewish organization for the latter to publish in English and other languages. There were quite a few private speculators about, but I did not have any dealings with them. However, my scholars so dragged things out that I had to chase them up. July passed, August, and still they were "discussing" it. I was demanding money for revolutionary work in Russia, setting a minimum price of 500 dollars (carriage out of Russia, the passage to America and the return to Russia), but stating that I wanted more. But they referred to the absence of rich representatives of their society and agreed to give 500 dollars from their own pockets. Time was precious, so I took the 500 dollars to get back to Russia more quickly. Living and the journey had cost about half that amount, so the rest could go towards revolutionary work in Russia.

In the two months of my stay in New York I had time to acquaint myself only superficially with the life of that monstrous city, resembling a huge workshop. American life is steeped in hardheadedness about business. The whole American way of life is coloured by an extreme selfishness. Everyone lives only to get rich quick or to dream of doing so.

New York City is situated on a peninsula washed by the Hudson River and the Atlantic Ocean, divided by a canal and a river into several parts, and with well-planned main streets stretching the length of the peninsula and transecting it. In the southern part works, offices and warehouses are concentrated while in the northern part are the dwellings of the best-paid section of factory and office workers. In the morning all trams and underground overhead railway traffic heads southwards in force, but in the evening uptown to the north. Every day hundreds of thousands of people rush back and forth from one end of the city to the other. The New York worker dresses smartly and lives and eats considerably better than his European counterpart.

During my brief interlude in New York I observed two strikes: one by tramway employees, the other on the buses. The action was led by the trade unions. The employers mobilized strikebreakers and the republican and even democratic authorities provided police to protect the "right to work". The working population declared a boycott of the trams and those operating them. The strikers took to photographing the strikebreakers, clashes occurred, the police took the strikebreakers' side and fired on the strikers. The sympathies of the working population, including even the children, were on the side of the striking workers and strikebreakers who drove their trams through working-class districts had a hard time. Little boys smeared the rails with soap and pelted the scab drivers with stones, while the adults threw them out of their cabs. The police fired in the air, waiting for reinforcements; a scuffle would take place. Disputes between labour and capital in America are bellicose. Scabs, spies and provocateurs from all kinds of Pinkerton-type bureaux join in on the employers' side. It is rare that a major strike passes off without provocations, arrests of union leaders and some bloodshed.

In New York I made the acquaintance of the editor of the social-democratic newspaper *The New York People's News*, published in German for German-speaking social democrats. I gave them a piece on the revolutionary movement in Russia. The comrades took an internationalist position within the left wing of the American Socialist Party, which was thoroughly opportunist.

America had not yet been drawn into the war and was preserving its neutrality by fulfilling contracts for the Franco-British-Russian coalition. The gold from war contracts flowed bountifully into the pockets of American businessmen. The newspapers were conducting a persistent campaign for America's entry, but Wilson confined himself to peacemaking for the moment. Even at that time, however, it was clear to everyone who wanted to see that American capitalists were preparing for war. They were cleverly working on so-called "public opinion", fostering militarist sentiment and preparing for conscription. Churches, demonstrations, newspapers, parliament, the Stars and Stripes, theatres, schools, cinemas, were all used to preach the defence of the "American homeland" and to demand the formation of an army and navy.

Although old immigrants from other countries were little concerned at the fate of the "American homeland", the generation that had grown up in America, those of pre-school age included, responded vigorously to this chauvinist bally-hoo. In one working-class district I saw an American window display, "Downfall of a Nation", which showed the invasion by unnamed enemies, the destruction of cities and other such horrors, and children would always greet the American flag with wild enthusiasm.

American organized capital kept firm control of the people. It also knew how to buy off the labour leaders. The president of the American Federation of Labor, Samuel Gompers, regarded himself as a friend of Wilson and was his accomplice in hoodwinking the workers.

The corruption of workers' representatives by bribery and other means had become a regular employers' tactic and did enormous damage to the workers' cause.

However alluring my comrades' proposal for me to remain in America and get to know its working-class life, I overcame all temptation and made preparations for my departure. Again a passport was required. As I had already used all my papers I had to reapply to the local consulate. There a clerk advised me to obtain a reference from a religious community, against which the consulate would be obliged to issue me a passport for the journey to Russia. The difficulty was that I was not a member of any of the communities and had no contacts with priests. But I presumed that in America priests also would above all be "businessmen", and I banked on the dollar doing its job. My supposition was justified. For two dollars the clergyman gave me a reference. I affixed a picture to it, handed it in at the consulate and arranged to collect the passport at the quayside when the ship sailed.

The New York comrades arranged a small send-off, and on 14 September 1916 I left the shores of America on the Danish vessel *United States*. The comrades asked me to send some party friends to America who could direct the work and the newspaper, and gave me money for the purpose.

This time I had a second-class ticket and was registered on the passenger list as a journalist. It was stuffy in the cabin and I could hear the noise of the engines. I complained, and was given an individual cabin in the first class. My isolation was most convenient, as I was carrying articles and letters from various American comrades and had quite a few documents on me which might attract the interest of the British police. I managed to hide them in the cabin.

About eight days later we were back in Kirkwall. A stern reception awaited us there. The ship was held for forty-eight hours and a personal search made of all passengers. Women travelling to Germany were searched especially rigorously. I still managed to get through without being searched, while my membership card for the Amalgamated Society of Engineers, of which I was a member, served as a passport, since my Russian passport had been "forgotten" at the consulate.

We were all very relieved to get beyond the British blockade. Twenty-four hours later the coast of Norway appeared, and after another twenty-four hours we were at Christiania, having spent two whole weeks from New York. My friends were no longer in Christiania (Bukharin was living in Copenhagen), and I continued to Denmark on the same ship. I stopped several days in Copenhagen to contact the foreign centre of the Central Committee and agree plans about work in Russia. And there too I found my old Russian pals.

Return from America
There were many Russians in Copenhagen that autumn. Here were gathered all the wartime speculators and marauders. They were mostly speculating in food and German manufactures (dyestuffs, medicines, office materials etc.). A layer of wealthy "goulashers" appeared, a peculiar variety of speculator in "military" tinned food who knew how to dispose of it in Germany. "Socialists" did not hang back from war profits either. Parvus, a German socialist well known in

Russia in his day, had already made more than a million and had begun to finance and establish businesses. Some Russian social democrats had no qualms about profiteering in pencils, medicines and other such trifles required by the Russian and Scandinavian markets. Some paid for this with deportation from Denmark, but the change of domicile did not hinder business. It was generally a nasty scene.

Already many comrades had gathered in the Russian social-democratic circle. At a meeting in the autumn of 1916 I met the liquidators, Sazonov-Rozanov, Piletsky and Dalin; the *Nashe Slovo* people, Chudnovsky, Uritsky and Zurabov; and Bukharin, Gordon and others from the Bolsheviks.

Lack of activity oppressed Bukharin, and I suggested he travel to America for party work. N.I. agreed and found himself a companion, Chudnovsky. Some thought had to be given to travel arrangements: and this was fairly complicated as the British blockade was becoming stricter. Bukharin was the type of impractical Russian intellectual for whom I had to think out every detail of the trip. Before his departure he thought of "legalizing" himself in Denmark and going to America not as Moshe Dolgolevsky but under his own name; but before confirming the possibility of legalization he had already booked a ticket to America in his own name. All his legalization moves failed: Stauning, the socialist minister, could not and would not help with it.

Nikolai Ivanovich had to remain Moshe, but this complicated his passage. The steamship office had already been paid the money and the name of Bukharin was by now familiar; they knew his face there. I again had to devise ways of getting out of an absurd situation. The trouble about cancelling the steamship booking in Bukharin's name was one of money; and anyway there were no spare places left. I decided to take Nikolai Ivanovich as far as Christiania and embark him there as Moshe Dolgolevsky. I would ask the steamship office for Bukharin's reservation to be forwarded to Dolgolevsky in Christiania, since "Bukharin" had supposedly cancelled it. This worked. Chudnovsky embarked at Copenhagen, while "Dolgolevsky" was to embark at Christiania. But our route there lay through Sweden, entry into which was barred to him on pain of a six-month stay in prison.

We decided to go by steamer to avoid arrest. We bought tickets and made straight for the vessel with our luggage and escorts. It turned out to be small tub laden with foodstuffs, and the sea was running high. It emerged that the steamer would be calling at other towns and settlements with prolonged stops and would not reach Christiania in under forty-eight hours. The voyage would not be cosy; tossing about on the waves would not be much fun and a lot of precious time would be wasted, so I started to think about how to get rid of the ticket and go by rail. I asked the captain whether we weren't running a risk of being caught by the Germans aboard that old steamboat. He stated that such occurrences did happen, and that he could provide no guarantees that it wouldn't happen to us. I gradually brought N.I. around to travelling by rail; I proposed that he became my brother for the time being and travel via Helsingør and Hälsingborg whence the trip across the Öresund takes only a few minutes. N.I. agreed, and we were left with the job of working out how to ditch the steamboat. I went to the office and asked the manager: are you able to guarantee us against seizure by the Germans? Well, of course, the manager got cross and could give us no guarantee. Then I asked him to help unload our things and exchange our tickets for train tickets. He kindly agreed, and a couple of hours later we were already on our way. We crossed safely over the the Swedish side, caught a quick glimpse of some sleuths, got into a carriage and a few minutes later moved off. In the morning we were in Christiania, where we awaited the arrival of the ocean liner. A couple of days later I saw comrades Bukharin and Chudnovsky off on their "conquest of America", then I made for Stockholm, intending to set off for Russia as soon as possible.

During my absence from Sweden work on the despatch of literature had completely fizzled out. Contacts were kept up, but the comrades in charge of this work had no money. It was essential to get moving as much literature as possible immediately so that it could cross the frontier as I travelled. More than ten poods were sent to Tornio and Karunki, presupposing arrangements for ferrying it over in various places.

I had meetings with all the comrades from the Swedish left social democrats: Höglund, Ström, Kilbom and others. In this period an event of enormous importance took place in the Swedish party: a split occurred. The young or "left" social democrats left the united party and founded their own central organ and party Central Committee.

Branting took advantage of his position to criticize and slander the "youth". The bourgeois press welcomed the critical onslaughts of the old central organ *Social-Demokraten*. But probably because of this criticism, the young social-democratic organization grew and tore the Swedish proletariat out of opportunism's embraces.

My meetings with Branting were of a purely working nature. Bearing in mind the military situation in the north and the variety of fortifications and garrisons in the frontier zone, I would notify him of my journeys on the frontier and about my work. This was necessary in the event of any misunderstanding at the border, suspicion of espionage or my arrest. We agreed that I could inform the local authorities into whose hands I might fall that Branting knew about my trip; and upon receiving some communication about my misadventure he would contact the appropriate minister. But I managed things so carefully that during many trips around border villages I did not once attract the attention of the authorities.

Haparanda, the border town of Sweden, was at that time a centre for espionage and snooping. Native Finns and Germans who had lived in Russia and Finland before the war, British, French and Russian and other intelligence agents and counter-intelligence agents were regulars at the hotels and restaurants, in barbers' shops and other public places. Every word travelling in or out of Russia was seized and conveyed to the right quarter.

But in Haparanda a secret Finnish "activist" meeting-point had been organized. It has a well-equipped passport office that supplied its supporters and German agents with the relevant papers conforming to wartime requirements. They had their own ferry for people, literature and arms. The organization was amply fitted out. I had managed to obtain information about this from my Swedish acquaintances living on the border, whom I had to deal with over organization and transport.

Military espionage was likewise making excellent use of the "sympathies" of various varieties of socialist who had turned into supporters of either the Entente or the Central Powers. German espionage had found agents from among the socialists of the small nationalities like the Estonians and Finns. One Danish socialist journalist, Kruse, made a trip to Russia on unspecified business, hovering around our exiles to obtain from them personal contacts in Russia. Then he would turn up in Russia to meet social democrats, purportedly bringing assignments from organizations or individuals abroad. His link with the German spy Kesküla was quickly discovered and the exiled comrades threw him out of their circles.

We had to be most careful and alert to any dirty dealings from the military: provocation and espionage. The disintegration of the socialist circles and their division into every conceivable "orientation" created a cover for sheer graft and the passage of certain members of the intelligentsia into the service of the bourgeoisie, with the appearance of serving an idea.

When I set out for the Swedish frontier, I took an interpreter, a worker who had a good command of Swedish, the exile A. Khavkin. En route we called at Lulea, and met local social democrats to obtain a few contacts at the far end of the Swedish-Finnish frontier. From there we set off for Haparanda.

My old friend, the master cobbler, had during the war turned into a staid entrepreneur and property owner, now wealthy from his shoe business and with his own house. His views had also undergone a certain modification. In his arguments he was becoming more respectable and approved of the right-wing stand. He no longer exhibited any special interest in my work and he was obviously afraid of being compromised in the eyes of the authorities and his customers. But that did not hurt me, as there were enough comrades prepared to help on the Swedish border. Part of the literature was sent over to Seskarö, the island in the Gulf of Bothnia, to comrade Löteberg. Another part we took with us in a wooden trunk to an address given by the editors of *Norskenflyammen*, at a hamlet some fifty kilometres north along the frontier from Haparanda.

Not far from the railway station we found a small farmstead and its young owner. He welcomed us in and, after reading the letter from the comrades in Luleå, agreed to help us. I decided, with the comrade's help, to make for Russia from there, and later to have literature sent by the same route. The farmer asked for two days to set up and prepare the route. A particular nuisance was the Tornio river, which was resisting the mild frosts and had frozen only in one or two places. We had brought some refreshment and plied our new acquaintance with it. Having settled upon a route, he went off to scout.

A couple of days later the farmer returned and joyfully announced that all was ready. He had found a route and a horse that would get us away. My main requirement was to be taken to Oulu. If one person could not do this he must hand me over to another driver so that I would not have to look for horses myself. I promised to pay one mark for each kilometre's travel and could pay more if necessary. But the Finns rarely exploited this.

We decided to set out at midnight. It was the second half of October 1916. I changed into clothes appropriate to a Finn, took a bag for the journey, underwear and literature and said farewell. We went cautiously across the fields to the river, often stumbling into holes. The Arctic night was not dark, and although the sky was covered with light clouds you could still see a long way over the snow. We crossed the river well apart from each other holding on to the ends of a long rope, as my guide did not trust the ice. We walked along the river for a long time. Finally we reached the bank; a track ran alongside through the snow. My guide pointed out that the track had been trodden by the frontier guards and gendarmes. We walked on under the cover of reeds and thickets and came out on to the main road to Tornio. After walking along it for a couple of kilometres we headed for a solitary farmhouse and roused the owner. As we rested, a horse was harnessed and off I was taken. Where and to whom I no longer cared, trusting entirely to the Finn's prudence and honesty.

The Return to Russia

We did not drive far along the paved road but turned off down a cart-track in an easterly direction. There was a little snow and the sledge leapt over the hummocks and dipped into the hollows, tiring out the horse. By dinner-time we had reached the farmhouse and stayed with a business-like Finn. The farm was on the forest fringe and had many outbuildings and much livestock. The lads were out shooting hare around the house. They did not know any languages other than Finnish and we had to pass the time in silence. We were treated to coffee, milk and something recalling our Russian yoghurt but a lot thicker.

A few hours later we set out but now with a different driver. I did not ask which road it was — I wouldn't have been understood, but I could see that they knew where they were to go. The road ran through a wood and was little used. The Finns had obviously selected the most secluded routes on purpose. From the border onwards I had not met a single horse or pedestrian. This driver did not take me far but stopped at a farm too. The building was old but sturdy; and while the forest was not far away, ploughed land lay all around. I could not understand how in the far north it could yield a crop. The householder welcomed us in cordially in Swedish and explained using his fingers that he had been expecting me for two days. That rather surprised me, but as I did not command sufficient vocabulary could not enquire how he had been informed. He took us into a log house. The interior reminded me of our own peasant homesteads. The same large living area with the huge stove, benches around the walls and clothing, horse-harnesses and other tackle hanging on the wall. But in some farmhouses there would be another section which was clean and where you would find bentwood chairs, a sewing-machine, a mirror and even a gramophone or accordion. The Finns are great coffee-lovers as we Russians are tea-lovers; so everywhere I would be treated to some, but I preferred bread and milk as I wanted to have some nourishment.

We left the farm at about six in the evening. It was comfortable to relax in a good sleigh after the ruts of the previous track. The driver did not ask where he had to go but followed his own route avoiding the main roads. We drove over the weak ice of a rivulet, sparsely vegetated rough land and cart-tracks. It began to grow dark. The autumn night was quickly coming on. Lights appeared in the distance; that was the little town of Rovaniemi twinkling. We kept straight towards it. The closer the lights twinkled, the clearer became the muffled noise of a river. It was very dark, there was a little snow but the clever horse knew the way and cautiously descended the steep bank as it made towards the sound of the water. After it had gone a couple of hundred paces the horse snorted and stopped. The distance was sinister and black. The driver got off and walked on ahead. I soon heard his whip-handle striking the water. The ice did not stretch the full width of the river. He shouted once and then again, evidently calling for a boat. An answer was heard out of the distant gloom. With a sign my guide told me to alight. The approaching splash of oars was soon audible and in a few minutes the bow of a large boat came up on to the ice beside us. One of the men got out and stayed with the horse while the farmer came with me to the other bank. A few minutes later the boat had crossed the noisy river and pulled into a landing-stage.

We walked up the bank and came out into a small street. We went into a large house, where a few people were sitting at a table. Conversation was palely lit by a paraffin lamp. They all turned towards us: the farmer was obviously talking about me. I was given a chair and they watched in anticipation and discussed among themselves. A young man arrived, dressed in town clothes, and put some questions to me in Finnish and Swedish. I replied in Swedish that I could speak and understand only Russian, French, German and English and knew no other languages. Then he asked me in German for the password; another approached me and flicked back his jacket lapel to reveal a badge. I said I hadn't a password or a badge. My words when translated stunned them all and I was questioned: where was I going? How had I got there? And who was I? I quickly gathered that I had landed myself on the premises of some organization that seemed to me conspiratorial in nature. Thousands of possibilities flashed through my mind but two were most likely: I had landed either among German spies or Finnish revolutionaries by courtesy of the bourgeoisie — the so-called "activists". I decided, however, not to manifest any of my suspicions. To the questions I replied that I was a Russian revolutionary, a member of the RSDLP and my name was Belenin. I was travelling to Russia on party business and I had arranged drivers and the route through a Swedish comrade on the frontier. "I hope that this will not go beyond the people present here and that I shall not be sent to the police," I added.

They listened to it all, interpreted, discussed and then announced that they would make a search of my belongings. I offered them my bag with my things and literature and the pockets of my clothes.

They looked for marks on my underwear and on my outer clothing as well. But everything on me was foreign and they attached no importance to the newspapers and pamphlets. Anyway, nothing suspicious had evidently been found on me and I re-packed everything. The Finn who spoke German offered to look after me. We left the mysterious house and went to another, smaller and fairly new one. He stated that this was his quarters. A few more questions were asked there about what Finns I knew. Out of caution I named two or three know to me only as Sejm deputies. My interlocutor proved to be an engineer who worked at a local sawmill. The conversation moved on to the war. The engineer was on Germany's side on this question. He wished for her victory and expected good fortune from this for Finland too. I did not have enough German to enter into a long argument; but I did express my conviction that the Finnish people would gain their freedom only through the overthrow of tsarism. The orientation towards Germany was only to replace one yoke by another. Finland's whole fate was tied up with the success of the revolutionary struggle of the working class in Russia and not with the victory of one or other of the coalitions.

The lady of the house treated us to coffee. I learnt from the engineer that I was free and he explained his original behaviour by the fact that they were wary of espionage. I asked him to find me a horse with the stipulation that driver would take me to Oulu, transferring me to another only with the clear understanding that I was to be driven to Oulu. The engineer called his landlord, who agreed to accompany me with his horse for some twenty kilometres. After midnight we reached a farmstead which evidently served as a post and coaching station. I was given a little room.

In the morning a young man came to me and introduced himself as a student. He spoke Russian well and had learnt of my exploits from the driver. I chatted for a long while with him about world affairs. He also proved to be supporter of the German orientation, though he called himself a Finnish revolutionary and democrat. He reacted contemptuously to mention of Finnish social democracy as he did not regard it as revolutionary.

I also learnt from him that a considerable section of Finnish student youth and intellectuals had declared war on the Russian government. Some of them had gone off to Germany to fight for Finland's liberation; others like himself had stayed on to organize a Finnish army out of young peasant volunteers and veterans of the former Finnish army. According to the student they were well organized and had agents and clandestine quarters throughout Finland. They obtained weapons from Sweden. They had fixed up a special route, in winter by sledge and in summer by motorbikes and bicycles, from the Swedish border to Vyborg. This route was used for transport, people and mail. According to him, they were particularly well organized in the north — the region where we then were.

During my stay at the farm various people came to see him who seemed like teachers. They showed their badges, gave the password and got their instructions from him. He informed me that he was the zone chief and showed me a map of Oulu province on which the routes and locations of their agents were pencilled in. I was involuntarily taken aback by such a rash exhibition of their whole organization, and my chance activist acquaintance spent the whole day rubbing the markings off the map.

We spent the whole day at the inn without going out. I was advised not to leave as the Finnish police were patrolling the roads. The next day he offered to accompany me for two days as he needed to make a tour of his district and our routes coincided.

The following day we set out on the road early in the morning. I was really glad that I had a fellow-traveller and interpreter. We arrived at a coaching station in the evening where we were allotted two rooms and given a good supper. My companion said he had had a report from his people that Finnish police and Russian gendarmerie were at large in the vicinity of our lodgings. When we went to bed he warned me that should the police swoop on the hotel he would fire. He laid out revolvers beside himself for the night and bolted the door.

The police did not disturb our sleep, however, and we set off again. As we progressed southwards the snow became less. By nightfall we had reached a small settlement and stopped at the log cabin of an old Finn, a soldier. The soldier was a great patriot — he retained his old uniform and worked with the activists.

From individual conversations and passing encounters I was becoming convinced that some cunning hand was skilfully exploiting the noblest sentiments and revolutionary moods of Finnish youth: the hand of robber imperialism. I tried by every means to prove the incorrectness of the path that the activists had embarked on. My remark to the student that they were working not for the good of the Finnish people but in the interests of German imperialism worried him.

I learnt that after finishing university he had gone to work at the customs house at Beloostrov. During the war he had been in Vyborg and in Petersburg also, where he had acquaintances in the household of Prince Oldenburg's family. It was clear that their secret service stretched right into the tsar's court. He dreamt of forming units in the north which could start then and there an armed struggle against the supporters of the tsarist régime in Finland.

The morning following the night at the soldier's house we parted. He persuaded the soldier to take me to a particular spot and hand me over to someone else who would transfer me to the next and so on right to Oulu. The soldier fufilled his mission punctiliously and handed me over to another man before dinner. The latter in his turn took me to a hamlet on the bank of the river Ii Yeki. The landlord was not in at the house that this driver had brought me to. I thought he would arrive and so I waited an hour and then another, but no one appeared. I asked the landlady in sign language when we would be going to Oulu, and in reply she gave me a newspaper and pointed to the railway timetable. It turned out that not far away, in all some twelve kilometres, there was the railway station of Ii Yeki from where she recommended that I leave for Oulu. But this did not enter my plans, as I did not carry the documents necessary for rail travel.

Having waited till about four o'clock in the afternoon, I decided to leave the shack and find a horse myself. I took my bag, bade farewell to the landlady and made off through the village. At the exit I met a group of peasants by a log hut. I enquired whether any of them spoke Russian. One put himself forward but he understood very little and badly too. I asked whether he was agreeable to taking me as far as Oulu. He was surprised at my wish and advised me to go by train as it would be cheaper and quicker. Seeing that I was getting nowhere I asked where the road to the station was and headed that way.

I did not know why but it was obvious that I intrigued the peasants. Two of the group followed behind me at a distance. I sensed that I had come under observation, but I decided that boldness and confidence would destroy all suspicions. There was no other way out for me. About two hours later I had reached the station. To approach it you had to cross a railway bridge over the river Ii Yeki; there was a footway for horses and people. The bridge was guarded both above and below by sentries. There was no room for dithering now. I set off towards the station. It turned out that I had arrived too early. There were not many people about and there were no gendarmes on the station. It started to get dark and the lamps were lit. The station began to fill up. I bought a ticket and learnt from the booking clerk that an express was due first which stopped only at Oulu but that after it came a local train calling at all stations. This was the one I needed. It would be dangerous to travel by the express as a check of the documents which I did not have would be made at Oulu. With the local train I would be able to get off a stop earlier and go on to the town on foot. While waiting for the train to arrive I decided to familiarize myself with the station's layout. All round was forest. The entrance to the station waiting rooms was from the platform only. A few minutes before the arrival of the first train a soldier with a rifle appeared. From his shoulder-tabs I could tell that he was from the counter-intelligence branch. He went into the station. I walked round the station and, concealing myself on the fire-escape set against the roof, started to watch the soldier. He began to check passports. The two peasants who had been following me were in the hall. I decided not to show myself when the express arrived and not to catch the soldier's eye at all. The express arrived and noisy passengers rushed out to the buffet. The officers and gendarmes travelling on the train appeared. The station sprang quickly to life. A whistle and it just as quickly emptied.

A little while later the local train was due to arrive I went up closer to the station. The soldier was walking up and down the platform, noticed and started to observe me. He was watching attentively and was trying as he passed to edge nearer. I felt that things were not so bright but I decided to wait and see what was to follow. He finally made an about turn and made towards me. As he came over, he addressed a question to me in Finnish: where was I going? I replied in Russian that I was going to Oulu. He was surprised at my knowledge of the language and started asking where I had learnt Russian to which I replied, again in Russian, "in Petersburg" overlooking the fact that by then it had been renamed "Petrograd". In the end of course this warrior demanded my passport and requested me to go into the waiting room. We went into the first-class one — it was empty. I did not look as if I did not have a passport but rummaged through my pockets and bag, but of course could not find it. I stated that I had forgotten it at a flat only ten kilometres away. As a local resident I did not require a passport anyway. This however did appear somewhat implausible to a representative of the counter-intelligence service and the soldier declared me under arrest and requested me to follow him into the third-class waiting room. There were many people in there. It would have been easy to call someone to his aid and so I decided not to leave the first-class one. A determination to escape quickly crystallized in my mind. Seeing my obstinacy the soldier opened the door into the third-class, stuck his head through and started to call someone, but I had quietly pushed open the outside door of the first-class, slipped smartly out on to the platform, ran round the station, leapt over a fence and hid myself in the darkness of the forest. At that very moment the train I had been waiting for arrived. The officer had evidently decided that I had hidden on the train, but by then I was already running through the forest.

When I came out of the forest I did not know in which direction it was best to go. The sky was overcast and it was impossible to determine directions by it. I strayed into the forest to examine which side of the trees were overgrown with moss from the cold northern gusts; but it was hard to establish in the dark. I decided to lie down for a while in a culvert under the track and wait for the train to pass. If it passed by in my direction then my path was certain. But if it did not, I would have to go back in the other direction. I had to wait a long while. They were obviously searching the train for me. But then at last I heard a whistle. A few minutes later two shining eyes started to gleam in the distance and the train rushed past in the same direction that I was walking in. I had found my escape route and became so overjoyed that I wanted to make the forest expanses resound with song.

It was some seventy kilometres to Oulu along winding roads. Assuming the possibility of a hot pursuit I decided to keep walking all night without a halt. I set out along the railway trackside. There was little snow and the frost was very light. It was uncomfortable to walk in Finnish boots without soles. I was tortured by thirst after the running, and hunger set in. It had been twenty-four hours since I had had anything to eat apart from being "treated" to Finnish coffee. I decided to knock on the door of a trackmen's hut in the hope of buying bread and milk but the trackmen, tired after a hard day's work, slept through my appeals. Tortured by hunger and thirst I crawled into barns and storehouses but found nothing, so I quenched my thirst and hunger with snow.

Behind Haukipudas station my way was blocked by a bridge. Going across it past the sentries at midnight was risky and I started to look for other ways. I went along paths, through back gardens, past and over outbuildings and finally ran across a main road of sorts. Where the road forked I took the branch that veered back towards the railway. This road brought me to a big river, the same one that the bridge went over. By the bank there lay ferry boats. There was a broad unfrozen stretch along the bank but beyond was a solid sheet of ice. I decided to wait until morning to find a boatman, and for the moment to settle down in some barn. I found a straw store where I slumped down till daybreak, when I went down to the ferryman's hut. A light was already twinkling inside. People were getting up. An old man replied to my request about how to cross by pointing to his feet, i.e. you could walk across. I asked him to show me the way and the old man took me down to the river, threw a board across the unfrozen strip and went across it to the firm ice. When we had crossed to the other bank he indicated the Oulu road, and he was most pleased with the mark I gave him for the crossing.

A warm day set in. The snow was melting, my boots swelled with water and their pointed toes curled upwards. It was very hard to walk and fatigue began to take over. I avoided encounters along the way, hiding in the forest at the sight of groups of people, riders and carts. At one small hamlet I found a shop, and bought some buns and apples.

It was only at two in the afternoon that I reached the offices of the Oulu social-democratic newspaper, after being on the road from eight o'clock in the evening of the day before. I found my acquaintances in the editorial offices in good spirits and after sitting down for a couple of hours while they found me some suitable lodgings I was no longer in any state to walk. My legs had become heavy and my toes were covered in blood blisters. The comrades decided to hide me outside the town on a farm with some social democrats for a couple of days.

Only after five days could I control my legs freely and relatively painlessly. We then decided to travel on. Comrade Uskila found a document to which my photograph had to be stuck and a local photographer produced a print as a matter of urgency and destroyed the negative.

I reached Helsinki safely. I found Wiik, Rovio and the other comrades. Rovio obtained a Finnish passport for me and a few days later I set off for Petersburg. The train was full of military personnel and bourgeois. We passed safely through Beloostrov: I was back in Petersburg by the latter half of October.

5

Back to Petersburg

I ARRIVED in Petersburg in the heat of battle. Powder was in the air of the Vyborg quarter. I stayed with some relatives beyond the Neva gate and hunted out the Petersburg Committee. At a meeting of the Executive Commission of the Petersburg Committee, I met Evdokimov, Antipov, Schmidt and "Anya" (Kostina). I acquainted them with matters abroad, shared out the literature that I had managed to bring with me, and learned about the most important events of the year.

After my departure abroad in February 1916 there had been a number of strikes in Petersburg. An especially bitter one happened at the New Lessner works, flaring up spontaneously over an economic issue. The main demand was for an increase in the labourers' rate to 2.50 rubles a day. The strike began on 21 March on the eve of the holidays and was thereby already doomed. However, despite the unfavourable situation, an unofficial committee assumed the leadership of the strike and to this end issued a series of appeals, some of which I have preserved:

> When you come into the plant don't start work but maintain your main demands! The sacrifices inflicted upon you by this strike shall not be in vain. From their experience of this strike, the plant-owners and manufacturers shall be convinced of our solidarity and organization and once having given the labourers here a rise the plant-owners will be compelled to agree to a rise in a whole number of other plants. We will not allow memories of the course of this strike to crack our solidarity. Remember: the rise we demand for the labourers is as vital to them as air and water! Pay heed to your leading committee — it is formed from your own representatives and representatives of the all the revolutionary tendencies in the plant. Pay heed to the voice and counsel of leading comrades and then you will be able to use the favourable prospects to advantage.
>
>   Leading committee of workers at the New Lessner works.
> 29 March 1916.

However, given the lack of a common trade-union centre and under conditions of police terror and the threat of posting to the front the difficulties of an economic struggle presented themselves a few days after the declaration of the strike. The leaders' chief mistake was a decision to accept sackings which reduced the effect of the strike to nil and disoriented the men who had stopped work. Moreover, a strike that raised the question of increasing labourers' wages could only be successful where there was a movement to hand involving all or at least a majority of engineering undertakings behind those demands. This there was not, and the stoppage that had started unfavourably with regard to its timing was furthermore not linked to wider action by other metalworkers. This is very starkly evident in a statement by the leading committee itself:

> From the leading committee of workers at the New Lessner works.
> Comrades, those of you who have received dismissal notices and have signed on for work are heatedly discussing: what should we do? What happens now? Other comrades who took part in the strike have been guided in their attitude to it for the eight days by announcements posted by the works management or even by rumours and stories originating in those same offices of bottom and top management. Hence all sorts of wrong and absurd opinions. Thanks to this, a part of the workers talk of a lost strike, envisaging all sorts of terrible things: call-up to the front and so on and so forth. But what in fact is the situation? Is there room for despondency? Or is the reason rooted in comrades' inability to take full account of the circumstances that have arisen in the course of the stoppage? If comrades would listen more to the view of the leading comrades and the view of their leading committee and carry out the decisions of their representatives and did not each act at his own risk and peril there would be no place for despondency. What we said at the general meeting and in the first leaflet should be firmly understood and borne in mind. We said: *more resoluteness, more organization*! Don't believe management rumours and announcements. Remember, your leading committee is guarding your interests with vigilance. It will indicate to you what to do and how when the time comes and only in that way will we tear from the capitalists everything that we have the power to win at the present time. We have said earlier and endorse now: the struggle is hard and the greater the degree of organization the greater the chances of winning the strike. Our resolution on not accepting dismissal has been violated and in the interests of the good orderliness of the strike we have been forced to recommend acceptance of dismissals to the remaining workers even though we understand that this will weaken our forces. The announcement about signing on for work appeared and, having seen the impossibility of restraining comrades from signing on, we were forced not to protest against it, realizing once again that it was not in our best interests. Comrades, a mistake has been made! So, if you want the strike to finish in victory for the workers don't repeat these mistakes in the future. Comrades, understand that, under compulsion from the military authorities and driven by the desire to wring out surplus value again as soon as possible and also the fear of the works passing into the hands of the state and a fear that demands will likewise be presented in many other plants, the management will be forced to start up the works again as soon as possible. It is in the management's interests to

break the workers' strength and organization by trying to intimidate them with all sorts of scares and smash their forces. Comrades, remember that all Petersburg workers have an interest in the outcome of our stoppage and the defence of our basic demands, that is, the reinstatement of all workers and the increase in wages for male and female labourers. It is not by chance that the Association of Factory and Plant Owners have advised shareholders of the G.A. Lessner works not to yield to this demand. Finally, comrades, remember that although there is no call-up to the front as yet nor mass arrests of leading comrades, there will be the very moment the works management is convinced of our weakness and our inability to defend our interests. Comrades! Today or tomorrow management will either put up a notice about re-starting work and will carry out a thorough purge by not reinstating many leading comrades or else it will distribute selective invitations to report for work to the remaining workers. Whether it is done this way or that, you should know that it is in your interests when you arrive at the plant, and don't start work, to send representatives to the works management to hold talks on reinstating all workers and paying the labourers' rise, for otherwise not only will you be still working under the old conditions but the management will exploit your lack of organization to worsen your working conditions yet more. Comrades, realize that eight days of the strike have passed and we are still saying: *the position is favourable and we will triumph and we can uphold our main demands provided you stand firm and remain solid*. There is no other way out for the management for it is forced to meet our demands. And the position now is just as it was at the start of the strike. By understanding and upholding your main demands — *reinstating all workers at the plant and the rise for the labourers* — we will have achieved something towards a percentage rise for the other workers too.

Throughout the strike, management has been feeling out our strength and the workers' solidarity but it has been forced to re-start the works as soon as possible: it fears the workers and therefore it is re-starting three shops today; but tomorrow when it is convinced of our lack of organization it will start up the remainder of the shops only after throwing out the most advanced comrades, using the police to make hundreds of arrests and sending hundreds of our comrades to front-line positions. Although this has not already been done don't help it to be done now.

Comrades!

Understand the gravity of the situation! All of you who have come to the plant can force the management not to smash our forces and break up our ranks. The management has no other way out and it will be compelled to meet our demands. Stand firm, act in an organized fashion and listen to the voice of our leading committee and advanced workers. By acting in a disorganized manner you will fragment the strike and assist its collapse. The sacrifices brought upon the workers by this strike must not be in vain. Have greater confidence in your own strength, don't rise to provocations and don't split our ranks! Don't further the prospects and

intentions of your class enemies, the capitalists, by your lack of organization! *Don't start work, send delegates to the management and demand satisfaction of your main demands: the reinstatement of all workers and the rise for the labourers!*
The leading committee of workers at the New Lessner works.
Petrograd, 31 March 1916.

This appeal, reproduced in typed and hectographed form, was distributed among workers when the plant was closed down. The impact of the strike in the working-class districts of Petersburg and even beyond the city limits was enormous. Manufacturers and the government replied with repression. The leading figures of the War Industries Committees were then playing a shameful strike-breaking role. Breido, the Menshevik and a member of the labour group of the War Industries Committee, was especially zealous. Two thousand men ended up on the street as a result of the defeat, and were blacklisted. Many found themselves in special battalions and at the front. A whole article was devoted to the strike in the third issue of the illegal *Proletarskii Golos*, a publication of the Petersburg Committee.

The Petersburg Committee undertook wide-scale agitation prior to May Day and issued a special leaflet. We managed to hold a lot of mass meetings and strikes at many of Petersburg's factories and works. The summer was also spent in organizing forces in separate actions that had by September acquired a mass character. And in October things came to street clashes.

As in previous years the movement started and found particularly organized revolutionary expression in the Vyborg quarter. On 17 October a strike began at the Renault works. The workers went off to bring out other plants. The police appeared on the scene and started dispersing them. There were especially large groups of workers around the New Lessner works. The barracks of the 181st infantry reserve was situated at the side of the works. Relations between soldiers and workers were extremely amicable. Soldiers were among the thronging workers. It was said at the time that there was a wounded soldier among them who was a holder of the George Cross. When the police started to lose their heads and assaulted the crowd with sabres and whips, soldiers from the neighbouring barracks who were looking over a low fence into the street knocked down the fence and joined the workers, beating up and driving out the police. Cossacks were called out to arrest the soldiers and workers. But the cossacks decided not to act and they were withdrawn. The soldiers' behaviour caused consternation among the military hierarchy. All sorts of top brass paid visits to the barracks; however, they were only able to arrest the "instigators" from the 181st regiment at night after a roll-call. 130 men were arrested and threatened with court-martial.

The strike and the whole movement bore an openly political character but it had begun spontaneously and was directly led by the masses themselves. A leaflet from the Petersburg Committee of our party was taken as a signal to strike, although there was no call for a strike in it. However, the workers' mood was so heady that the news that the Petersburg Committee had merely issued a leaflet could have been taken as the call for a strike. The Stürmer government was at that time waging a struggle against the Duma bloc. Both sides were branding each other as "traitors". It was forbidden to print even Duma speeches by bourgeois representatives and this aroused an extraordinary interest among all the people. The speeches had probably never been sold in such quantities as in that period. Their basic theme was the government's inability to organize the war or, as was then said, to organize the "defence of the country". There was quite a bit of bravado in their speeches but no principled, class lines reflecting the needs of the hour.

N.S. Chkheidze, whom I often met at N.D. Sokolov's, replied to my criticisms by saying that they too were "Zimmerwaldists" and opponents of the war; and that the war had become a factor which it was essential for social democracy to exploit, though without breaking from patriotically minded democrats.

The Petersburg Committee hastened to wind up the spontaneous strike which had flared up. A special leaflet was issued on this occasion which ran as follows:

> Russian Social-Democratic Labour Party
>
> Workers of the World, unite!
>
> Once again our comrades, the Petersburg workers, are exhibiting their courageous will-power and their political wisdom to the whole world as they come out on to the street with the cry of "Down with the war!" No one can hurl the reproach at them that they are leaving their jobs merely through narrow personal considerations. No! Indignant at the tribulations of the silent peoples who for twenty-five months have been allowing their government gang to annihilate millions of lives and the capitalists to loot the fatherless poor, Petersburg workers are openly and loudly declaring that it is necessary to put an end to this torrent of rapine and death. The excruciating absurdity of this lunatic war waged by the ruling classes with the cold-bloodedness of murderers, is now beginning to be understood especially clearly by the soldiers, our previous plant and factory workmates.
>
> For this government is drilling them and keeps them on the streets day and night turning the city into a strongpoint; forcing them at a signal from its hired serfs to sow death among the people to blame only for having the audacity to tell the truth straight to its face.
>
> Soldier comrades, you have been sent to Russia's frontiers on behalf of

those who are crushing you in the vice of their power. But here your rifle barrels are aimed at unarmed workers and your bereaved mothers and sisters all so that the capitalists can rob them without hindrance. Such fratricide they call the defence of the fatherland; but concerted action by our soldier brothers can during these days serve as a sign that they are with us.

Worker comrades, explain to the most backward and ignorant of your people what this interminable war is bringing to the people: make collections, link up more closely with the soldiers but don't let yourselves be fooled by those who want to call you to a premature slaughter by rumours and attract police action and provocations.

Worker and soldier comrades, prove that the hopes of your enemies who are waiting for you to come forward into a clash with them now when your forces are not yet rallied are in vain. Every day brings the storm closer to the heads of the government and the ruling classes. The scarcity of the most essential items of food, the rapacious greed of local bosses, the heaps of paper money and the breakdown of the transport system are embracing Russia ever more widely. So let the coming hour of the people's judgment find our ranks closed and ready for a lengthy and stubborn struggle!

Read our appeals, hold meetings, pass resolutions, aim to organize demonstrations and stoppages but don't take every demonstration and every protest strike as the opening of the final round in our hard war against the tsarist monarchy. Long live that war which began long ago though at times ebbing! It will yield us real victory if we prove able to prosecute it fully equipped organizationally. Go back now to your benches so as to leave them again to lead the final assault by a general strike in alliance with the army to topple autocracy and establish a democratic republic, the eight-hour day and the confiscation of landed estates.

Long live the revolution! Down with the war! Down with the monarchy! Long live the democratic republic! Long live the international revolutionary proletariat! Long live socialism!

Petersburg Committee of the RSDLP

The workers went back to work, but not for long. A few days later the Petersburg Committee raised Petersburg to the defence of sailors of the Baltic Fleet who were threatened with a court-martial. At the beginning of 1916 there were numerous raids and arrests in Petersburg, Kronstadt and Helsinki among sailors and individuals in touch with them. A major public trial of the "Military Organization of the Petersburg Committee of the Russian Social-Democratic Labour Party" was held. The voluminous Bill of Indictment, consisting of fifty typed pages, describes the Petersburg Committee's work among the sailors in reasonable detail. The Okhrana's secret service was pretty well informed. It began as follows:

From the autumn of 1915 reports started coming into the Kronstadt gendarmerie headquarters that there was a marked increase in the activity of revolutionary organizations of social-democratic tendencies among the crews of vessels of the Baltic Fleet. These are endeavouring to place as many of their supporters in the fleet who would train the ships' crews for actions in pursuit of a variety of demands when the war comes to an end. The aforementioned activity, although not succeeding in organizing systematic propaganda, has, as events have proved, nevertheless exerted a powerful influence on the crews' excited mood and this in the end overflowed into major disorders on the battleship *Hangut* on 19 October 1915 the participants in which, namely twenty-six ratings, were sentenced by the Naval Court-Martial of 17 December of the same year and duly punished.

At the same time there arose similar disorders on the cruiser *Riurik*.

The existence of propaganda was confirmed by the participants and by disorders on other vessels that arose from the crews' dissatisfaction with their food and officers bearing German surnames.

The Petersburg Security Department has received reports parallel to this material about the emergence of a military organization of the Russian Social-Democratic Party among ship and shore-based crews of the Baltic Fleet.

According to these reports social-democratic circles have been formed on each warship whose leading personnel sat on a general directing committee. The latter, by arranging gatherings ashore in teashops and restaurants, directed its energies chiefly towards explaining current events to the sailors in a desirable light with the purpose of creating a climate of discontent among them.

This approach apparently succeeded in winning some influence on the sailors, creating among them a highly restive mood for which no other reason could be observed. But the movement's ideological leaders tried in every way to restrain the sailors from sporadic disorders in order to bring a situation about where a general action could take account of the possibility of an active movement from the part of the working class which might bring decisive influence to bear on changing the political system.

No actions planned for a set date have as yet been noted in the secret service reports. All the revolutionary work shows itself primarily in the organizational field. Having thus succeeded in creating a desirable mood aboard the vessels of the fleet, the leaders are now experiencing difficulties in restraining isolated actions and in this regard the openly expressed discontent on board the battleship *Hangut* made an unfavourable impression on them.

Although the circles arose on the ships independently and outside of the influence of the group functioning in Petersburg that styles itself the Petersburg Committee of the Russian Social-Democratic Labour Party, the leading committee of the naval organization has none the less from the time of appearance sought opportunities to join forces with the "Petrograd Committee" which it in fact achieved through one of the active leaders of the workers' movement who was the representative of the Vyborg party district on the Petrograd Committee, the peasant Ivan Fedorovich Orlov.

The charge was made under section 1 of article 102 and paragraph 2 of article 317 of the Naval Penal Code. The shrewd behaviour of the defendants in court aroused the admiration of friends and the involuntary respect of the judges. But the Petersburg Committee decided not to confine itself to the eloquence of a legal defence but conducted agitation for mass defence by means of a strike. On 26 October, the day of the trial of our sailor comrades, over 130,000 workers left the furnaces, benches and stifling vaults of the prisons of labour for three days.

The government and the Association of Factory and Plant Owners decided to punish the workers with a "gentle" lock-out and closed down the striking enterprises on 26 October. But that did not intimidate the workers and in response to the lock-out, workers from other factories and plants who had not taken part in the 26 October strike decided to support the comrades locked out by going on strike also. The Petersburg Committee issued an appeal, calling for a struggle to get the factories reopened. But the lock-out was lifted on the very day the leaflet came out, 1 November. The plants and factories were reopened without any further consequences. It was clear that the government feared to put tough measures into effect lest they produce more storms in reply.

The Central Committee Bureau and Party Work

All around revolutionary work was seething. All circles of the population were being drawn into politics because of the high cost of living and the food queues. People had no compunction about insulting the authorities on any pretext. The atmosphere was laden with struggle. We managed to attract a lot of new personnel into work for the Petersburg Committee.

The Central Committee party workers whom I had organized in the autumn of 1915 during my first wartime visit from abroad had all been knocked out of action. Several were in jail while others were in exile or awaiting it. When I arrived in Petersburg the second time, in the autumn of 1916, I could only find K.M. Shvedchikov who was expecting banishment. The job of forming a leading centre had to be started again from scratch. Nevertheless the work hitherto conducted had not been in vain. Many contacts of the old apparatus remained and that eased matters considerably. With the help of comrade Tikhomirnov (Vadim) we managed to set up a network of illegal flats for meeting in and for storing literature. Tikhomirnov also got journeys over to Finland into operation to pick up illegal material.

It was harder to pick comrades for the Central Committee Bureau itself. There were so few organizers on the Petersburg Committee that to take them off it even for vital work could be contemplated in emergencies only. I managed soon afterwards to seek out some comrades who had escaped from exile, Skryabin and Zalutsky, and the three of us constituted the collegium of the Central Committee Bureau. By that year it was significantly easier to find co-workers. The turning-point in the mood of the people and the growth of opposition among even the bourgeoisie drove into our ranks no small number of student activists.

But we had to work under extremely tough conditions. We proved able to group many active comrades around us. But owing to lack of resources we did not succeed in expanding the work very widely. We were very poor. From 2 December 1916 to 1 February 1917 only 1,117 rubles 50 kopeks flowed into the funds of the Central Committee Bureau. We had to carry out all work within these means. If we sent an organizer out to the provinces we could not guarantee him even one month's support; consequently we had to rely upon the initiative of chance visits by comrades from different areas or strokes of luck for our contacts. The Bureau spent very little on maintaining its staff. The majority had their earnings but underground workers even in February 1917 could not receive more than a hundred rubles a month. The supply of literature required a great deal of funds, but we were unable to assign very much to it.

No less difficult were conditions of personal existence. From the very first days of my arrival, when I at once became the object of intensive trailing by spies, it was plain to me that settling down with my own flat, a valid passport and other such luxuries was in such a situation to court real disaster. To have any possibility of countering the stratagems of the agents I had to have as many lodgings as possible. Comrades helped me to find places, and I had a particular spot for each night. These were dispersed in various parts of Petersburg, including its extremities; for example, on the one hand, on the Grazhdanka and on the other, at the Galley Harbour and also in between them in the city centre. My life was turning into a perpetual wandering. It was hard to write, read and at times even to think as often when tired hospitable comrades engaged me with their political programmes and enjoyable conversation deep into the night. You could survive like that for two or three months but my physical energy did not allow more.

Petersburg proletarians tried to alleviate my existence in every conceivable way; but they could not rid me of the sleuths and were in no position to offer me any greater security and comfort than what they themselves had at their disposal. The Jewish worker, Shurkanov, formerly a deputy to the Third Duma, was especially sweet and ingratiating. He would express his "charm" and affection towards me by embraces and went as far with his concern for me as to offer to place his own flat at my disposal, and declared his desire to equip a "special" room concealed from extraneous observers. Although I had not suspected any treachery in this friendship the offer was not taken up and throughout my peregrinations I did not once stay overnight with him. His behaviour and general style did not as a whole predispose me towards his friendship and I called at his place only in cases of extreme necessity when a comrade had fixed to meet me there. After one such meeting once not long before the revolution I landed myself in such a web of spies that I was forced to roam the back gardens of the Vyborg and Lesny quarters till almost dawn when, with frost-bitten hands, I stumbled across the Eiwas worker, N. I. Nazarov, on the Grazhdanka at five in the morning. I had however broken free of the ring of observation and reached a lodging place minus the sleuths.

This situation dreadfully constrained our work. As before the Vyborg quarter was in the lead, and brought to the fore for general party work the outstanding energies of the workers, Chugurin, Alexandrov, Kayurov and many others. The Central Committee Bureau consisted of a "trio": the writer of these lines (under the alias of A. Belenin), P. Zalutsky and V. Molotov (Skryabin). The work was shared out between us as follows. Zalutsky was a member of the Petersburg Committee, carried out work on it and served as its link with the Central Committee Bureau; Molotov took charge of literary matters and organized the Central Committee's illegal printshop. To myself fell the organizational work and contacts with abroad and the provinces.

The Bureau's staff centre was at M.G. and D.A. Pavlov's at 35 Serdobolsky Street. Mariya Georgievna was the "custodian of the press" and of the Bureau's small archives and other papers and literature. There were rendezvous points at different places in the city. The ferrying of literature from Finland and its storage and distribution in Petersburg and around the provinces was left to the leading worker, comrade Vadim (Tikhomirnov). He had managed to organize a small group of young lasses who operated on this side, made trips over to Finland and distributed literature to specific addresses.

Relations with the Petersburg Committee were of the best. Chernomazov had long ago been removed and schemed against me among party workers in the Vyborg quarter, to no avail. Work was undertaken in unanimity and progressed with huge steps.

Smitten by the reverses at the front, the Russian bourgeoisie began to shift to the left. Its representatives, Milyukov, Guchkov and the rest, launched attacks on the ministers. The demand for a "government of national salvation" arose from the bowels of the bourgeois opposition. A campaign to back up this slogan was initiated around the Duma. The bourgeoisie had dreams of dragging the working class into this campaign also, and found a handy tool for realizing their aims in the persons of those workers who did penance to the War Industries Committees. But the party's Petersburg Committee, taking stock of the lessons of the revolutionary struggle of 1905 and the Russian bourgeoisie's militant imperialism, conducted a campaign against subordinating the struggle of the working class to governmental alliances of Duma liberals. The Petersburg Committee issued a leaflet on this topic in which it contrasted the slogans of revolutionary democracy with the slogans of the bourgeoisie:

> Workers of the world, unite!
> Comrades, all through the war, at the opening sessions of the State Duma, its members have sworn their allegiance to the tsar's government with expressions of most loyal subjects and by kissing the ministers' hands. Today, the militant deputies, while remaining as before cringing hangers-on of the tsar, have raised a hue and cry and started a row with the government. Over what? They declare that a cabinet change is required to continue the war to the end. Now that the masses of the people, exhausted by the excessive burdens of a war sanctified by the capitalists, are beginning to lose patience and are preparing to move against the oppressors, liberal smart dealers are trying to utilize this popular movement to satisfy their own bandit-like appetites. They must have their ministry of public confidence but what can it bring to a mutilated people? Milyukovs instead of Stürmers. They were talking of saving the country but are quite ready to lead it to new deaths and ever more fresh sacrifices.
> No! We should always remember that those who are calling on us to wage war to the end are considering us least of all and are bothered least of all about the true fate of the nation. The replacement of one lot of murderers by another will not force us to cease our struggle against a revamped cabinet. Particular hope is being placed in those self-seeking liberals by that bunch of chauvinist workers who until now have found only words of condemnation of our revolutinary action. Yet now it is addressing an appeal to us to fight for a "government of national salvation".
> Those "workers' politicans" who have abandoned us at the hardest moment of the onslaught of war and are going to the aid of the government and bourgeoisie in carrying out this slaughter, who condemn our revolutionary efforts not to lay down our weapons of struggle against the war and the oppressors, and keep silent about the seizure of our deputies torn from us, these "workers' politicans" are now calling on us to follow their slogans! Deliver the salvation of the country into the hands of those who want to turn the long months of blood-letting into years and

are ruthlessly strangling the workers' movement!

Comrades, surely dozens of years of bloody experience in the workers' movement shows quite clearly who is really able to fight against this piratical monarchy?

By rallying our forces and broadening agitation among the ranks of the peasantry and in the army, we shall forge a genuinely revolutionary hammer. The anguished people will finish off the government with its own blows.

We know only of this first task. Through the toppling of the tsarist government to the formation of a provisional revolutionary government of workers and poor peasants! Of this government we shall demand the immediate ending of the war; the immediate convocation of a Constituent Assembly; the introduction of civil liberties so as to create the conditions for waging a struggle to bring about true people's rule, the Democratic Republic; the confiscation of landed estates; putting into the hands of the working class its most powerful weapon — shortening its working hours by promulgating the eight-hour working day!

But now we must be on our guard! The governments and ruling classes, choking themselves in the torrents of blood they have let loose, will exert every effort for the outcome of the war to bring them further enslavement of the peoples and a strengthening of their power. The workers of all the world, and the workers in the countries at war primarily, must aim their blows against their own governments. When they have disarmed them and enabled the peoples to put a stop to this war by carrying through political overturns, we shall be able to save the country from doom in the most real way of all.

But remember, comrades! As long as the capitalists are prospering out of the people's life and as long as they remain lords and masters, in their chase for profits they will have no second thoughts about tossing the peoples over and over again in the conflagration of war. Only the destruction of the capitalist system and its replacement by a socialist one will put an end to war and human suffering.

Therefore, by developing the revolutionary muscle of the international proletariat, we Russian workers shall be devoting all our energies to the realization of socialism. We shall support the comrades of Britain, Germany and France in their readiness to conduct a struggle for the overthrow of capitalist governments once we have thrown off the fetters of the tsarist monarchy.

Forward without respite! Down with the war! Down with the tsarist government! Long live the Provisional Revolutionary Government! Down with the tsarist monarchy! Long live the democratic republic! Long live the revolution! Long live socialism!

Petersburg Committee of the RSDLP

November 1916.

At the end of autumn and the beginning of winter party work in the Petersburg region concentrated on explaining the causes of the high cost of living and also on agitation over the food supply crisis. It was a time when prices of foodstuffs were rising madly, which caused housewives' riots in the Petersburg markets; bread was starting to disappear and the government was compelled to take the path of state intervention in the grain trade. A timid attempt was made at a state grain monopoly but the grain lords proved to be the big landowners.

All public organizations were concerned with solutions to the food question. And each of them provided remedies for salvation from famine in line with its own nature. The landowners stoutly resisted any sort of regulation or constriction of their "freedom" and tried to gain control over the first state measures on grain supply to the army and the cities. The industrialists were for their part extremely interested in settling the problem and actively sought to concentrate supply to factory employees in their own hands.

In short, all these groups approached the problem from the standpoint of exploiting the food crisis for their own class interest.

The Labour Group of the Central War Industries Committee also took part in the discussion of this question. It made a request to organizations, chiefly the co-operatives, to provide information about the workers' food consumption. Replies were sent to the Labour Group's enquiry, but these were not published anywhere. Our party workers in the south obtained for me a copy of a reply which offered something distinct in principle from all the others. This reply belonged to the Kharkov or Ekaterinoslav comrades. Among other things it said:

> If a guaranteed supply of basic foodstuffs for workers is to be organized we insist that management and distribution be transferred wholly into the hands of the consumers themselves, i.e. the workers. If the delivery is to be undertaken separately for each enterprise then a special works committee must be set up elected by all the workers in the enterprise; but where organization is on a city-wide basis then an appropriate organization of representatives of workers of all the city should be formed.
>
> As interested parties, we consider that the transfer of the whole business of food supply to workers exclusively or even predominantly into the hands of the employers is not in any instance permissible and for workers offensive in the highest degree. We are sure moreover that food supply in the hands of employers will be used to justify reduced wages.

The political issues of the hour had determined this reply. It was important for the working class and urban poor to take over the supply business if only to make it subject to control, as the schemes of the landowners' government for "priority feeding" amounted to dividing workers and merely improving the lot of one section at the expense of another. Hence the "universal suffrage" and the equality of all in the sphere of food distribution proposed by the comrades above.

The Social Movement and Social Democracy

Stirred by the growth of our party's illegal organizations, I sought to attract intellectuals to the Central Committee Bureau and the Petersburg Committee, but in vain. All the "former" Bolshevik social-democratic intellectuals and writers had settled into organizations attached to the Union of Towns, the Union of Zemstvos, the War Industries Committees and so forth. Many of them, for example Steklov, Shary, Dansky, Krasin, Krasikov and others, would not touch illegal work. I managed to attract only a few out of the whole mass of intellectuals from the old days.

During this visit, I would often call at A.M. Gorky's, meeting people of interest at his place and obtaining from him information and money for our work. Aleksei Maksimovich himself dreamed of forming a party of the bourgeois intelligentsia in Russia, a radical-democratic party, as in his opinion the existing ones did not and could not satisfy it.

In December 1916 a variety of congresses of organizations working for the "defence of the country" were held in Moscow: the Union of Zemstvos and the Union of Towns with the participation of the War Industries Committees, the commodity and corn exchanges, the co-operatives and the "workers' delegations" (from the hospital funds, co-operatives and trade unions). These congresses adopted a whole series of liberal anti-government resolutions. One was carried at an assembly of delegates of provincial zemstvos held on 9 December 1916: it contained a number of attacks on the "individuals" who held supreme power in a tight grip and had infected the nation's conscience and were continuing to undermine "the roots of our political system". The resolution spoke about "chaos growing daily", and proposed "Salvation through practical patriotism and a vital sense of responsibility to the homeland. When the authorities become a hindrance to victory, responsibility for the fate of the homeland must be assumed by the whole country. . . . The government . . . is leading Russia along the path of destruction." Such was the position of "zemstvo liberalism".

The bourgeoisie, brought together in the Union of Towns, also adopted a resolution demanding "responsible government" and invited parties to form a broad alliance for supplying food to the populace and the army. But these resolutions were enough for Stürmer to dissolve the congresses. After their dispersal, the delegates became, in words, even more left-wing, and passed the following resolutions:

> Conference of representatives of Public Organizations.
> 11 December 1916.
> The banning and breaking up of the congress forces us representatives of public organizations of all classes of the population who have gathered for

the food supply conference, to register their indignation and resolutely protest against the habitual policy of the old régime which is dissipating and disrupting the country at a time which requires from the people the utmost concentration and unity of forces.

The fatherland is in danger! The food breakdown is growing daily. The ill-conceived plans of the incompetent authorities, which are not linked together by any system, are making this crisis more and more fearful. A spectre of famine is menacing the army and the nation. The government that has given us Sukhomlinovs, Myasoedovs and Stürmers, has from the very start of the war prevented the army from accomplishing its difficult task. The country has paid for the mistakes and crimes of the authorities with millions of lives and fifteen provinces under occupation. From the outset of the war, Russian society forgot all the earlier sins of the government and devoted all its energies to a joint struggle with the government against the external foe. But in their strivings to preserve their archaic privileges and prerogatives, the unaccountable authorities have put a toy in the hands of a bunch of shady rascals and have continued in the rear to conduct a treacherous struggle against society and the nation. This shameless and criminal régime which has disrupted the country and rendered the army impotent cannot be trusted by the people either to prosecute the war or to conclude a peace.

In these fateful days which are deciding the destiny of the nation, the political system that has brought the country to the brink of collapse must be done away with. The hour has struck. The reuniting of all strata and classes of the population in a cohesive organization capable of leading the country out of this blind alley, is becoming the urgent task of the hour. The State Duma must, by finding backing from a newly reorganized people, unflinchingly and courageously carry the great task now begun through to the end. No compromises and no concessions.

Our last words are to the army. The army, its officers and men, must understand that, by destroying and dissipating the nation's life-blood, the government is striking an irreparable blow to the common cause. The army must understand that the whole country is ready to rally together to lead Russia out of the disastrous crisis that is at hand.

This resolution was given wide circulation. Because of the constraints of censorship, all resolutions, speeches and letters from individual statesmen and other proclamations as a rule attracted unusual interest and were eagerly copied out by any means to hand. Manuscripts dealing with the war, the food crisis, the current situation and so on were passed from hand to hand. I managed to retain a portion of them but most I sent abroad.

Alongside the proclamations, appeals, speeches by deputies and other such documents, the following declarations also passed through workers' hands in the final months of 1916. The first document, knocked out on a typewriter, is an address "To All Citizens" which ran as follows:

The disgusting and senseless self-destruction of nations is running into a third year. Several million people have been killed or maimed, some hundred thousand millions' worth of public funds squandered irreversibly, whole countries devastated and all the working population of Europe placed under arms or posted to munitions plants.

To what end? For the liberation of nations from the yoke of Germany, or so they say. "For the liberation of nations from the yoke of Britain," the Germans tell us. Only ignoramuses can repeat this lie put about by the ruling classes. In this war the bankers of London, Paris and Berlin are in fact deciding the question of which of them shall rule the world by exploiting the manpower of their subject and allied nations.

Industrialists and landowners of all countries are no longer content with the share of unearned wealth given freely to them every year by the workers and peasants by being underpaid for their labour and overcharged for the goods they buy. They are aiming to invest the incalculable capital funds amassed in this way to produce further and large profits. And as no one's own country can alone, either through the poverty of its population (Russia) or the saturation of its markets (Germany and Britain), swallow up all the additional output of goods, the need arises to unload these goods abroad while refusing the sale of imported foreign goods at home, better and cheaper though they might be.

The interests of the capitalists of the individual countries collide. But the interests of the capitalists are the interests of the governments because modern governments, monarchs, presidents, ministers, deputies, civil servants, the military and the clergy are all mere henchmen of capital as are the newspaper hacks, diplomats, spies and that whole colossal gang of lackeys and toadies styled "public opinion".

Enjoying as they do the protection of their own ministers, their own courts, their own church and police and resting as they do on their paramount position in the economy of the country (as the owners of all the means and instruments of production), the capitalists in their internal policies are guided by one ideal: cutting wages for the workers, increasing rents to the letters of land and housing, inflating the prices of commodities and stifling any attempt at popular protest.

By relying on that same government and on the soldiers who have been stultified and drilled until they have lost all human semblance, the capitalists in their foreign policy are pursuing but one aim: that of fortifying for themselves at all costs rich markets for dumping surplus goods and investing surplus capital. Lackeys of German stockbrokers are trumpeting about the liberation of Poland with the same "honourable patriotic awareness" with which Mr Milyukov is calling the Russian people to the liberation of Galicia, Armenia and Tsargrad (Constantinople). The difference lies merely in that each lackey exerts himself only on behalf of his own master.

Over many years, Britain which had already seized the finest colonies, and Germany which still had virtually no colonies but had enormous surplus capital at its disposal, were preparing for a battle between themselves and sought allies. Countries whose propertied classes had grounds for fearing competition from British capitalists or which found themselves beneath the heavy clout of London joint-stock companies, joined Germany; but states fearing rivalry from German industry concluded military pacts with or gave support to the "Entente Cordiale" with Britain. The whole world split into two camps, jealously following each other and contending with feverish armaments, ready on any odd occasion to push mankind into self-destruction.

It is an idle question to ask who started the war. The capitalist cliques of all countries had been preparing for it. . . . The blame for this crime, unprecedented in its ferocity and number of victims, lies with all of them. Asquith, Briand, Bethmann and Trepov, Schiemann and Milyukov, D'Annunzio and Rolland, all those innumerable lackeys, prophets and bards of the capitalist classes who have uttered their phrase "war to the end". . . .

Citizens, you, workers and peasants, you, proletarians of mental labour, where is your voice, why does it not sound out loud and clear? Or is it that your conscience, shaken beyond limit and your ideas confused in contradictions, are now incapable of prompting decisions to you that are worthy of men and citizens? Or are you convinced that the liberty and economic well-being of Russia is unthinkable without the conquest of Galicia, Armenia and Tsargrad (Constantinople)? Surely you cannot after these twenty-eight bloody months feel able to share the false assertions of the venal rags that this war is a war for the freedom of humanity or that this war is the last war? Surely you must realize that even if the capitalist bands of the belligerent countries do not drown Europe in blood but conclude a peace, they will only be preparing for a new struggle to seek new allies and rearm themselves with the last copper of the people? Not only Britain and Germany, in the shape of their banks and companies, are making claims to world dominion; the American and Japanese capitalists are equally pretenders to this; and however the war turns out, it is only the beginning of horrifying world conflicts in which Russia will play its customary role of hireling of this or that coalition of industrial powers.

Freedom and the peaceful co-operation of nations is a great goal worthy of sacrifices. But that is not what inspires the businessmen of capital. India and Egypt are groaning under the yoke of the "British liberators". Morocco and Tunisia testify to the liberalism of France by the history of their uprisings. "Liberated" Tripolitania has been converted into a torture chamber by the Italians. Crushed Galicia and Armenia, downtrodden Finland, the ashes of Turkestani settlements, the gallows of Ireland and the annihilation of the Chinese people, call out for vengeance. In what way is this company of "liberators" better than the German oppressors?

A durable peace between nations is possible only when all the means and instruments of production, which currently serve as sources of unearned income for their private owners are expropriated by the state and declared public property like bridges, railways and waterways. Every able-bodied person will have to labour and every worker will receive from society the full value of his labour. The entire output of industry will be deposited in public stores and distributed among the peoples at prices equalling the value of labour expended in the production and distribution of these products. The multi-million taxes that are today in this country paid out to the capitalists either as deductions from wages or surcharges on goods will be lifted from the peoples' shoulders. Only any surplus of products, after meeting the needs of all the consumers of the country, will be exported abroad, in exchange for essential goods produced in other countries. Every undertaking will produce only to satisfy demands presented to it by the country. In such conditions there cannot be the artificial surplus of products which are at present dumped by the capitalists on foreign markets and form the principal cause of international conflict: surplus capital seeking profitable investment in overseas territories. Capital is generally created by the under-remuneration of the worker's labour and the customer's overpayment for the finished product. If the labouring people receive the full value of their output and the consumer pays for the product only what it is worth where can the profit that constitutes free capital be taken from? And who will be there to strive after profit if the production and distribution of material values lies wholly in the hands of the freely organized peoples and not of gangs of bankers?

Citizens who have believed the lies of your rulers, who have given the lives of your children and all the property of the nation over to the hands of self-seeking groups, you who are blinded by the ringing words "freedom of the peoples", are suffering the unequalled shame of your country; you are seemingly refusing to see that you are ruled by hysteria-mongers and rogues, conscious provocateurs and traitors, Rasputin and Pitirim, Protopopov and Rodzyanko, the harbingers of freedom, the Romanov dynasty acting the part of defender of oppressed mankind, Milyukov and Shidlovsky as the spiritual leaders of Russia.

Where are the limits to the moral decline of our country's governing classes, where are the bounds of our social downfall? The fields are emptying, socially useful enterprises are closing. Everything that is still being produced in the country is growing scarcer with the growth of worthless paper money, of no use to anyone, and is being eaten up by the armies. The left-overs are snatched up by profiteers and rot in store-houses awaiting a further rise in prices. While almost daily ever fresh taxes are imposed on the shoulders of the impoverished people and new loans are agreed at the expense of the people's labour.

Citizens! Does it not seem to you that an ominous dividing line has been reached; the capitalist world is outliving itself: will mankind perish directed by a plutocracy or is it still capable of inaugurating a new era of free labour and international solidarity?

On the battlefields the idea of the state as an association of capitalists has disappeared in favour of domestic violence and external conquest. But on the shed blood of the peoples there is asserting itself the idea of a new state as an organization of toilers for a just distribution of material benefits, equality in the exercise of obligations and equal participation in management. At this hour of greatest peril we, in full unity with the

Italian, Serbian and Bulgarian socialist parties and in fraternal solidarity with a considerable section of the French, German, British and Austro-Hungarian proletariat, call on the labouring classes of Russia to take the destiny of the homeland into their hands.

Remember, citizens, that every hour of the war will carry away hundreds and thousands of lives and this involuntary sacrifice by the peoples on the altar of capital, this senselessly shed blood, calls out to our conscience. We cannot delay, it is criminal to idle. A general political strike and uprising, the toppling of the government and the Romanov dynasty, the confiscation of all socially important undertakings and the establishment of peace — such is an objective worthy of all the limitless sacrifices and privations through which Russia is bound to pass.

The shame of centuries must fall; namely our autocratic régime. The Russian people is well able to manage its affairs without the diktats of crowned wiseacres. All the stooges of the court and the government, all those ministers of the moment, bribe-takers and provocateurs must receive due retribution according to the deeds they have committed. All the capital funds plundered for war contracts and profiteering must be subjected to confiscation.

Citizens! At an hour of national peril in 1789 France proclaimed the idea of popular power and triumphed. At this time of danger to all mankind when the capitalist cliques are threatening to turn the world back to the days of Attila with endless wars, we call you to loftier tasks.

It is insufficient to proclaim a republic and an assembly of people's representatives freely elected by all citizens of Russia. It is necessary to bring it about that this assembly declares all private enterprises, factories, plants, mines, roads, means of communication, housing, stores, estates, monastic and state lands, forests, properties and so on that are of social significance to be state property and transfer its management to workers' and peasants' associations, co-operatives, local democratic management bodies or special committees — all under the direction of the whole people in the shape of the Assembly of people's representatives.

When we summon you to an uprising in the name of the Republic, we have in mind the political emancipation of the Russian nation. The first thing, though, that the Assembly of the Republic is duty bound to do is to transfer all the means and implements of production belonging to the capitalists into the hands of the toilers, that is, to carry through the economic emancipation of the people.

Once having realized an economic and political revolution within its own country, the Russian people will propose a peace on the basis of liquidating standing armies and navies, of solving international disputes not by wars but by a court, of lifting customs tariffs and promulgating the full freedom of international commerce. If the labouring people of other countries are not yet in a position to support us and if the armed bands of these or those capitalist countries threaten us with attack we shall fight for the salvation of our free Republic and for the true liberation of the people from the yoke of capitalist gangs. But when our armies go into battle not under the eagles of the Tsar but under the red banner of the Russian

Socialist Republic, there will be no forces in modern society capable of halting the victorious onward march of such armies.

Citizens! The hour of ruin for our country and the whole of the world's culture is approaching! It is in your power to make it an hour of triumph and a great rebirth. Let us close ranks and stand up as one against the exploiters and butchers for our free Republic, free labour in socially-run fields and factories and eternal peace between nations. The war has shaken their power to the roots. Their strength lies in our cowardice and sloth for they have no other strength. One concerted outburst will give us victory over capital and all its underlings. Mobilize all democratic forces, form strike committees, organize meetings and circles, fight the prejudices about the aims and tasks of this war, reproduce our appeals, propound everywhere and by all available means the correctness of our views, seek to make our voice penetrate the barracks, factories, countryside and the front. Prepare for the great day of the uprising when Russia will need all your experience, courage and perhaps even your life itself.

A Petrograd Group of Social-Democratic Workers.

Similar groups of social democrats which had no permanent link with the overall city organization existed in large numbers in Petersburg. Several of these circles kept apart and isolated through fear of provocateurs. Well known to me were two groups of activists which for a long while did not join the network of Petersburg organizations out of their mistrust of Chernomazov. But these circles still undertook work; because of their detachment from the local centre, it did, however, bear a makeshift character.

The other document is a resolution on the tasks of democracy. It was produced on a typewriter. The resolution defined those tasks as follows:

The Tasks of Democracy.

The bourgeoisie as a whole, and especially ours in Russia, has demonstrated that it is incapable of organizing industry and the distribution of material benefits. Where it rules it is destroying the productive forces in the process of periodic wars instead of developing them.

Where, as in our country, the bourgeoisie is not in power, it is afraid out of fear of revolution to take power in its hands thereby dooming the country to its ruin in the general world scramble. Only the world proletariat can save the values of human culture by acting at once to terminate this bloody slaughter of nations.

Peace must be general and not the separate one that our nobility would like to conclude, afraid as they are of the route of German junkerdom from which our own reactionary forces could derive support in event of a revolution in Russia. A new and victorious Russian Revolution could provide the impetus to the world proletariat but this could only be successful given the existence of a firm class organization of the proletariat. The task of democracy is to end the war. The task of the Russian working class is to liberate democracy compelling it to carry out the tasks laid before it, by waging an organized struggle against autocracy.

The ruling class, who are the culprits for the current war, have laid all its burden upon the masses of the people who are suffering incalculable bloody sacrifices and at the rear are groaning under the oppression of the financial system. By financing not only the overhead costs of the war but also a part of general expenditure by a colossal increase in taxation on the essentials of life and an unlimited issue of paper money, avoiding the need to tax property, are, in step with the falling exchange rate of the ruble, reducing their debt obligations and interest payments in real terms and increasing the monetary valuation of their property also in step with the falling ruble and its newly enhanced profitability.

These same indirect taxes and endless issues of paper money are causing a frantically racing cost of living which is bringing about the pauperization of the broad masses of the peasantry and especially the urban petty bourgeoisie on a hitherto unseen scale, giving rise to a continual reduction in the basic necessities which a worker, for all the prolongation and intensification of his labour, can acquire for his earnings.

Successive state bond issues which in turn render property taxation unnecessary are imposing colossal interest payments on future generations and threaten to turn today's war taxes into permanent taxes increasing many times over thereby crushing the proletariat and peasantry with their burden and prolonging today's forced-labour régime for all time which, taken together with the high cost of living, will lead to the impoverishment, subjugation, degradation and degeneration of the broad masses.

The exceptional rise in state expenditure consequent upon the rises in prices, the reduced real return on the issue of paper money and bonds caused by the falling value of the ruble and the plainly imminent bankruptcy of the state are, in conjunction with the growing danger of indignation by the masses of the people bent down under the double burden of excessive toil and the scarcity and expense of food products, beginning to threaten the ruling classes with, from their point of view, a premature ending to the war business that has been so profitable to them and, given a favourable outcome, promises even greater profits. Unsuccessful and ever more feverish moves by the ruling classes to solve the "food question" flow from their desire to postpone the onset of a crash and are now leading to a temporary divergence of interests among them: one group of exploiters is, by heaping all the responsibility for the present high prices on the other group, seeking to protect its own war profits by a certain restriction of the war profits of the other group.

From the outset the landlords have responded to the attempt by the industrialists to retard the rise in landowners profits, by setting fixed retail prices for farm products, with passive resistance: a refusal to sell grain until their guaranteed prices are raised and, if the fixed prices remain held down, countering with a demand for the extension of fixed prices to industrial products consumed by the broad masses.

A reconciliation of the divergent interests of landlords and industrialists will be achieved either by a measured return to the free market and free price-setting and by a number of measures (new taxes, requisitioning etc.) that will force the peasant to put his grain on the market or, if fixed prices are extended more widely and are observed, by the setting of fixed rates for labour as well, which will guarantee the landlords and the industrialists high profits and threaten severe penalties (posting to the front, jail, hard labour or corporal punishment for refusal to work for the fixed rates).

The food supply conferences and congresses organized by the Union of Zemstvos and the Union of Towns have to arrive at such an accord between landowning and industrial interests: the former, with their war profits somewhat curtailed, will not permit the operation of fixed prices to be prolonged but will only allow the war to continue to the moment when its termination holds out hope to the ruling classes of more favourable results than at the present time. The admission of insignificant delegations from consumer associations and certain workers' organizations to the conferences and congresses is to present the appearance that the landowners and industrialists, the real bosses of the congresses, enjoy backing from all sectors of the people.

The total lack of many essential items resulting from the extreme reduction in the number of workers employed in productive labour, the acute scarcity of a range of other equally necessary items, all these famines, whether of sugar, flour, firewood or paraffin which break out now in one and now in another locality because of the complete dislocation of transport, the corruption of officials from the bottom to the top ranks and the senseless measures undertaken by them (local export bans, local, arbitrarily devised prices and so on) which lead to the lunatic rise in the cost of living regularly alternating with shortages of goods, all this has prepared fertile soil for speculation which though not creating the current food crisis, has taken advantage of it and thereby in some instances brought about its further aggravation.

As the executive committee of the ruling classes, the government has come under attack from all sides also for tolerating in its ranks almost open traitors who are increasing the bloody and material sacrifices of this war and making an unfavourable end to it unavoidable, and for the fact that it is incapable of reconciling the divergent interests of the different groups of exploiters to various restrictions placed upon them; it is rapidly driving the state towards utter military, financial and economic exhaustion and bankruptcy.

The government is seeking to protect itself from these attacks by taking every step to divert the attention of the masses of the people from the fundamental causes of the current situation and directing it towards certain secondary and tertiary phenomena like for example, small traders stashing away a few dozen poods of flour or salt. Beset by mounting external and internal problems, it will seek to turn the rising popular indignation towards pogroms, pogroms launched against this or that uninfluential group of bourgeois which plays a minuscule role in the soaring cost of living, upon minority nationalities which, as such, play no part in causing high prices and themselves fall into exploiters and exploited, and upon numerically small groups extracting benefit from the growing cost of living on the one hand and the broad masses suffering from that same high cost of living, on the other.

In their efforts to put off a complete food supply collapse which would make continuation of war impossible, the ruling classes want to split off workers producing destructive materials into a special privileged group which would experience the fewest food supply difficulties existing among the hungry population and, by corrupting it by this separation, to divorce it from the working class and the broad masses of exploited.

VI
The Beginning of the End

THE TSARIST government's contempt for liberal exhortations and pleas for reform reached its peak in the autumn of 1916. By its actions, the government gave the opposition some good trump cards, but when it came to open and resolute struggle, even if only within the confines of the State Duma, the disgruntled bourgeoisie proved to be so cowardly that it would grant any concessions. Fear in the face of the revolutionary workers' movement was stronger than any logic.

The irreconcilability of the government and its absolute inability to tackle the economic breakdown or emerge victorious from the military operations, undermined the prestige of the authorities in the eyes of even the widest circles of philistines. Left-wing liberal circles were forced to take an illegal line of work so as to retain the support of petty-bourgeois layers which were patriotically and oppositionally inclined.

The documents and proclamations printed below were reproduced from the resources of the establishments where they happened to be received. In the plants it was done by the Hospital Funds and, less often, in the office. In the plants they were passed round from hand to hand till they were in tatters. Enthusiastic amateurs existed who would copy out whole pamphlets by hand.

After the dissolution of the congresses of bourgeois public organizations, certain radical circles of the Petersburg bourgeois also took the path of illegal activity. Setbacks at the front, territorial losses and the growth of a revolutionary mood in the army and factories forced even the torpid Russian bourgeoisie to rise in open opposition to the predatory rule of the tsar's camarilla. It threatened an assault, but only for the sake of the war and to smash their competitor, the German merchant. At the end of December a special leaflet was circulated around Petersburg which came out of the Meeting of Representatives of Public Organizations held in Moscow on 11 December. One of several, this leaflet was addressed exclusively to workers. In it the bourgeois organizations spread the tale then current that agitation against the war was conducted by "German spies", hangers-on of the tsar and other such elements. The proclamation represented a model of the deception with which the bourgeoisie sought to entwine the mass of the people and thereby drive them to the slaughter:

To Workers.

You are the ones who stand at the benches. You are the ones who in stifling workshops forge the shells, our means to victory. Workers, we are addressing you. At a moment of exceptional external struggle, Russia is also undergoing an acute domestic crisis. A worthless government, composed of and headed by those same protégés of the old régime who are engaged not in a war with the enemy but a struggle against public and workers' organizations, has brought to the greatest state in the world dislocation of all its living organs. The problems in the sphere of feeding and supplying the population, which are connected with the war and inevitable while its lasts, have been compounded by the incompetent and possibly deliberate actions of the government into a scene of inconceivable breakdown, profiteering and pillage. And then, certain leading figures of the working masses start telling us that all this mess which besets our lives is a consequence of the war and that therefore the war must be ended. They further add that the war is being waged by the government and not the people and that the war must be ended in the interests of the international community of man.

Workers! Fight these exhortations by every means, open the eyes of others, cry out until you are hoarse that the war must be prosecuted at all costs not so much in order to destroy all the German people but to smash its militarism which lies with oppressive weight upon the democratic classes of Europe; cry out that the war must be continued to smash the German hearth of reaction, that same reaction that is supported in Russia by the accursed autocracy which torments the country. Realize that victory over Germany represents the definitive victory over the Russian autocracy. Realize that our government is lying when it says that it wishes to defeat Germany together with the people. It is lying because Germany always has and will support the vilest reaction in Russia for its own interests.

And so for the war, for its slogans of liberation which can be realized only with complete victory over Germany, we have the French Republic, now streaming with blood, ruined Belgium, freedom-loving Britain and the advanced section of Russian society; against the war are Germany and the secret yearnings of our ruling strata, the true enemies of our Russian liberty. In Russia itself the best forces of the Russian intelligentsia, the most eminent members of the State Duma, all Russia's zemstvos and towns, all the public organizations, the pillars of the Russian liberation movement, Plekhanov, Burtsev and Kropotkin, are all for continuance of the war; against the war are the toadying obscurantists of the autocratic régime.

So, however can you workers at such a moment and with such a line-up of forces, again put forward the demand "Down with the war" and thus unwittingly play into the hands of the autocratic system? No, it is impossible that anyone within whom there beats a Russian heart and whose soul grieves and mortally longs beside the motherland or anyone who has comprehended the exceptional gravity of the present moment will not march behind the banner which was raised in Moscow by the finest sons of Russia.

War to the end regardless of further sacrifices.

But every human life is immeasurably dear to us to avoid more millions of sacrifices being made in vain and so that our army is never again left without shells, it is written on our banner:

Down with the criminal government, down with the protégés of autocracy!

And so that the war brings us truly to victory and the war takes as few as possible victims from us, and to alleviate as far as is still possible our fatal domestic mess to which the government has brought our country, it is written on our banner:

Long live a ministry formed from the finest public figures and accountable to the people!

Workers! Moscow is Russia's heart. Let us rally our ranks around her banner and let us remember that in our alliance lies woe for Germany and woe for our government, and now:

Long live the army, the protectress of Russia.
Long live great and free Russia.

A group of united citizens of Petrograd.

Arrange widest distribution.

Our adversaries were hoping to lure workers over to their side with such slogans. However, two and a half years of war and the behaviour of all the bourgeois parties had taught Petersburg workers a great deal. They did not trust the allusions to their erstwhile mentors. Plekhanov, Kropotkin and others who had latterly taken the path of aiding the bourgeoisie and were lauded by them for it, were duly regarded as having deserted the workers: that was how the Petersburg proletariat saw it and that indeed was how it was.

This phenomenon was typical not only of Petersburg but of many other Russian cities too. As I toured several localities, Moscow, Nizhni-Novgorod and elsewhere, I encountered the same picture. Comrades arriving from other places reported the same thing. Illegal leaflets and proclamations were no longer shunned but sought, asked for and read with interest and trust. Hatred of the government had plumbed the very depths of society and this terrified the bourgeois liberal top dogs. The government sensed this and prepared for struggle, arming the police and training them in machine-gunnery, artillery and so on. But the interests of the ruling classes were divided and even among the bigwigs surrounding the tsar's throne there was no unity of views. Rasputin's murder led to the disintegration of the court and the break-up of the reigning camarilla. The downfall of the monarchy was now inevitable and close at hand.

The Central Committee Bureau's Links with the Provinces

On this visit to Russia I managed to establish relatively close contact with the provincial organizations. There was regular communication with Moscow, Nizhni-Novgorod, Kiev, Tula, Voronezh, the Donets Basin and certain plants in the Urals and Siberia.

Work in Moscow was progressing considerably better this time. Student youth was beginning to stir, and in working-class districts work was proceeding well. The organization was run by V.P. Nogin, P.G. Smidovich, I.I. Skvortsev and others. Through M.G. Pavlova I came to know R.V. Mostovenko, whose flat I personally availed myself of for lodging and rest. Things were not going too badly in Nizhni either. The Sormovo organization had grown stronger and even sent a certain proportion of dues collected as a contribution towards the Central Committee. Besides our organization among refugees, the Bund was also active there, as was an organization of the left tendency of the Socialist-Revolutionaries. In December 1916 the last-mentioned group succeeded in publishing a printed leaflet directed against the "hereditary blood-suckers" of the tsarist government with its landlords and capitalists. This organization's slogan was "down with the war", coupled with a call for an armed uprising.

I managed to obtain a number of reports on the workers' situation and the state of our party's work in the Donets Basin which provided the following picture.

From the very start of the war all the ore-miners were exempted. None of the mobilizations affected them. This circumstance had an enormous effect on the course of the workers' movement in the Donets Basin. It appeared that all that half-starving mass was so stultified with patriotic feeling that it did not so much as notice what was being done all around or rather what was being done to it.

But the capitalist joint-stock companies took advantage as never before of this convenient moment, and as workers sang patriotic songs, the working day was lengthened in all enterprises (the "stint") and workers were forced to work overtime. The managements of the mines incessantly fined workers for the slightest manifestation of protest against rough treatment, with the result that only a few wretched coppers would remain out of their meagre earnings. For all their harsh conditions the workers showed no sign of protest during the first year of the war; their awareness seemed to have been drugged, and became no clearer. A wave of chauvinism took hold of a considerable section of those workers, who took collections for defence and in aid of war victims, refugees and so forth.

Ever-rising prices forced workers to start giving thought to their own situation. To the rescue came their friends, the intellectuals who, from as far back as 1905 and 1906 enjoyed great prestige among the masses. Propounding the idea of defence, they called on workers to organize co-operatives that were supposedly to ease the tough economic plight which was as much hitting at workers as the population as a whole. At first workers indeed did resort to this remedy. Throughout almost the entire basin the co-operative movement grew, new consumer associations were formed and the old ones strengthened. Workers took part in them to use the legal opportunities for meetings, but even at consumer association meetings voices of brave and irreconcilable fighters for complete freedom could be heard, though their message at that stage did not encounter any support. By the beginning of the second year the picture had changed a little: here and there in the plants and mines small cells and grouplets were organized where questions of current affairs were discussed and where even the first news of the Zimmerwald conference percolated through. As it later turned out, all these cells were to become adherents of the Zimmerwald resolutions. We should note that these grouplets were not interlinked and did not even know of the existence of others similar to themselves.

In February and March 1916 there appeared two leaflets at one of the Gorlovka mines, calling on workers to organize, which quite graphically portrayed the political and economic state of the country and put forward the slogans of the RSDLP majority. These leaflets had also been distributed at other mines and although very badly hectographed they were nevertheless read with great eagerness, the more so because this was the first sign of an awakening movement, and no more positive initiative was to present itself elsewhere until the very outbreak of the strike. In early April the first wartime strike in the Donets Basin broke out, involving twenty neighbouring undertakings with some fifty thousand workers in all. The signal for the strike was given from the mine where the leaflets already mentioned had appeared and another twelve mines joined the strike in a single day. In the very first days they set to to organize themselves and everywhere identical demands were advanced for a 50 per cent wage rise and, in one or two places, the abolition of fines for not reporting for duty. These rises were predetermined by the ever rising cost of living. The mining companies refused to meet the demands. Thereupon at a general meeting of all the mines a decision to strike was taken until all demands were met. The strike started off quite calmly and workers continued to assemble at now one and now another mine to discuss the situation. At all these meetings workers engaged in no adventures. At one, a strike committee was elected. But meanwhile the custodians of law and order went into action after their own fashion: two companies of soldiers were despatched from Bakhmut, ostensibly to protect the mines. But on the second day, following an order to disperse a meeting, the soldiers refused to undertake "protective" roles of this type. A detachment of mounted police was sent out in their place, and at first confined itself to merely a presence at all the meetings. On the tenth day, an official came from one of the mines with the special mission of negotiating with the workers. All the workers duly gathered. He addressed them in a brotherly way, pointing out to them that, as he said, it was criminal to go on strike at such a critical moment, that the Jews, those enemies within who desired the downfall of the homeland be it by spying or by revolutionary propaganda, were inciting them to this crime and that workers, as sincere orthodox folk to whom the fatherland was dear, must fight this enemy of the Russian people and pay no heed to their hostile speeches, especially as the workers were earning good money and had no need to go out on strike. The workers grew restive, for none of them had anticipated such speeches. Voices were heard to say that this was not 1905 when the myth of Jewish domination made such a terrible impact, that nowadays they were well able to distinguish their friends from their enemies, that economic demands were not punishable under the law, and that the strike had come about by virtue of the very low wages which you just could not manage on with the high cost of living. Realizing that his assignment was not to be crowned with success, the official started to threaten postings to front-line positions. The workers replied that if their demands were not met they would go themselves to the military governor. The official threatened them once more with shootings and jail but drove off with nothing gained.

After his departure there were several attempts by the police to arrest the more prominent workers, but in vain. At all the mines workers organized a guard who would raise the alarm as soon as they caught sight of police approaching their workmates' dwellings so that a crowd would come running out and drive the police off, even springing arrested workmates for them.

The general situation was getting worse and worse. There was no money and holidays were approaching. Although the companies had not yet stopped allowing credit in their retail stores, workers started being refused in many of them. The workers did not know how to proceed. With their last money, two telegrams were sent to workers' deputies in the Duma but alas, no reply was received. One more effort was made: a little money was collected, a representative was chosen and sent to Petersburg to consult with the deputies, but he was never seen again, as if he had vanished into thin air. The governor of Ekaterinoslav paid a visit to the mines after the holidays were over. He, just like the official on the special mission, addressed the workers in an emotive "brotherly" speech, rebuking them for a mindless strike.

He conceded that wages were low in view of the rising price of basic necessities, but the workers could make an approach to him, for he would at once mediate with the company for a 30 per cent rise. Then voices called out: "We won't go back for 49 per cent, we demand 50 per cent." The furious "mediator" started to threaten legal proceedings, saying that this was no longer an economic strike but a rebellion pure and simple and that people were shot for rebellion. The whole mass of workers stood there as if frozen to the spot, and shouted "Fire!" Even mothers with babies did not shift from the spot. "Better to be shot down right here than to die of starvation," shouted the workers. "Let's have another Lena and serve as an example to others who have to fight for their rights." The governor went wild, the police were standing by, and the most terrible outcome was to be expected. But the governor refrained this time, although he had left instructions with the police which they were subsequently to fulfil to the letter. The governor drove off and in order to avoid any excesses or clashes with the police, the workers took the decision not to assemble on May Day but to gather on 2 May to decide how ultimately they should proceed. May Day passed off quietly and there were not even any arrests.

On the morning of 2 May workers started to collect at the pre-arranged spot but found soldiers there. They had to occupy a nearby knoll. When a section of the workers started to move off to forewarn workmates who had not yet arrived, the knoll was unexpectedly surrounded by police who started demanding that the workers disperse. Noticing workers from the Gorlovka mines approaching some people on the knoll started to go to the aid of those arriving. At that moment the police turned around to face the Gorlovkans and made straight for them. The Gorlovkans turned back and ran for some nearby gulleys. But having got that far, the crowd was now delayed by having to cross the gulleys. At that point the pursuing police, led by a superintendent, caught up. Upon command of the latter, two volleys were fired but both appeared to be deliberately into the air. Then the infuriated superintendent burst into the crowd and started to fire in all directions with his revolver. Simultaneously another two volleys rang out and the police took cover. The crowd which caught up from behind found four dead and twenty wounded on the site.

At the other end of the settlement, a police detachment swooped on a crowd going to warn workmates due to arrive and beat them up with whips, while a desperate brawl broke out with other workmates who had by now drawn near and the others had wanted to warn, as a result of which one policeman and several dozen workers were seriously injured. The injured were taken off to Rudnik hospital and the dead put in the morgue. All four dead proved to be family men, one of them left seven children and a sick wife. Workmates collected 44 rubles and some kopeks to help the bereaved families, and bought shrouds and wreaths. But when they arrived to dress out the dead, the police would not let them into the mortuary in spite of requests from relatives and the bravery of the crowd which had to be driven away by threats of further shootings. When they arrived for the funerals the next morning the morgue was empty: by night the police had removed the dead and buried them in an unknown place, refusing even to show relatives the graves.

Mass arrests were carried out on the night of 4 May. Feeling defeated, the workers no longer resisted.

The strike was to last another seven days, during which workers agreed to end the strike but did not enter into negotiations with the company. On 11 May they reported for work at all the mines on their old conditions. Subsequently, however, a "financial ration" was awarded amounting to a 25 per cent pay supplement. From that month onwards, strike action overflowed throughout the Donets Basin, mostly finishing in defeat for the workers.

The strikes were accompanied everywhere by sweeping arrests, sacking of workers from the plants and the deportation of workers in their hundreds to front-line positions. Thus, in the May of that year, a strike flared up in the town of Mariupol at one of the richest plants; this ended in defeat after two weeks, being crushed by mass arrests and the sacking of hundreds of workers. In July a colossal strike flared up in Lugansk which ended in a bloody massacre and mass arrests.

Simultaneously with the strike wave, strong political groups began to be formed, the cells rapidly gaining strength rather as if workers wanted to recover the precious time lost. They started to seek links between each other. This was now easy. During the strikes all these grouplets and cells had become acquainted with each other. At this juncture they all united to form the social-democratic organization of the Donets Basin, whose statutes and programme were those of the RSDLP majority.

Relations with Other Parties

Comrades arriving with reports from the localities regretted but one thing, the lack of literature, demand for which was extremely great and whose supply from abroad was limited. We had to distribute Petersburg Committee publications and hastily prepare literature for publication inside Russia. But there were serious obstacles owing to lack of funds.

The Petersburg Committee had well equipped its illegal printshop in Novaya Derevnya but it was seized along with several thousand copies of the pamphlet *Who Needs the War?* by A.M. Kollontai. Many of our technical workers were seized together with the printshop. I soon afterwards managed to establish that "Aleksei the printer" had ratted on the printshop. The Petersburg Committee took immediate steps to isolate and boycott this man. But this whole fiasco did put a brake on Petersburg Committee proclamations for a while.

As the activity of the Central Committee Bureau developed, a great variety of reports on the revolutionary struggle of the working class started to come in. The publication of a newspaper became a crying need. Comrade Molotov made intensive investigations in quest of premises and staff for the organization of an illegal printshop. In anticipation of this, we decided to publish *Osvedomitelny Listok* ("Information Bulletin"), reproducing it on typewriters and sending it out to our organizations even if only in single copies for them to duplicate it in accordance with the requirements of their forces. It was planned to issue the first number of the Central Committee Bureau's *Osvedomitelny Listok* after 9 January.

At the end of 1916 I learnt from N.D. Sokolov that comrade E.D. Stasova was arriving from exile for treatment and I at once hastened to meet her and bring her into the work. Comrade Stasova undertook a part of the secretarial work that did not require trips around the city's rendezvous points.

In spite of ever mounting repression, mass arrests and the loss of party workers, our illegal organization developed and strengthened. The most powerful illegal organization in Petersburg was our party's Petersburg Committee which brought together some 3,000 members, but the majority of Petersburg workers could be regarded as sympathizing with its anti-war policy. Out of our party's legal organizations there remained in existence only the Workers' Group of the Insurance Council, which was also the all-Russian centre of the hospital funds and its journal, *Voprosy Strakhovaniya*. The activity of these institutions was inhibited in the extreme and many members of the Insurance Group were in jail or exile.

Closest to the Petersburg Committee in its tactics and attitude to the war was a group known by the name of the "Inter-District Organization" of the Social-Democratic Labour Party. There numbered in this organization a group of "non-factional" social democrats, former Trotskyites and Plekhanovites, but the organization did possess the resources and opportunities to publish leaflets and even a small four-page newspaper, *Vpered* ("Forward"), of which two issues appeared. The membership of the Inter-District Organization never went beyond some 150.

At the end of the summer of 1916 the Petersburg Initiative Group of Menshevik Social Democrats was resurrected and in the August a leaflet came out opposing the "War Industries Socialists" and disclaiming any responsibility for the Labour Group of the Central War Industries Committee, forbidding its supporters to enter into any pacts with them on matters of the workers' movement and declaring the Gvozdevites to be instigators of a new split. The organization issued four leaflets during 1916: the first was devoted to the War Industries Socialists; the second to the general nature of the war and the position of the working class, with the slogans "down with the war" and "long live peace"; the third leaflet consisted of an eleven-point statement on the food crisis; the fourth leaflet was issued for 9 January 1917 beneath the slogan "down with the war, long live peace, long live the democratic republic and the constituent assembly".

There were also many diverse national social-democratic groups in Petersburg, some of which affiliated to our party organization with the status of districts within the Petersburg Committee. Of other non-social-democratic organizations there were the Socialist-Revolutionaries. Their Petersburg organization had a majority of leftists, Chernov supporters. According to Aleksandrovich, the deputy Kerensky also joined them, renouncing his previous position of national defence. The Socialist-Revolutionaries carried out work in various districts with some success, but they were unable to create a strong organization.

After our organizations, brought together by the Petersburg Committee, the strongest without doubt was the defensist Mensheviks' organization. The latter made highly practical use of their semi-legal status, publishing the periodicals *Delo* and *Ekonomicheskoe Obozrenie*, and staffed hospital funds and labour groups of the War Industries Committees.

At the offices of the Central War Industries Committee on the Liteiny in Petersburg, their "Labour Group" had its premises, where defensists gathered from all over Petersburg, reports were made and members of Chkheidze's Duma faction, the "non-party Socialist-Revolutionary" Kerensky and others would go. The meetings were often well attended and representatives of the Petersburg Committee would go along there to pursue the fight against "Gvozdevism". After one such visit we lost comrade Evdokimov, who was put in jail.

This organization had intellectual resources and funds at its disposal, thanks to its proximity to capitalist moneybags. The tsar's government however undervalued the defensists' patriotism and believing that it could not split the Petersburg proletariat any further, started persecuting them, liberal and patriotically-minded workers as they were.

After the congresses of the "public organizations" in Moscow broken up by the Stürmer government, the "Labour Group" became a tool of the liberal-organized movement around the Duma, following the slogan of "national salvation".

With the existence of a whole multiplicity of groups and party organizations, the growth of the revolutionary movement demanded unity of action from these organizations. The danger of fragmenting the movement was, though small, still present. With this in mind, the Menshevik social-democratic Duma faction in the figure of N.S. Chkheidze proposed to our Central Committee Bureau via N.D. Sokolov to discuss the question of co-operation and co-ordinated revolutionary actions. The Socialist-Revolutionaries made a similar approach through Aleksandrovich. The Bureau considered the proposals and took the decision that it could only enter into an agreement on the matter of co-ordinated action with organizations that had adopted the position of a consistent struggle against the war and its supporters and were not party to any agreement with the liberal bourgeoisie.

An appointment between myself, Chkheidze and someone else was arranged at N.D. Sokolov's at which I raised in practical terms the question of a break by Chkheidze and the rest from the Gvozdevites and of an open condemnation of their policy, and furthermore demanded their firm backing for the working masses' revolutionary anti-war movement both from the Duma tribune and outside it.

In front of witnesses, Chkheidze disowned solidarity with "Gvozdevism" but sought to justify his visits to the Labour Group of the War Industries Committee as being for information purposes only. A vacuum was developing around the Duma faction by that time. Their policy of continual wavering did not meet with support from any of the illegal social-democratic groups. The performances of the Chkheidze faction in the Duma were so pale that they could not evoke any response or support from revolutionary-minded workers' circles.

I also had an appointment at N.D. Sokolov's with Kerensky. The topic of the conversation was the attitude to the war and co-ordinated action. A.F. Kerensky called himself an internationalist, accepted the platform of the Zimmerwald left and renounced his patriotic aberrations. I put to him the same terms of a break from the "Gvozdev-Guchkov" bloc as it was perfectly well known to me that he too was taking part in the work and meetings of the war industries socialists. I moreover demanded more clarity on the attitude to the war, a definitive break from the "defence of the fatherland" and a public statement on the matter.

All we members of the Central Committee Bureau and Petersburg Committee organizers, however, put little faith in the sincerity of Chkheidze's and Kerensky's statements. The latter were all in very close touch with the bourgeois opposition and we suspected that these people were, in the guise of making "contacts", intending to latch us on to the movement "around the Duma" which was being prepared among bourgeois intellectuals and democrats from the autumn onwards. The most extreme slogans of this movement were "accountable government" and "a government of national salvation".

The Bourgeoisie's Struggle for Power

The autumn of 1916 was marked by open public activity by the organized merchant and industrial bourgeoisie. The Russian bourgeoisie followed the bourgeoisies of all the other belligerent countries, and adopted the war as its own, considering it to be a highly profitable business, proclaiming a "union with the government" and encouraging the reconciliation of classes. However, the policy of barbarian tsarism which was not only undertaken in the interests of merchant and industrial capital but also had its own purely dynastic aims, frequently subordinated the "final ends" of the Russian bourgeoisie to the interests of the court and thus sowed anxiety in the business hearts of our country's merchants and manufacturers. While striving for an alliance with the government and understanding all the "evil" sides of the tsarist, bureaucratic-police system of government which crushed any public initiative or self-activity whatever, the bourgeoisie decided to erase the pernicious effect of the tsar's policy and to take over by itself the conduct of the war.

A number of public organizations, with auxiliary functions to the military and civil organs of the state, had been created by the liberal bourgeoisie. These organizations acquired the character of class organizations of the bourgeoisie, were more mobile than those of the government and quickly assumed an enormous importance in servicing the requirements of the war. The government tolerated these organizations as a necessary evil and was even compelled to concede them increasingly wide-ranging rights. The all-Russian Union of Zemstvos, the all-Russian Union of Towns and the War Industries Committees united around themselves all the so-called "enfranchised" section of Russia. Thanks to their liberal parentage and the government's hostile attitude towards them, all these organizations proved able to draw upon organizational forces within the democratic intelligentsia and through it to gain a foothold in the populace as well.

All these public organizations formed by the liberal merchant and industrial bourgeoisie presented by the end of 1916 powerful strong-points of a Russian bourgeoisie united around the issue of the war. In spite of holding such fortresses in their sway and being brought together by the black-and-yellow banner of the "progressive bloc" in the State Duma, our bourgeoisie did not so much as dream of using them against the tsarist government and its régime. All the liberal representatives of the commercial classes and war industries were advocates of a constitutional monarchy. Democracy scared them just as much as socialism. They were truly afraid of revolution, many times more so than of German imperialism.

Nicholas II's policy aroused resentment not only because it did not fully answer the immediate interests of the merchant and industrial bourgeoisie but also because that whole tsarist system of governing Russia was dealing irreparable blows to the monarchy itself. The bourgeoisie, in its relations with Nicholas II and the House of Romanov as a whole, was in entire agreement with a certain section of the Russian aristocrats and court retinue who looked on with "heartfelt anguish" as their beloved but degenerate monarch and all his minions fell under the spell of "dark forces", political adventurers and charlatans. There were among the aristocrats groupings which took part in all the backstage "manoeuvres" of public activities and implored Tsar Nikolai to make concessions to the "finest men of the country". Nikolai II was however deaf to all entreaties and would not agree to moderate his autocratic power.

The critical situation within the country, the unceasing danger at the front and, most important, the blatant aspiration of certain court circles for a rapprochement with Germany and reports of possible backstage peace negotiations with Germany, worried the "patriotic" progressive bourgeoisie to the utmost. During the enforced Duma recess a snap cabinet reshuffle took place: it was no mere change of faces but a demonstration of the tsarist autocracy's firm intention of maintaining its rightward course irrespective of the black-and-yellow bloc and so-called Russian public opinion. To buttress the attacks by the progressive bloc in the State Duma, preparation for a struggle was being made by all the bourgeois organizations: the all-Russian Union of Towns, the all-Russian Union of Zemstvos, the War Industries Committees, Chambers of Commerce, all sorts of commodity exchange committees and finally even the Congress of the United Nobility. However, the liberal bourgeois and liberalistic monarchists, at the same time as preparing a struggle against the tsar's feudal chieftains, courtly parasites and bureaucrats of the best vintage, were also holding backstage negotiations with representatives of the same "dark" government forces. Among the intelligentsia very many rumours and stories circulated around Petersburg about all sorts of secret deals done in the wings of the State Duma. We did at that time manage to obtain a virtually verbatim account of one such conference where a deal was attempted. The conference took place on 19 October 1916, prior to the opening of the State Duma. (The opening of the autumn session of the State Duma was held on 1 November.) The conference, held at the house of the State Duma president, N.V. Rodzyanko, had an inter-factional nature. All its participants, from Shulygin to Milyukov, had reacted negatively to Protopopov's entry into the Stürmer cabinet. As a colleague of the president of the State Duma, Protopopov was regarded as a member of the then celebrated "progressive bloc" and his joining the government was considered a betrayal. At this conference of Duma members, the allegations by now circulating throughout Petersburg, that Protopopov was an adventurer who did not even enjoy the support of his personal friends in the Duma, were confirmed.

The arena of the bourgeoisie's struggle for its own rule was the State Duma. For the opening of its work, the bourgeoisie had already succeeded in concentrating the attention of very wide circles in the country on this parliamentary duel of the knights of Russia's liberalism versus the monster of our nation, the government of the tsar. Within the Tauride Palace itself, the seat of the Duma, the great day was awaited.

In Petersburg, reactions to the speeches anticipated in the Duma were fairly mixed. The intelligentsia, officialdom and the philistines were expecting a thunderstorm. The working population, understanding the class essence of the Duma, nurtured no exaggerated illusions about a parliamentary contest.

1 November and the days following were indeed red-letter days for the liberals. The forms of the parliamentary struggle lagged in no way behind those of Europe. The government took the step of forbidding the printing of the deputies' declarations and speeches, but this only led to all of them being illegally issued. Their intervention opened with the declaration of the progressive bloc read out by Shidlovsky.

The declaration stated on behalf of five factions of the Fourth State Duma that "the great struggle for our just cause [i.e. the war] must at all costs be carried forward to a victorious end". The progressive bloc saw in the actions of the tsarist government many grave impediments to a successful conclusion of the war. The authorities' ill-conceived and haphazard regulations were threatening the whole of the country's economy. The declaration stressed the government's isolation and the ever growing mistrust it aroused. It even treated the patriotic upsurge of the "public organizations" with suspicion and was conducting an open struggle against them. The declaration then passed on from the government's convictions and warnings of possible evils to its own proposal that it "leave" and make way for those who énjoy the trust of the "whole people". A peculiarity of this declaration lay in its address to the army and navy included at the end. The phrases concealed a desire to win over the sympathies of the officer-corps of the armed forces to the State Duma. Though the bourgeoisie was far removed from the idea of involving the army in the settlement of political questions, it was most important for it to have support among the military staff and the officer caste. This objective was relatively easily achieved.

The focus of attention in the first sitting of the State Duma was the speech by the leader of Russian liberalism, P.N. Milyukov. His speech provided the programme not only for the Cadet party but also for the whole bloc.

The orator's basic theme, underlying all his speech from start to finish, was the government's inability and reluctance to tackle all the difficulties flowing from wartime conditions. Especially heavy points were made against the head of the government of the day, Stürmer. The latter was made the symbol of the Germanophile tendencies in court circles and was suspected of direct treachery. The predatory, conquering greed of Russian liberalism, which demanded the Straits and Constantinople, also expressed itself quite sharply in Milyukov's speech. The speech gave rise to a multitude of interpretations and prompted talk of a duel and the prosecution of Milyukov by Stürmer; the fall of the Stürmer cabinet, which followed soon after, was also attributed to it. Its publication was prohibited but that did not prevent its eager distribution by illegal means. The working population made use of all the material in the speech that implicated the tsarist government together with its civil service and ministers.

After Milyukov, Chkheidze spoke. All the indecision of the Chkheidze faction was evident in his speech. He could not find a single objection to the overtly imperialist designs expounded in the declaration of the bloc. In Chkheidze's speech, Russia's militant proletariat would not find anything to guide them in the struggle they were waging throughout the land. At a time when the appetites of the bourgeoisie were finding a voice in the rhetoric of Milyukov, Maklakov and others, the people who called themselves social democrats were not merely incapable of reflecting the struggle against the war being waged by the proletariat of our country but actually behaved quite as if no such struggle was in fact in progress. Yet our Duma social democrats were at that time most fond of "showing solidarity" with Karl Liebknecht. Solidarity with Karl Liebknecht was not taken by them to mean following the same path as his and working in a revolutionary anti-war direction in one's own country; Chkheidze and the rest confined themselves to "hailing" his courage. But the chauvinist press was likewise full of articles that hailed his struggle "in an enemy country", thereby aiming to deceive the workers. So the solidarity expressed by Chkheidze was drowned in the general flood.

Even in moderate working-class circles, Chkheidze's speech produced perplexity: in it no one could trace any of the revolutionary tension that the working class breathed; still less was there any socialist clarity, in relation to the war in particular. Revolutionary workers' circles and Bolshevik social democrats had anyway long ago ceased to regard the Duma faction as a guiding revolutionary centre.

The offensive opened by the liberal bourgeoisie against the government was rounded off "from the left" by the Narodnik (Socialist-Revolutionary) deputy, A.F. Kerensky. In the first days of the November session, he put a question on the ban on publishing Duma speeches, military censorship and the predicament of the press. On the fundamental questions of domestic and foreign policy and on the question of the war itself, this representative of the party of the Socialist-Revolutionaries had, however, no opinion of his own.

The bourgeoisie succeeded very rapidly in shifting the struggle for power far beyond the bounds of the Tauride Palace. The start of the winter of 1916 was noted for a series of elaborate congresses that opened up wide possibilities for the bourgeoisie to step up their offensive. The policy of the tsarist government was not even encountering backing among the most true and loyal nobility. The congress of representatives of noble societies which took place on 28 November endorsed the moderate demands of the progressive bloc.

This period of the war, with its liberal cravings for power, was witness to a peculiar form of political agitation: the publication and illegal circulation of letters between one dignitary and another. Letters from Chelnokov to Rodzyanko, Guchkov to Alexeev, and others were that autumn passed round from hand to hand. In the end, up spoke also our organized prop of the throne of the fatherland, the nobility. The president of the united nobility, A.P. Strukov, addressed a letter "by way of appeal" to the tsar in which he "indicted" the State Duma, citing the untold harm that its public activities were causing. This letter and also the tactics of the Duma formed subjects for discussion at the Congress of the United Nobility on 28 November 1916.

A section of the nobility headed by V.N. Lvov formed the "left" at this congress. Our merchant and industrial bourgeoisie also spoke through the left section of this congress. An assessment of the political situation from the standpoint of this social class was contributed by V.N. Lvov in a speech which was circulated quite extensively among the Petersburg and Moscow bourgeoisie and intellectuals.

This speech by V.N. Lvov typified the anxiety of the noble estate for the fate of the tsarist fatherland and its own age-old privileges. All the nobility from the right to the "left" wing was moved by but one desire: to save the House of Romanov at any price, to safeguard it from the disintegration, corruption and decomposition of the top ruling circles and shield it from the eyes of the people. Unmasking of Nicholas II's system of government and exposing the ineptitude and venality of its lackeys was of course considered by the nobility to be dangerous demagogy.

At the beginning of December congresses were convened of the public organizations connected with work for the defence of the country. Having lost its support among even the ranks of the united nobility, the government withheld permission for the opening of the congresses. The leading figures of the Unions of Zemstvos and Towns had to make improvised arrangements at short notice. The All-Russian Union of Zemstvos organized an assembly of delegates from provincial zemstvos for 9 December. At this assembly G.E. Lvov made a speech "on the current situation". His speech was fraught with the landowners' anxieties for the fate of the monarchy and the privileges of noble and bourgeois society linked to it.

The driving force of the liberal zemstvos was the war and the thirst for plunder that went with it. They saw the road to Russia's "salvation" in "smashing" the enemy and acquiring Constantinople and the Straits. It was such imperialist appetites which stirred the patriotic hearts of the liberal zemstvos.

Representatives of the Union of Towns gathered the same day but separately. The government took police measures against this congress. In place of the opening of the congress, a police charge-sheet was served. Representatives of the public organizations were this time no longer afraid to hold illegal gatherings. In reply to the police ban on congresses, the representatives of the zemstvos, towns and other organizations gathered on 11 December in a joint conference which adopted a motion of protest against the government's action in dissolving the congresses.

Support for the Fourth Duma

As was to be expected, the tsarist government sought to neutralize the progressive bloc's plans for agitation. All opposition speeches by deputies were systematically deleted. On many days newspapers were published with blank columns in place of the reports of State Duma sittings. This state of affairs did not, however, disrupt the militant programme of the parliamentary bloc. The deputies' speeches, which were reproduced by a variety of means, were quite amply distributed among the population.

Duma progressive bloc politicians sought and found a basis in working-class circles among the defensists and through the War Industries Committees. In those days the war industries socialists were conducting strenuous agitation around the plants of Petersburg. The creation of a united front against the government formed part of this agitation. The workers' interests, their class tasks and attitude to the war around which struggle was unfolding, were left out of account by our social-patriots. All their efforts could be reduced to a drive to win support for the State Duma. In November the following resolution was put out by them around the factories and plants:

> The government, which has now even come into sharp collision with the majority in the State Duma, is openly leading the country, already groaning under the yoke of war, to utter dislocation, ruin and downfall. The salvation of the country lies in the free and broad organization of the masses of the people; but the free and broad organization of the masses of the people is possible only with a radical change in the existing political order. The country may perish, fall apart and starve but the people will still not be freed or organized for it is lack of organization and fragmentation which forms the best guarantee of the rule of the noble-bureaucratic clique. Such is the essence of government policy. The ban on publication of speeches at the first sitting of the Duma and the reduction of the Duma to an inarticulate department of state indicates that the Russian government is ready for a new betrayal and is preparing to carry out a new *coup d'état*: to abolish the 3 June Duma because the Duma will not consent to keep quiet about the crimes of the government.
> Russia is undergoing an unprecedentedly grave and threatening time. The mass of the people and the working class above all, must direct all their resources of mind and will to intervene skilfully in the movement now embracing all layers of the population and exert decisive influence upon events.
> In consideration of the situation that has come about, we declare that to save the country from a government which is driving it towards its doom, the following steps are necessary: (1) immediate and decisive transformation of the existing régime and the organization of a Government of National Salvation, founded upon the people, the Duma and all the existing public, labour and democratic organizations; (2) immediate declaration of a universal and complete amnesty and as a priority, the release and restoration of civil rights to the exiled social-democratic deputies of the Second and Fourth Duma.
> In adopting this resolution, we consider it necessary to send it at once to the State Duma, demanding that it conduct the most resolute struggle against the government's power regardless of the threats.

However, this resolution did not have any success. Our Petersburg Committee of the RSDLP was obliged to develop counter-agitation and issued a special leaflet exposing the Duma's lickspittle policy, the falsity of its slogans and also the treachery of the war industries socialists. Here is the leaflet:

> Workers of the World, Unite!
> Comrades, throughout the war, the State Duma, whenever opening its sittings, vowed with an outpouring of the most loyal sentiments to be faithful to the tsarist government and exchanged kisses with its ministers. Yet now the militant deputies, while remaining as before hangers-on of

the tsar, have raised a stir and a row with the government. What about? They declare that a change of ministers is required in order to continue the bloodbath through to the end.

When the masses of the people, exhausted by the immeasurable burden of a war sanctified by the capitalists, begin to lose patience and are ready to march against the oppressors, liberal leading lights then attempt to exploit this movement by the people for their own thieving appetites. They need a ministry of public confidence. But what can that bring the tormented people? Instead of Stürmers, Milyukovs, who talk about the salvation of the country but are ready to lead it to new deaths and demanding ever fresh sacrifices.

No! We must always bear in mind that those who are calling us to wage war to the end are least of all considering us and are least of all concerned about the fate of the nation. The swapping of some murderers for others will not make us halt the struggle against a revamped government. That bunch of chauvinist workers which until now has found only words of condemnation for our revolutionary actions has set special store by the lustings of the liberals for power. It has addressed an appeal to you to fight for a "government of national salvation".

These "labour politicians", who have abandoned us at the toughest point of the war's woes so as to assist the government and the bourgeoisie to carry on the war, condemn our revolutionary urge not to lay down arms against the war and the oppressors and keep silent about the kidnapping of our deputies, are now, though rejected by us, calling on us to march behind their slogans and to surrender the country's salvation to those who wish to turn the long months of bloodshed into years and are ruthlessly strangling the workers' movement.

Comrades! Haven't ten years of bloody experience of the workers' movement quite clearly demonstrated who will really fight against the predatory monarchy? By rallying our forces, extending our agitation into the ranks of the poor peasantry and into the army, we shall forge a veritable hammer of revolution: at its blows the government which so torments the people shall perish.

We know of only this primary task. Through the toppling of the tsarist government to the formation of a Provisional Revolutionary Government of workers and poor peasants! We shall demand of such a government the immediate termination of the war, the immediate convoking of a Constituent Assembly and the realization of political liberties so as to provide the conditions for conducting a struggle for the realization of genuine democracy, the Democratic Republic, the confiscation of landed estates, and, in order to put into the hands of the working class its most powerful weapon, shorter working hours, establishment of the eight-hour day! But today we must be on our guard!

Governments and ruling classes, choking in the streams of blood flowing through their own making, will strain every effort for the outcome of the war to bring them continued enslavement of the peoples and the reinforcement of their power; the workers of all the world and first and foremost the workers of the belligerent countries must direct their blows against their own governments. Only by disarming them and assisting the people to put an end to this war through carrying out the political overturns, will we lead the country away from its doom in the truest possible way.

But remember, comrades, as long as the life of the peoples is being sapped by the capitalists, as long as they are masters of the world, they will not stop in their chase for profits to hesitate to throw the peoples over and over again into the conflagrations of wars. Only the destruction of the capitalist system and its replacement by a socialist one will put an end to wars and human sufferings. That is why we Russian workers will, through development of the revolutionary potential of the international proletariat and the formation of the Third International, devote every effort to the realization of socialism. We will support our comrades in Britain, Germany and France in their readiness to wage a struggle for the overthrow of capitalist governments once we have removed the fetters of our tsarist monarchy.

Forward without respite! Down with the war! Down with the tsarist government! Long live the Provisional Revolutionary Government! Down with the tsarist monarchy! Long live the Democratic Republic! Long live the revolution! Long live socialism!
Petersburg Committee of the Russian Social-Democratic Labour Party.
November 1916.

In its call for the unity of workers, soldiers and the poor peasantry, the leaflet counterposes the slogans of revolutionary social democracy to the false liberal positions of the defensists. The Petersburg proletariat did not allow itself either to be intoxicated by the poison of nationalist venom or to be carried away by the false slogans of the "government of national salvation", and would not follow the progressive bloc in the State Duma to which the defensist elements of bourgeois democracy were summoning them.

The Labour Groups of the Central and Area War Industries Committees had finally and irrevocably turned into adjuncts of the pseudo-liberal bourgeoisie. The tsarist government's attitude to the activity in the State Duma and also the attitude of the various classes to this activity prompted the "war industries socialists" at that time to address a special appeal to the Duma which is highly instructive:

> Blank spaces have been appearing in the newspapers in place of Duma reports for a week now. Government repression against deputies' freedom of speech is turning the State Duma into a mere office divorced from the people and reducing the effect of its work to a minimum. We cannot allow ourselves to be flattered by the fact that one section may still, despite the barbs of censorship, learn of the content of the deputies' speeches. That is only an insignificant part of the population. For the enormous majority remain in complete ignorance of what the State Duma is doing. The country can freely acquaint itself with the activity of the Duma, exert influence upon it and mobilize its forces around it under one

condition only: that of free and open circulation of the deputies' speeches among the population at large.

The originally concentrated attention paid by the mass of the public to the Duma when they found blank spaces instead of speeches in the press will gradually subside and be replaced by apathy. An atmosphere could develop which would be extremely dangerous for the interests of the country and all its progressive forces and extremely favourable to reaction and its schemes.

In view of the aforesaid, the workers' representatives in the Central and Petrograd Area War Industries Committees consider continued work by the Duma *under such conditions to be impermissible*. To continue Duma activity in such conditions is not only incompatible with the dignity of a representative institution but also highly damaging and dangerous, creating an undesirable precedent by placing a tool in the hands of reaction whereby it can at any moment turn the Duma into a harmless talking shop.

In maintaining that the situation created, which has effectively destroyed the Duma as such, cannot be tolerated any longer, the workers' representatives on the Central and Petrograd Area War Industries Committees demand in accordance with the sentiment of broad layers of the working class, that the Duma majority adopt every possible means, not discounting the most extreme, to acquaint the population and the army with the work of the State Duma by the free and wide circulation of Duma reports. While not expecting any results to come from its formal question tabled on this matter, the State Duma is however in duty bound on the one hand to revoke immediately the regulation on war censorship issued under article 87 and on the other to undertake the task of the widest possible distribution of Duma speeches by relying upon the backing of the public organizations.

This is supreme obligation of the Duma. Without this stipulation and without the immediate restoration of public knowledge of its work, the Duma will inevitably find itself once and for ever cut off from the country and deprived of any basis on which to further its activity.

The social-patriots drew the "lesson" from the attempts by the liberal bourgeoisie to threaten the government (while at the same time seeking a new deal with it behind the backs of the people and at their expense): that the conditions in which the government had imposed on the sycophantic and posturing bourgeoisie was "effectively destroying the Duma". As a solution they demanded that the Duma majority adopt "extreme measures" . . . to circulate the speeches of Milyukov, Rodzyanko, Maklakov, Shulygin and other such heroes.

Such was the policy of the leaders of the all-Russian centre of the "War Industries Socialists". The attitude of the Petersburg proletariat to these circles of social-patriots was distinctly negative. The Mensheviks themselves were forced to dissociate themselves from their own children who had ensconced themselves in the War

Industries Committees. It should however be borne in mind that only a year after the beginning of the election campaign for the War Industries Committees, when the split and nationalist poison had been introduced into working-class ranks, the Initiative Group of Mensheviks renounced the defence of its own representatives and issued the following appeal:

> Russian Social-Democratic Labour Party
> Workers of the World, Unite!
> Comrades, the world has never before seen such a horror, such sufferings and destruction: the whole air is saturated with the charred and rotting bodies of humanity and blood flows without end. And there seems to be no sign of a dawn through this thick bloody mist. There is only the further involvement of hitherto neutral countries in the bloody carnage. Rumania has now been dragged in by its international adventurism. Instead of blood circulating through the veins of mankind, it is watering the fields and forests and turning the seas and rivers crimson. To untie the knot of this world-wide tragedy at this crucial historical moment, it is essential to gather together all the living resources of international socialism beneath the banner of social democracy; the organization of our forces for the struggle against the imperialists, the predators of human life, and the struggle for the speediest end to this slaughter is a vital one.
>
> But not all is gloom. There are bright features also in the life of the people of the world. We can already see a tiny strip of light gleaming on the horizon of international social democracy. We can see for example that in Germany, Britain and France, a minority which takes the standpoint of the International, is becoming stronger and more powerful. That strip of light is widening as this minority grows. And the day is not far off when this light will overwhelm the gloom of congealed blood and illumine the minds and thoughts of the social-nationalists. But this light that will bear with it joyful tidings for the world has not as yet perturbed our defensist committee-men. Under the banner of an independent national socialism they are continuing as before to do deeds that are destroying international solidarity.
>
> Comrades! You will remember that when we Petrograd workers sent them into the War Industries Committees, we gave them a mandate in which they were empowered to demand the calling of an all-Russian workers' congress at which our attitude to the current situation and to the War Industries Committees would be set out. We considered their term of office to be temporary and in no way authorized them to speak in the name of the entire Russian proletariat. We granted them only a provisional mandate and stated quite categorically that we were the most fervent opponents of the war and stand for its immediate termination.
>
> But they forgot that! They forgot that the Petrograd proletariat had in no way authorized them to speak on their behalf over the heads of the electors the language of national socialism and the language of defensism. They "overlooked" the fact that one particular political group, although covering itself with the banner of the then united Menshevism, together

with its electors did not for one moment adopt the standpoint of defence but repeatedly demanded that the mandate be fulfilled.

Using the cover of the impossibility of calling an all-city meeting of electors and conferring incidentally and only now and again with individual representatives of the college, they kept repeating and go on blandly repeating: "We are carrying out the wishes of the proletariat which sent us here." They are thus blasphemously covering their anti-labour policy with the name of the broad masses. Instead of a continual emphasis on the negative attitude to the war adopted by the broad masses and their advanced elements, they "proudly" uphold the banner of imperialism, the banner of defence, the will and desires of the proletariat notwithstanding. They are thereby introducing disruption into the workers' ranks. While the banner of the International, the banner of international class solidarity, has been surrendered by them to Guchkov for the archives as an out-of-date and worthless rag.

More than that, comrades! They are flouting the decisions of Zimmerwald and Kienthal and will not recognize our own comrades who are striving to resurrect the international class association. They are dreaming aloud of recalling Martov and Axelrod. In renouncing these decisions, they are renouncing the necessity for a struggle to achieve a peace. Organized Mensheviks who take the stand of the International have therefore discussed the question of our present attitude to the group in the Central War Industries Committee in all the districts and at an all-city meeting and resolved by an overwhelming majority of votes to recall the Labour Group of the Central War Industries Committee. In bringing all the aforesaid to the notice of the broad masses, we declare that the Labour Group of the Central War Industries Committee has not to this day heeded the voice of organized workers and that that voice has remained but a hollow sound for the committee-men.

We therefore state: 1) we renounce any responsibility for the activity of the Labour Group of the Central War Industries Committee; 2) We shall not enter into any agreements with them on matters of the workers' movement; 3) We declare the group to be the instigators of a new split.

The Petersburg Initiative Group.

Workers at many plants and factories carried resolutions for the recall of their representatives from the War Industries Committees. Protests were passed against their speculative play on the name of the working class and the workers' mandate. The Petersburg proletariat had never, in its revolutionary majority, supported the "Labour Group". The workers' negative attitude to the "war industries socialists" found echo in even the committee's own publications. Thus, in *Byulleten Rabochei Gruppy* no. 4, we find the following:

> The Labour Group must stress that the demands for the Group to walk out of the Central War Industries Committee emanate exclusively from comrades who reject a defence standpoint. We must therefore reject the demand for a walk-out as one of the facts of the unceasing struggle of the

THE BEGINNING OF THE END

two ideological currents in Russia's working class. The Labour Group has serious grounds for refusing to walk out if only from considerations of principle. A legitimate outcome to the conflict between the two viewpoints cannot in any event be achieved by a formal removal of one of the parties from the base whose views it is implementing in practice. One or other viewpoint will not triumph as a result of whether the Group leaves the Central War Industries Committee or stays in it. The only difference will lie in the fact that the organizational soil provided by staying in the Central War Industries Committee will disappear from beneath the feet of a particular section of the working class.

Leaving to one side the argument over principles, it is also necessary to take account of the value of the practical and organizational work, a part of which is reported on in the current *Byulleten*. Only if the ideological dispute ends with the victory of the opponents of the Labour Group's position, will we be able to say that the price of even this great practical work cannot compensate for the violation of principles. But the argument has not yet reached this stage and therefore to wind up practical work in the name of purity of principles whose correctness has yet to be demonstrated would be an act unheard of in the history of the workers' movement.

The Labour Group must emphasize that the demands for its departure originate from limited circles in the working class and it cannot give them more consideration than demands from a number of other workers' organizations which are giving ever closer suport to the Labour Group, taking part in its work and supporting it organizationally and ideologically. Even discounting the important factor that the demand for a walk-out has been presented by groups which differ from the Labour Group over its basic position on the question of war and peace, agreeing to leave our posts would still mean a sharp break from the numerous comrades scattered throughout Russia who regard the Labour Group as a vital and extremely valuable instrument in the hands of Russia's working class. To agree to the proposal of the recallists would mean heading for an open break with several dozen workers' organizations, prominent leaders of the working class and all the international tradition of modern democracy. We cannot make a break from broad circles of our ideological sympathizers just to meet the demands of a small number of ideological opponents.

Such in broad terms is the purely practical standpoint of the Group on the question of its recall. In conclusion it should merely be noted that the struggle by certain elements against the Labour Group has in recent days assumed an extremely acrimonious nature that entirely excludes the possibility of a comradely pact. Leaflets have been published in which the Labour Group is portrayed as a bloodsucker sucking the blood of the working class and so on. A number of wholly fictitious doings have been attributed to the Group and to advance the aims of a struggle against the Group, distorted accounts by newspaper reporters, refuted at the time, have been put into service. The Group has here to note that it is very difficult to find time to deal with all these distortions and that it has not always been possible to refute them for reasons of censorship as these newspaper inventions are utterly and completely composed in highly patriotic terms so that any refutation will naturally be regarded as "treacherous conduct".

The role of "leader of the Petersburg proletariat" was not being fulfilled by the social-patriots. All the liberal bourgeoisie's hopes for workers' support for the progressive bloc's "parliamentary" struggle against the government were dashed against the revolutionary class resolve of the Petersburg proletariat.

As we have said above, the government responded to the progressive bloc's behaviour in the Duma with a tightening of military censorship of Duma speeches. On 10 November the chairman of the Council of Ministers, Stürmer, was replaced by Trepov. The Duma sitting was put off till 19 November. A "declaration" was awaited from the new chairman of the Council of Ministers. The interval was to be explained by the need for time to prepare Trepov for the role.

In spite of rumours that spread around Petersburg about a further postponement of the convening of the Duma, the sitting was resumed on the date set by the government. Trepov, the new chairman of the Council of Ministers, made a statement on the opening day. The appearance of the representative of the "renewed government" was greeted by a hostile demonstration by the social democrats and Trudoviks. When Trepov attempted to read out his declaration, his voice was drowned by noise and shouts of "down!" Such a welcome had not formed part of the progressive bloc programme, and the Duma left found itself on its own. The majority of the Duma bloc had by now wearied of the break with the government and saw their "triumph" in the replacement of Stürmer by Trepov, and did not wish to create any animosity. The progressive bloc now found a convenient opportunity to dissociate themselves from the left and the Duma president, Rodzyanko, proposed to punish the demonstrators by suspension from eight sittings. The motion was adopted. Four deputies, Chkheidze, Kerensky, Skobelev and Khaustov, were suspended. The suspended members were, in accordance with standing orders, allowed to speak in their own defence.

The suspension of the left section of the State Duma members gave rise to a series of protests. No campaign was however undertaken among workers in the factories on this occasion. This indicated to the deputies and defensist organizations closely linked with them that they had no base of support in the mass of the workers, even less in the thick of the Petersburg proletariat – in fact they had never sought such a thing, always preferring the parliamentary game. Concentrating energies and attentions around the Duma was moreover not one of our tasks. The suspension was a very convenient gauge of the falsity of the tacit agreement fixed up between the Mensheviks and Narodniks on the one hand and the progressive bloc on the other. For a while the incident did cool the defensist ardour of Duma "support", and the lesson taught them by the bourgeoisie was most instructive.

From the Activity of the Russian Social-Democratic Party (Bolsheviks)

In spite of telling blows dealt to our underground organization by individual and mass arrests, exile to Siberia and postings to front-line positions, the work of our organizations did not ebb and by the end of 1916 their overall expansion could be observed. Once freed from war hysteria and also from the apathy and pessimism brought on by the war, many new forces were driven towards us and several who had left party work during the war returned to the bosom of the party.

The strongest organization we had was the Petersburg one. Throughout the war the Moscow organization suffered from the lack of a general leading organizational centre. The cause of this was the espionage of the Moscow branch of the security police (Okhrana) and especially by its so-called "inner light". Moscow comrades understood this perfectly and had their suspicions about one or two people, but were nevertheless unable to get the organization established. The Central Committee Bureau then directing all-Russian work had to resort to forming such an organizing centre from the top downwards by means of appointments made in consultation with Moscow party workers, and created a Regional Bureau of the Central Committee of the RSDLP(B).

The contacts of the Central Committee Bureau with its seat in Petersburg and its close link with the Petersburg Committee were expanding greatly. Contacts were established on the arrival of workers from the industrial centres and by trips made by our representatives to the localities. Lack of financial resources did not permit us to support the organizations and we often had to rely solely upon the occasional trip or chance visit. We would receive not only simple reports on the work of the organizations but also material evidence in the shape of leaflets produced by the most diverse means.

In November the Central Committee Bureau received the reports from the areas. For conspiratorial reasons, the cities sending in information were protected beneath more general titles.

A provincial capital in the central industrial district (Tver). A city committee was elected as early as the autumn meeting of local party workers in 1915, but it was only able to resume active work in March 1916 when a group of new party workers arrived to assist the ailing committee. Discussion-group activity was promptly set in motion but there was no co-ordination in the work for the lack of a centre. The committee did not disband but did nothing. The strikes which broke out in the second half of April ended in a victory for the workers at two undertakings. The strike movement ended at the end of May with the rout of the organization. Over that period the organization had managed to issue three leaflets on the war, the War Industries Committees and May Day. Work was resumed at the beginning of June. A new centre was formed; a plan of work was drawn up (the main point lay in stepping up agitation). Work was made harder by the fact that no people remained at the centre who were rich in knowledge and experience. Discussion-group work had not ceased even by September. . . .

A city on the Volga (Nizhni-Novgorod). In September 1916 we eventually managed to organize a city committee. There are two district committees: one for the outskirts and one in the main factory district (Sormovo). There are now four circles active in the outskirts. In the factory district there are fourteen; the organization thus amounts to 150 to 200 members (those paying dues on the basis of at least one per cent of their earnings are considered to be members). The resources of the organization are apportioned for the requirements of the districts, literature and the all-city committee, with ten per cent being allocated to the Central Committee. The Central Committee Bureau has been sent an advance of 25 rubles to cover illegal literature. There is a dreadful shortage of literature. As yet we have not had many issues of the central organ. The pamphlets "On the War" and "On the High Cost of Living" come only in single copies and those are hard to get hold of. We haven't even seen *Kommunist*. All the work in the organization, including purely propaganda work (there exists a college of propagandists of six members), is at present being undertaken exclusively by workers. The main shortcoming of the organization is the almost total lack of theoretically knowledgeable and experienced people. The local intellectual forces do not take close part in the work for a variety of reasons. Given the presence of a few experienced propagandists and also literature, work could be expanded more widely. The appeal of the organization has been very great. At the present time a reorganization in the factory district is being carried out by the committee. It is proposed to split into two. Deep discontent with the current state of affairs with the high cost of living is mounting in the factory district: a new struggle for wage rises lies ahead. (The Central Committee Bureau has already been notified about the summer strike). Foreseeing the possibility of a strike, the liquidators and defensists have taken steps to avert it. They have started implementing their Guchkovian ideas about conciliation courts and have proposed that workers form joint commissions with employers' representatives to deal with questions of food supply and wages. These commissions have now been set up. Our organization proved unable to open workers' eyes to the true nature of these employers' commissions in good enough time and workers took the bait. Now they are awaiting the outcome of these commissions. There have been no results so far. But to a question of a wage rise the manager answered with a categorical refusal. The matter will not therefore be settled without a strike. The city committee put out in the middle of November a hectographed proclamation on the food crisis in which the link between the high cost of living and the food crisis and the war is brought out and a call for a struggle against the war and the Russian government made. A copy has been sent to the Central Committee Bureau. Although the liquidators along with the employers have succeeded in duping workers over the business of the commissions, their influence is pretty slight. Thus, the proposal by the Central Labour Group of the War Industries Committees that they contribute information on the workers' situation and so on encountered a sharp rebuttal from the latter. The workers stated that they did not regard the group as representative of workers and therefore refused to have any dealings with it. Around the plants, signatures are currently being collected beneath the statement in support of its aim. A considerable number have been already gathered. The sheets are still going round the plants. Many are now signing them who had earlier declared themselves in favour of participation in the War Industries Committees.

Kazan, 5 November 1916. There has been a student demonstration. To start with, a meeting was held in the university lobby where speakers got up to criticize the government and make speeches on the war. A resolution against the war was carried demanding peace and advancing the slogan of revolution. After the meeting a crowd of some 800 to 1,000 people went on to the streets and, singing revolutionary songs, headed for the prison where more speeches were made; afterwards, on the way to Theatre Square the crowd gradually broke up. The police did not intervene. The demonstration lasted about an hour and a half.

Kharkov. The organization numbers some 120 members paying dues regularly. Among young Latvian Bolsheviks there is a tendency to work together with the Russians and not in isolation in the way evident among members of Latvian social democracy, the majority of whom work separately from the Russians. This is to be welcomed. In September Kharkov workers suffered some casualties from the collapse of the strike at the Union General Electric Company works.

After staying out two weeks, the workers went back following numerous arrests. Since September the idea of publishing an illegal newspaper has been mooted. The Kharkov organization has now succeeded in producing the first issue of a hectographed paper: *Golos Sotsial-Demokrata*. The newspaper will come out weekly. They have in mind to publish a journal alongside this as soon as the equipment can best be set up. But for the time being they are only able to produce a newspaper in hectographed form. In reviewing these last two months it should be said that the local Mensheviks always oppose deciding this or that question at broad meetings preferring to settle them at group meetings as they are afraid of defeat and are keenly aware of their scant influence among the proletariat. Kharkov workers have refused to participate in the War Industries Committee in the most decisive fashion. In the course of such work, our party has been deprived of two active comrades who spoke publicly at a meeting and were arrested on exit. In the first days of November the Central War Industries Committee's Labour Group or, as they are called here, the "Gvozdevites", sent the following letter to the management committee of the workers' club with a request for a reply: "How many arrests have taken place during 1916? Over what?" and so on. They asked for all the material to be sent to them. The management committee considered this matter at a meeting; a preliminary question was put to it: do we recognize the Gvozdevites as representatives of the workers and is it desirable for workers to have any dealings with them? . . . About forty people were present at the meeting of the management committee. With long debates the meeting dragged on past midnight and it was resolved that as Petrograd workers did not recognize them but regarded them as political adventurers, Kharkov workers would for the same reason not wish to have any common business with them and so it was resolved not to answer their letter or even to send them the resolution lest they then claim that Kharkovans had momentarily recognized them as representatives.

The strike movement in the industrial centres and in Petersburg developed in the autumn of 1916 with hitherto unseen strength. The burdens imposed by the war could be keenly felt. The condition of the working class deteriorated from day to day. The movement which had its origin in the economic demands of one or another group of workers would turn into a political struggle. The workers' mood was so buoyant and revolutionary that strikes arose at the mere appearance of a leaflet. Solidarity strikes were particularly widespread during that autumn. News of a struggle by comrades had only to reach workers at another factory for the latter to rush off to make contact and give firm backing at the necessary moment.

THE BEGINNING OF THE END 185

In December I wrote a letter to our Central Committee which was based in Switzerland and to V.I. Lenin and G.E. Zinoviev personally. In this I reported briefly on our work and the state of affairs in the country. I am including it in full omitting only the coded section which concealed the illegal addresses of the time.

Petersburg, 2 December 1916.
Dear friends,
At last I have a chance to share some news and documents with you. I feel you will be moaning about the long-standing lack of news but I think you will have guessed the reasons, which are not of my willing, namely, lack of personnel. My journey was full of unexpected adventures and lasted nearly three weeks because of that. I only got here at the end of October (old style). I shall report all the details when I have more time to spare. I found all my friends and acquaintances in fine fettle. However our losses started as early as 5 November. That day and night there were raids on all the hospital funds and a few hospital fund staff were arrested. On the night of 16 November mass searches were made on workers and intellectuals of all tendencies but the majority of these individuals were "old" ones, already on the Okhrana's books. One member of the workers' group of the Insurance Council, G.I. Osipov, and one or two people attached to the marxist press, were arrested. Many of my personal friends disappeared in those arrests.

A total absence of patriotic euphoria is generally discernible in the mood of the working masses and democrats. The high cost of living, the vicious exploitation and the barbaric policy of the government have all proved convincingly to the masses the true nature of the war. The cry of "war till victory" remains the slogan only of the war industries. Working men and women, soldiers and ordinary "residents" openly express their dissatisfaction with the continuance of the war. "Will all this soon end?" can be heard absolutely everywhere. The workers' movement is marked by an upsurge of strikes throughout the country. There have been strikes in Moscow, Petersburg, the Donets Basin (Kharkov and Nikolaev), Ekaterinburg and Baku. You will receive the details. This summer in Petersburg passed off amid a considerable lull. The high cost of living has assumed catastrophic proportions. The lack of foodstuffs has angered broad circles. People have been entirely preoccupied with how to get hold of this or that item. They have gone in for co-operatives, bulk purchasing and so on. Prices have gone up five or ten times compared with last year's. Clothing and footwear are becoming almost unobtainable. What used to cost (suits and so on) thirty to forty rubles before the war now costs 150 to 200 and so on. By autumn the state of affairs was getting even worse and there were days in September and October when there was no bread in working-class districts. And you no longer need talk about meat. The same thing is evident in Moscow. At the beginning of October the Petersburg Committee launched a mass campaign for a struggle against the "food supply" breakdown by organizing protest meetings and so on. The meetings took place around the plants amid great spirit behind the slogans of "down with the war" and "down with the government". Leaflets have been issued. The appearance of leaflets in a plant was taken by the mass of workers as an invitation to strike and this rapidly involved all the Vyborg district. There have been demonstrations. A strike which had started on 17 October against the wishes of the organization lasted two or three days. During it there were many clashes with the police. One of these should be taken note of as an indication of the mood of the mass of the soldiers. The barracks of the 181st infantry reserve are situated beside the New Lessner works. When the strike began, police charged in to break up the workers who were coming out singing. In the crowd were soldiers whom the police threatened with all sorts of reprisals. Many started arguing; the police attempted to make arrests but the crowd beat them back. There was at that time drilling in progress in the yard of the 181st infantry reserve barracks and the soldiers there, attracted by the noise, went up to the barrack fence where they were invited by workers to help them against the police. The reservists and young soldiers quickly responded to the workers' appeal, knocked the fence down and went into the street to join the mass of people and then started to throw stones at the police (the soldiers had no weapons with them). The latter fired back as they retreated. Shortly afterwards cossacks arrived, ringing the plant and placing sentries all round the barracks. The regiment had been placed under arrest.

Then rumours spread round the city that many soldiers had been arrested and would be going before a drumhead court-martial. It was difficult to verify these rumours but a court-martial of Baltic sailors accused of membership of the RSDLP(B) military organization had been fixed for the 26 October. In the dock of the district court-martial were seventeen petty officers and three civilians. The Petersburg Committee decided to give support to the sailors and declared a general protest strike for that day. Taking part in the strike were 116,000 workers, all educational establishments and many small workshops and printshops, the number of whose employees could not be estimated. The strike had a big impact on the trial and the sentences were relatively "mild". Four men were convicted: T.I. Ulyantsev, an engineer on the cruiser *Rossiya*, to eight years' hard labour; I.D. Sladkov, a petty officer at the Naval Artillery School, to seven years; I.V. Brendin, a petty officer on the cruiser *Rossiya*, who retracted all of his testimony given at the preliminary investigation, to seven years' hard labour; and I.N. Egorov, a deportee, to four years' hard labour. All the defendants acted most properly in court.

The protest strike lasted between one and three days and led to repression. The Association of Factory and Plant Owners decided to punish workers with a lock-out; many plants closed down: Ericssons, Lessners, Renault and others, for example. The Petersburg Committee decided to start a struggle against the lock-out by agitating for a general strike. A leaflet was put out but the employers quickly stepped in and the military authorities ordered the plants to reopen their shops. This was effected by 1 November.

The mood of working-class circles started to liven up after that strike. The strike had the beneficial effect on the "food shortage": bread, meat and other items began to appear in abundance.

Following these and more general events, attention became riveted on the Duma "circus". The progressive bloc came out against Stürmer. Publication of the speeches of accusation made at three sittings (1, 2 and 3 November), and especially the first, was prohibited, but they were widely distributed around Petersburg in manuscript. Many believed in the sincerity of the State Duma majority's struggle against the government, at whose head marched the Cadets of 1 November.

But reality was soon to expose the Cadets' inconsistency, for their words of opposition little matched their fawning deeds and the backstage games they are up to.

The Cadet accompanists of our time, the Gvozdevites, have already begun their agitation for support for the State Duma and its demands. A special resolution has been drafted which demands a "government of national salvation". It was carried at a small number of plants and delivered by a "deputation" to Rodzyanko.

A couple of days later the majority of the bloc ejected their previous and current friends, the factions of Chkheidze and the Trudoviks, from the Duma. The poor Guchkovite boys were most demoralized at such a turn by the "saviours of the nation" and started to agitate against the bloc while still "supporting it".

The Petersburg Committee is circulating its own resolution on its attitude to the Duma around the plants. The cabinet reshuffles and Stürmer's replacement by Trepov are considered by the Cadets to be a "great" victory. This already satisfies a considerable portion of the bloc and it is striving towards "joint" work with the government. The Cadet party at its own meeting decided to maintain a hypocritical tactic: not to compromise in words and say that "nothing has changed" but for the sake of "preserving the unity" of the bloc to work in practice with the government. In relation to them, our organizations are maintaining the old tactic of exposing the falsehood of Cadet liberalism.

Local party workers have promised to supply more detailed accounts of the state of the work and the life of the organizations and the workers' movement. Here work has been set up fairly well but we do experience a shortage of personnel. Our mutual relations are of the very best and most comradely. I go to meetings of the Executive Commission every week and sometimes meet them more often. I have made reports and there have been discussions. There are comrades who are wavering on the question of the "right of nations" to self-determination and the United States of Europe. Justified criticisms about the lack of leading articles are being sent to the central organ. These demand that the Central Committee representatives in the Zimmerwald groupings be more specific. We have had all Central Committee publications here since the September ones. . .
The War and the Cost of Living has been published in five thousand copies. It has become most difficult for me as I have been obliged to turn my hand to everything: writing articles, organizing, liaising with people,

preparing reports and attending committee meetings. I live between the earth and the sky. I live on the move. Literature and people are demanded from all sides and the Central Committee is moaned at. The idea of the need for an all-Russian conference crops up more and more often. Bear this in mind and prepare reports and resolutions on the current situation.

8 December: Forgive the patchwork style of my letter, dear friends. I have received various bits of information from various parts of the provinces, copies of which I am enclosing for you. Delegates from the provinces arrive very frequently at the Petersburg Committee requesting literature and information. There is an uproar over the shortage of people, literature and directives. Everyone is demanding that the Central Committee Bureau arrange a conference. The Executive Commission has already elected people for a joint discussion with the Central Committee Bureau on the agenda and reports. The Central Committee Bureau's resolution concerning the differences among the collaborators on the central organ has been adopted by the Petersburg Committee's Executive Commission.

You can judge the mood of the provinces and all Russia by the following incident conveyed to us by comrades coming from Kremenchug. A large crowd of "queuers" had collected around a shop for sugar – the majority were women. A row broke out between the women and the guardians of order, the town constables. The row led to the constables being beaten up and the shops being looted. Soldiers were called out to "restore order" but they refused to fire. Cossacks were called in but they too kept out of the way. Then the authorities put their last forces into action, the mounted police guard. The latter complied and opened fire on the crowd. This disturbed the cossacks and soldiers and they rushed upon the mounted police and broke them up. After that the crowd joined up with the cossacks and soldiers and started to attack the police stations and the police chief's own quarters and he was injured, though managing to hide in time. They wrecked the army offices and killed the local army chief. Many shops were wrecked. This spontaneous mutiny lasted two days, but then fresh forces arrived and the crack-down began with the customary ferocity. Many were killed and wounded.

It is reported from the Donets Basin that our organizations there are growing stronger. A regional conference was recently held by the regional committee. There are many working prisoners-of-war (Austrians) in the area. Relations between them and the workers are very good. The prisoners-of-war are organizing themselves and are seeking to join our organizations. In various places managements have attempted to squeeze out free labour by bringing in prisoners-of-war (in the pits) but have run up against protests from the prisoners-of-war themselves who declared that they would not go down the mines even on pain of death if they were displacing dismissed workers.

The enfranchised bourgeoisie is planning congresses and has already sent out invitations to various workers' organizations like the hospital funds, co-operatives and the War Industries Committees (the

Gvozdevites). The government tends to oppose the congresses. But it is not alone in opposing them, for the progressive bloc is now also against them. We managed to discover that on 16 November a conference of the bureau of the bloc was held with delegations from the public organizations, namely, the Union of Towns, represented by Chelnokov and Shchepkin; the Union of Zemstvos (Prince Lvov) and the War Industries Committees (Konovalov) under the chairmanship of Meller-Zakomelsky, a member of the Council of State. Milyukov was the reporter for the Progressive Bloc. He sang the praises of the bloc and the public organizations for their display of "unity" as a result of which such a brilliant victory as the removal of Stürmer was won. After such a "celebration" for the bloc there ensued the "bread-and-butter" business during which the bloc's task was to follow a zigzag path. "Society must be prudent in its demands to the Duma lest it bring about a breaking of the unity of the public front". . . . Shingarev dotted the i's, declaring in his comments on Milyukov's speech that the progressive bloc could not make demands and therefore it would be proper to refrain from organizing congresses and conferences, for it was not known what their mood would be. They could present demands to the Duma, but any further aggressive policy towards the Duma would be impossible. Shidlovsky stated openly that an aggressive policy by the Duma could lead to its dissolution and dissolution to "revolution", which of course they feared most of all. That is all the information there is for you at the moment; reports on this affair will be carried in *Proletarskii Golos*, which is soon to come out.

Personally I stand for exploiting the election campaigns for the congresses and for publicly presenting there an independent declaration, but for opposing participation in "organic work". . . . Colleagues in the Central Committee Bureau are in solidarity with this. It has also been carried by the Petersburg Committee. But there have already been one or two instances of boycotting the elections. A leading article should be printed in the central organ against the boycott system. It is necessary to follow the same line that the Petersburg Committee adopted in relation to the War Industries Committees in the autumn of 1915. A boycott is clearly advantageous to the Gvozdevites as it gives them links with the provinces and assists in the deceit about their representative status.

The Russian government's attitude to the Duma and the German peace proposal has perturbed broad circles of the general public and intellectuals. Even the patriotic element is discontented with the Duma's decision and its unwillingness "on principle" to accept a basis for discussion of the peace proposals. Our organizations have used this fact as a graphic illustration of the predatory ideals of the Russian bourgeoisie and government. To the "peace" plans of the ruling classes of the belligerent countries we are counterposing the need to turn the slaughter against the government. A proclamation of the Petersburg Committee to this effect is coming out in a day or two.

The Bureau also proposes to issue a leaflet and it may manage to establish a periodical central organ. Work is in hand in this direction.

It is reported from Kharkov that differences have arisen there over the current situation. Certain comrades there take the position that we are living in the era of the social revolution. I shall shortly be seeing one or two people from there and shall clarify their intentions.

The soldiers' mood is extremely tense. Rumours of mutinies in the army are circulating. It is reported that there are disturbances in Dvinsk, but it is not known over what. It has been announced that the tsar has "relieved" the commander, General Alekseyev, for his "opposition views" and has appointed General Gurko in his place, but Gurko was replaced by someone else on 2 December. By 6 December the Congress of Nobility, the Duma-ites and the Council of State made ready to be received by the tsar. Our tsarist retainers had already got their speeches prepared when they were unexpectedly "beaten": the tsar had departed for the front and refused to meet them. He had clearly demonstrated by his address to Pitirim and by bestowing an order on General "Kuvaka" his displeasure with the bourgeoisie. . . . "Society" is as a whole full of rumours and gossip. It is reported that back in the summer there had been a conference of certain military circles on active service, corps, divisional and certain regimental commanders where the question of overthrowing Nikolai II was discussed. By and large, even avowed monarchists are extremely disturbed by all the doings of the tsarist autocracy.

14 December. There were raids at the end of last week. The printshop of the Petersburg Committee has been seized; 6,000 copies of the pamphlet *Who Needs the War?* and 3,000 copies of the fourth issue of *Proletarskii Golos*. Twenty-four people were arrested at the printshop and in the stores. There have been further arrests among the printers: all in all, major losses whose extent has yet to be clarified.

Thoughts of workers are now revolving round the question of "peace". Slogans are demanded. We are thinking of putting a resolution out. Reports are demanded. The mood is very uplifted, especially so in Moscow. The "congressites" there have gone into struggle against the police authorities. The Duma in its tactics lags behind the mood of the bourgeoisie. There's no time to write any more. I must send this off as I'm heaped up with work. I firmly shake your hands.

Yours, Aleksandr.

The Sailors' Military Organization

Revolutionary work among the sailors of the Baltic Fleet was full of heroism. Party activity among sailors had never entirely ceased since the days of the first (1905) revolution. It had been only temporarily retarded by repression and had not disappeared. During the war revolutionary work received a boost. Thanks to the mobilization many proletarian elements and sailors with a revolutionary past had poured into the fleet. Screening crew members in wartime was far more difficult than in peacetime.

The Petersburg Committee maintained the closest links with the

THE BEGINNING OF THE END

fleet's military organizations. All work on the vessels and among shore-based and fortress companies was carried on by the sailors themselves. It was impossible for an outsider, newcomer or civilian to have a stable existence in the fortified zones of Kronstadt, Viipuri, Tallinn and Turku. The Petersburg Committee had made several attempts to send people to work among the sailors, but was unsuccessful and was therefore compelled to recommend the sailors to build the organizations with their own forces.

The upsurge of the workers' movement in Petersburg which could be noted in the summer and autumn could not help reflecting itself in the mood of the proletarian elements in the fleet, crushed by the harsh wartime discipline. In the autumn of 1915 a fairly strong social-democratic sailors' organization took shape. All the biggest vessels and shore companies in Kronstadt, Helsinki, Petersburg and other zones of the Baltic coast were linked up by the "Chief Committee of the Kronstadt Military Organization".

In spite of the extreme caution and conspiratorial skill shown by party workers in the military organization, their activity soon fell under the surveillance of internal and external Okhrana agents. Shortly after organizing the committees, the party workers themselves, members of our party, conducted a mass campaign of agitation both oral and printed, distributing literature received from the Petersburg Committee. The agitation fell upon highly fertile soil: discontent with the war and the soldiers' conditions deeply stirred the men between decks. Leaflets and pamphlets were read till they were in shreds and were distributed widely.

The buoyant revolutionary mood among the crews soon overflowed into open indignation. On 19 October the crew of the battleship *Hangut* expressed their anger at the régime in force aboard the ship, and also at the bad food. The indignant crew seized some of the officers and contacted other vessels, seeking aid. This unorganized outburst of indignation was quickly isolated and quelled. The naval authorities took brutal reprisals against the vessel's crew. Twenty-six men stood trial and the whole group was transferred to shore work and disbanded. The trial was held on 17 December 1915, passing two death sentences and sentencing another fourteen sailors to hard labour for varying terms. But even such savage repression could not kill the revolutionary spirit in the fleet. "Disorders" of varying proportions occurred aboard many vessels even after the reprisals against the *Hangut* sailors.

In the December of 1915 the precise contacts between the sailors and the Petersburg Committee were identified by the efforts of the Okhrana. Agents of the gendarmerie were among the sailors joining political circles. The links between the Petersburg Committee and the

Kronstadt sailors were "illuminated" by the provocateur V. Shurkanov (the ex-Duma deputy). The Petersburg Committee members who kept the contact, K. Orlov and V. Schmidt, were closely acquainted with V. Shurkanov and frequently arranged venues at his flat. This was the way in which the Okhrana had set itself up throughout almost all the work of the Petersburg Committee's military organization.

A memorandum by Colonel Globachev to the director of the police department was compiled from information obtained in this way:

> Over a recent period the existence has been noted by the special agents of the Department under my charge of a military organization of the Russian Social-Democratic Labour Party among ratings of the Baltic Fleet operating along the following lines:
>
> Functioning on board every vessel are social-democratic cells that elect their own committees, each vessel's committee having its representative on the leading committee. The aforementioned cells have arisen quite independently, owing to the existence of favourable soil in the sense of the high degree of development of the ratings and the presence among them of individuals who prior to entry into military service had already become skilled in underground work.
>
> By arranging gatherings ashore in cafés and restaurants, the vessels' leading committee has directed all its energies chiefly towards explaining current events to the sailors in a desirable light with the purpose of creating a climate of discontent among them. Such an agitational approach in the hands of the experienced leaders of the committee has already had some influence upon the mood of the ratings, and according to the secret agents in question there is at the present time on nearly all ships a mood of excitement and extreme nervousness, despite the fact that no other grounds for this exist – all shipboard life is following its normal course.
>
> The ideological leaders of the underground work on the warships have tried in every way to restrain the sailors from sporadic unrest, in order to bring about a situation where a general action could take account of the possibility of an active movement from the part of the working class which might bring crucial influence to bear upon changing the political system; no actions planned for set dates have as yet been found on the people named and all their work is concentrated in the organizational field. Having thus succeeded in creating a favourable mood, the underground are now experiencing difficulties in restraining isolated actions and in this respect the openly expressed discontent which took place in August or September of this year on the battleship *Hangut* as a result of which one part of the sailors from that vessels were sent to Arkhangelsk and the other part of the sailors court-martialled, made an unfavourable impression upon them.
>
> The cells and committees aboard the vessels arose quite independently without the assistance of the group now functioning in Petrograd which styles itself the "Petersburg Committee" of the Russian Social-Democratic

Labour Party; according to secret reports which have come in, the leading committee of the naval organizations has from its inception sought opportunities to join forces with the already mentioned Petersburg Committee, which in practice it only recently achieved through one of the active leaders of the workers' movement who was a representative of the Vyborg party district on the "Petersburg Committee". Having made contact with the military organization, the aforementioned party worker surrendered his mandate for the Vyborg district and is currently sitting on the Petersburg Committee as representative of the military organization. All matters relating to the latter are passed by this party worker via a sailor of the twelfth company of the Kronstadt Naval Support Company, Pisarev, whose exact identity has not yet been established, and from whom the former receives party rendezvous points. On 29 November this year an unknown sailor was despatched by Pisarev to Petrograd to that same representative on the "Petersburg Committee" with a message for a rendezvous signed by "Otradnev"; Pisarev possibly signs himself thus, but another sailor could possibly be concealed behind that name.

At the moment one of the leading military committee's primary concerns is to make contacts with vessels lying at Helsinki and finding premises in the town of Kronstadt where it is intended to arrange for some woman to meet the sailors in the guise of a laundry-woman. In connection with the above, an assignment was given by the committee for the also as yet unidentified sailor, Brendin, one of the foremost party workers who was going off for six months' sick leave in Helsinki. He was also given rendezvous points for a member of the "Central Committee" of the Russian Social-Democratic Labour Party, one "Albert" who had settled in Helsinki as clerk in a local dock office.

One of the first manifestations of the activity of the leading committee will be a meeting of sailors in Kronstadt fixed for 6 December.

Steps towards continued secret observation of the military organization have been taken by myself.

Copies of this report have been forwarded with nos. 229 and 230 to the Heads of the Kronstadt and Finland Gendarme Administrations.

I have the honour to report the above to Your Excellency.

Colonel Globachev.

Arrests of a considerable proportion of the active members of the groups of sailors leading the military work were carried out on 28 December 1915.

Heading the military organizations as members of its leading centre, called the "Chief Committee of the Kronstadt Organization", were I.F. Orlov (Kirill), Timofei Ulyantsev, Ivan Sladkov, Nikolai Khovrin, Nikifor Brendin, Mikhail Stakun, Nikolai Pisarev and Vladimir Zaitsev. "Krill" Orlov maintained the contact with the Petersburg Committee, with right of membership of it.

The Chief Committee's links with the ship and shore companies were extremely broad. It had its people aboard nearly every warship and on many there were whole groups called "committees". The arrests on 28 December and subsequently over the same case disrupted the organization's work in part only. Even the Chief Committee was not arrested in its entirety, for example Vladimir Zaitsev was spared arrest.

The plan of the military organization was well thought out. By dint of the peculiar conditions of military work, democratic and elective principles of representation were somewhat restricted by comparison with normal social-democratic organizations.

Alongside personal contacts between the committees and their centre there also existed coded correspondence. During the arrests part of these agreed formulas fell into the hands of the gendarmes. As all servicemen's correspondence passed through the hands of the officers, letters were written in a coded form that bore a realistic everyday appearance. The document below, while not exhausting all the complexities of the sailors' conspiratorial methods, does provide a good illustration of its general lines.

> (1) The date indicates from which point to start deciphering.
> (2) If it is mentioned that uncle has been round and that we have been over at his place then you are to understand that everything is going brilliantly.
> (3) If they write that mum is alive and well, you are to understand that things are going brilliantly everywhere.
> (4) If something remarkable happens on one of the ships you must write about the successful events in this way: A brother or sister (mention the ship's code name) states (underline what he or she has said) that he or she has been at home and that there they cannot endure the shortages and are praying to God for the enemy to be defeated swiftly. That will mean that things are going very well on that ship – if things are going badly, put it round the other way.
> (5) If you or we need help then you should write this: dad (put the ship's code name) wants to buy a foal from the stud (don't put the price).
> (6) If you have things on all ships in order write that there has been a bumper harvest at home and if things have not been too successful write that the spring crop has been poor.
> (7) If any ship needs help or literature to be sent, write the ship's code name and then mention afterwards that you have received a letter from your little brother and he writes that everything at home is sorting itself out and he doesn't feel any hardship at all.
> (8) But if it is very hard to get help, write that dad has bought a foal from the stud.
> (9) If things at your end have been tied up all right or those between the army and ourselves, write that you have been out for a walk and had a very nice time but if things haven't been tied up all right, a very miserable time.

THE BEGINNING OF THE END

(10) If you have hopes of making new contacts, write that you have hopes of having an even nicer walk.

It was extremely risky to name ships, crews and other units in the letters and therefore the comrades were compelled to resort to code names for all ships and shore establishments. The Chief Committee devised a special code for these names and put it in the charge only of organizers of the committees. The names were sometimes changed.

The whole plan of organization of work in the navy was literally the doing of the navy proletarians themselves. All the military organization lay with the sailors themselves and therein lay the organization's insuperable strength. The first point, which defines the tasks of the military organization, speaks of its complete subordination to the Petersburg Committee. This point was extremely important as anarchistic tendencies and impulses to hold independent demonstrations and other actions had emerged among sailors, including the proletarian ones; this arose from their isolation from the workers' movement as a whole. The organization had to counter such phenomena and especially the idea that the navy could "by itself", independently of the general struggle, lead a victorious revolution.

In December 1915 there was among the organized sailors of the Baltic Fleet a desire to express their attitude towards the celebration of 9 January in some way or other. Certain hotheads proposed to hold a "demonstration". However, the Petersburg Committee took account of the overall situation and also the lesson of the *Hangut* and declared itself firmly opposed to political action by sailors and recommended its members not to expose themselves in any way at that stage but just carry on with work of a general nature.

The trial of those arrested on 28 December 1915 was held on 26 October 1916. Petersburg proletarians reacted to it with a political protest strike in which some 130,000 working men and women took part. This trial did not in any degree kill off revolutionary work among the sailors. After the December arrests, work in the navy did not halt. This provided the clearest evidence that it was not sustained by merely the seventeen instigators who were now lying in jail. The military authorities took advantage of these arrests to introduce and reinforce every type of repression, but these measures only provoked the crews yet further.

In the report of the Chief of the Kronstadt Gendarme Administration made on 9 October 1916 on behalf of the Commander of the Rear and the Chief Commandant of the Port of Kronstadt, Colonel Trecak admits that "after the liquidation on 28 December 1915 of the RSDLP groups which had arisen on the battleships . . . and other vessels of the Baltic Fleet at Kronstadt, their criminal activity which had come from the Petrograd Committee to the Baltic Fleet *was paralysed but by no means eliminated*".

The memoranda of that same sleuth-in-chief, Trecak, report also that proclamations of the Petersburg Committee were already being distributed around the garrison again in January 1916, i.e. immediately after the arrests, the "liquidation" notwithstanding.

The secret service had established that in February fresh people had already re-started contacts with the Petersburg Committee and literature supply from it. In the month of April Petersburg Committee leaflets devoted to the Putilov works affair and also to May Day turned up among sailors and soldiers.

Through the observations of the external secret service and the "inner light" (provocateurs) it was established that as early as July 1916 the "Chief Committee of the Kronstadt Military Organization" had been reconstituted. Many of the gatherings of organized sailors, and in particular those held in cafés in Kronstadt, were "observed" by the secret service, and the authorities were by August already contemplating new plans for mass arrests and further "liquidations".

In a secret memorandum dated 2 August 1916, the Chief of the Petrograd Okhrana divulges information obtained from provocateurs to the Chief of the Kronstadt Gendarme Administration, reporting that "in the Kronstadt Committee, things are set up thoroughly and conspiratorially, and its participants are all silent and prudent people. This committee has its representatives ashore also."

The following "plan of action" was uncovered by the same internal secret service. When, with the onset of the frosts and shipping movements hampered, there would as a result be plenty of sailors in Kronstadt, they planned to mount an uprising; when they had partly killed and partly arrested the officer corps, they would present a demand for the overthrow of the existing government, a change of the political system and the termination of the war: "The Petrograd proletariat must support this uprising and to notify it of its commencement, the fleet will, once ridden of its officers, sail from Kronstadt and fire a few salvos towards Petrograd. If severe measures against the workers ensue and the government starts to fire on them, the fleet will raze all Petrograd not leaving a single stone."

This report, obtained as it was from provocateurs, suffers from gross inaccuracy. The "Chief Committee" of our military organization was mature enough not to adopt such an exclusively conspiratorial plot. This sort of plan could not have found any backing from the Petersburg Committee. There had been talks back in 1915 between party workers about the Baltic Fleet's possible role in the open revolutionary movement. In these, stress was always laid upon the armed forces' ancillary role, which although perhaps crucial, would always be subordinated to a workers' rising. Isolated political action would not have been of any use to the workers' movement, and it had no proponents in the Petersburg Committee or the Central Committee Bureau.

It further reported that "the Kronstadt Committee of the Military Organization is so confident of its strength and regards its tasks as soundly planned that it does not even desire outside help. . . ." The report is correct in one thing only: the "Kronstadt Committee" had after the arrests become stronger than in 1915, but it by no means took the line that "it could do everything".

According to the same information, the Kronstadt Committee was asking only one thing of the Petersburg Committee: to print a leaflet in 100,000 copies and to send them one party worker.

In conformity with an instruction of the Director of the Police Department, Major General Klimovich, a fresh "liquidation" of instigators was carried out with the agreement of the military authorities. On the night of 8-9 September, thirty sailors were searched and seven of them arrested. There were also searches in Petersburg in the quest for the "military group".

But these arrests did not destroy revolutionary work nor even less "scare" the sailors. Literature was distributed as before and propaganda openly conducted. In the autumn of 1916 the workers' movement had attained a sweep unheard of in wartime and the proletarians in the forces responded to the summons of their brothers-in-arms.

All these protracted proceedings by the gendarmerie actually evoked a negative reaction from Admirals Viren and Nepenin. They sensed full well that all these arrests, searches and spying were only exciting the mass of the sailors in a revolutionary direction and so frequently refused to authorize such measures. Two months later, the Chief of the Kronstadt Gendarme Administration intervened to press the commandant of the fortress into banishing all unreliable sailors to forward positions or "remote military zones" of the Russian Empire. There was no other solution, for arrests no longer availed.

The Government and the War Industries Socialists

Notwithstanding the valuable services rendered by the defensist Labour Groups organized under the aegis of the War Industries Committees, the "renewed" government in the autumn of 1916 embarked on a struggle against the Labour Groups which had gone over to a path of revolutionary opposition to the government. In many areas semi-legal "action groups" of the Labour Groups of the War Industries Committees were formed by social-democrat defensists

(Mensheviks) and Socialist-Revolutionaries. This rallying of even moderate and patriotically-thinking elements worried the tsarist government.

The "new" Minister of the Interior, Protopopov, launched a general offensive against the Central War Industries Committee and against its Labour Group especially. In a letter addressed to the Chief of the Petrograd Military Region, S.S. Khabalov, Protopopov sought to portray the "Labour Group" as "covert defeatists" trying to exploit their legal status for revolutionary activity.

In conclusion Protopopov recommended that Khabalov adopt appropriate measures against the Labour Groups and reported how the Chief of the Kiev Military Region had solved similar problems most successfully by reorganizing the group and divesting it of the means to maintain contacts with workers. Khabalov's attempts to interfere in the activity of the Central War Industries Committee encountered a certain rebuff from the policy-makers of the War Industries Committees, and "reorganization" along Kiev lines was not achieved.

The bourgeois leaders of the War Industries Committees were briefed on all the activity of the Labour Groups and defended them from police incursions. The industrialists defended the activity and inviolability of the Labour Groups not so much because they liked Labour Group members' faces as out of entirely realistic political calculation. The most moderate elements of workers and patriotically-minded intellectuals were grouped around the "Labour Groups", namely, those who placed national unity in the name of victory above the principles of class struggle and international solidarity.

By taking advantage of the privileges of legality and the overt sympathy and patronage of the liberal bourgeoisie, the social-patriots from the Labour Groups sought to monopolize political activity undertaken on behalf of our country's working class. This was to the bourgeoisie's benefit, and it accordingly found both a place and representative functions for the groups which spoke its native language of "defence of the homeland and culture", thereby introducing a split into working-class circles.

The tsar's government had in the autumn of 1916 successfully repulsed the verbal assaults of the progressive bloc and, capitalizing on the irresolute nature of the State Duma, opened an offensive against "public opinion". The "public opinion" of the War Industries Committees centred around the Labour Group of the Central War Industries Committee, and Protopopov in consequence struck his first blow in that direction. The provocateur activity of Abrosimov and others assisted him in his campaign.

In the middle of December, a conference of local Labour Groups of

War Industries Committees was held. The conference was run under the direct leadership of the Mensheviks' central organization, the Organization Committee, one of whose members, Batursky, took part in the preparatory work for the conference. From material from Okhrana files and reports published by the group itself it is clear how far removed the defensists' policy was from the actual revolutionary struggle of the working class. On the basic question of the attitude to the war, the social-patriots continued to see "our task of the defence of the country as one of the principal means to achieve the liquidation of the war on conditions acceptable to democracy".

At the end of November news arrived that the Central Powers were prepared to conclude a peace and therefore our defensists considered it obligatory to meddle in that diplomatic game and declare that "the international proletariat must actively intervene in the wheeling and dealing over the liberty and dignity of the peoples now in progress behind their backs". While advancing such a standpoint for the "international proletariat" the defensists spoke in other terms to its own country: "The position of the Russian proletariat, confronted as it is with the danger of the military rout of the country, is highly complex as a result of the necessity for combining practically the realization of our international tasks of a struggle against the conquering ambitions of the possessing classes with a struggle for the destruction of the political régime that has brought the country to catastrophe." The conference demanded but one thing of the bourgeois Konovalovs and the tsarist government: "definitive statements on the aims of the war and the terms for peace".

The general leftward shift in the country and the intensifying strike and political movement of the working class compelled even the defensists to alter their tactic of rejecting struggle. The conference of 13-15 December was, in its resolution on "the political tasks of the working class", driven to make the reservation that "the working class will not renounce . . . the slogans behind which it has marched towards Russia's total de-feudalization for eleven years." However there immediately followed another reservation and a dilution of the very slogans behind which the proletariat had fought in 1905. The immediate task of the hour was considered by the defensists to be "the final removal of the existing régime and the formation in its place of a provisional government resting for support upon the freely and independently organized people". Behind this verbal window-dressing there lay concealed not a revolutionary content but merely a play upon the slogan they had given in November: the formation by the State Duma of a government of national salvation. The defensists were pinning their hopes on the State Duma becoming the "centre of an all-national movement". The burning desire of the defensists to adapt to the slogans and demands of liberal bourgeoisie showed clearly through all their key resolutions.

However, the change of tactics did force the Labour Groups to take an illegal path as well. Thanks to provocations, the government was well informed on all the activities of the Labour Group and took steps to "neutralize" it. The unpopularity of its members among workers together with the latter's negative attitude to the policy of "War Industries socialism" eased Protopopov's task. He was confident, and Okhrana briefings confirmed it, that the liquidation of the Labour Groups would call forth no protests from the working masses, who had refused to follow them; he therefore took measures for their arrest.

The Activity of the Bureau of the Central Committee of the RSDLP(B)

The all-Russian centre directing day-to-day social-democratic work had been organized by myself on the assignment of our party's Central Committee as early as my trip to Russia from abroad in the autumn of 1915. But one year later there remained of the comrades who had launched the work on an all-Russian scale only isolated individuals, and in 1916 I again had to select comrades for running the technical side of the work of the Central Committee Bureau. This time the job of drawing in collaborators was accomplished far more rapidly. The choice of party workers was much wider than in the previous year. There was no longer that odd Chernomazov-Starck rivalry to establish contacts from the Petersburg Committee as there had been during the first period of organizing the Central Committee Bureau. With the agreement of the leading party workers on the Petersburg Committee (comrades Zalezhsky, Shutko, Antipov, Evdokimov and others), we were able to bring comrades Zalutsky and Molotov into this leading centre.

Sometimes, though not often, representatives of the Petersburg Committee and organizers from the Insurance Council (workers' group) attended our meetings. We have not been able to preserve the minutes of our work. Nor has much of the material relating to the practical work of that time survived. We would meet at different ends of Petersburg. Often business was decided in the deserted streets of Lesny district, the three of us "going for a stroll" in the dark evenings.

Among my papers I have kept half a sheet of paper with the agenda and decisions of one such meeting of the Central Committee Bureau. Judging by the nature of the resolutions this "protocol" relates to November 1916. The following items were placed on the agenda: (1) Relations with the Central Committee (abroad). Resolved: to send everything from the provinces via the Central Committee Bureau. (2)

Relations with the provinces. Resolved: addresses and contacts held by the Petersburg Committee to be passed over to the Central Committee Bureau. (3) Educational and organizational tour of the provinces. Resolved: to be undertaken by the Central Committee Bureau. (4) On literature from abroad. Resolved: to get equipment (for reproduction). To centralize literary work — decentralize reproduction — make tours to organize the machinery. (5) Publication of *Izvestiya Byuro Tsentralnogo Komiteta*. The resolution is unrecorded, although one was carried. It consisted of comrade Molotov being charged with the organization of the technical side and finding premises, staff and equipment. (6) Resolved: to publish the leaflet "Against the Defensists" on behalf of the Central Committee Bureau. (7) Chinese at Lessners. The question of yellow labour. Resolved: defer to next meeting. (8) Enquiries from Moscow about setting up work. Resolved: send V. (this initial stood for V.M. Molotov) with an allotment of 250 rubles. (9) The "unifiers". (10) Declaration.

The Central Committee Bureau would assemble not less than once a week. Brief encounters and meetings were far more frequent. At our meetings matters not only of a Russian nature were discussed but also international questions and the work of the foreign section of our Central Committee. At the request of the editorial board of the central organ *Sotsial-Demokrat* and a group of party literary workers, the exiles G. Pyatakov, N. Bukharin and others, the Bureau examined the questions of the differences on the national question which had arisen abroad and carried the following resolution:

> Having listened to comrade Belenin's statement concerning the differences among the collaborators on the party press over particular points in the party's programme and tactics, the Central Committee Bureau deems it essential to bring the following to the attention of the central organ's editorial board abroad: (1) the Central Committee Bureau in Russia, in stating its full solidarity with the Central Committee's basic line as carried in the central organ, *Sotsial-Demokrat*, expresses its wish that all Central Committee publications be edited in a strictly consistent fashion in complete compliance with the line of the Central Committee adopted from the start of the war. (2) The Bureau declares itself against the conversion of Central Committee organs into discussion papers. (3) The Bureau finds that the divergences between contributors and the editorial board of the central organ *on particular questions of the minimum programme* must not form an obstacle to the participation of these individuals in the Central Committee's publications and it proposes that the editorial board of the central organ accept their collaboration on other questions standing outside the area of disagreement. (4) The Bureau proposes that in order to clarify and eliminate the differences, *private publishers* should be used both inside Russia and abroad to issue special collections of discussion articles.

We were confronted with the problem of the "unifiers", who were fighting against the factional situation prevalent in Russian social democracy. In the first year of the war, an article was issued illegally by them, handwritten and hectographed, giving historical data on the splits in the parties of other countries. On the basis of this "fight for unity" within the party there appeared a new political organization of social democrats which assumed the title of the Inter-District Committee. This organization was born in 1913 and had a certain link with the "Central Group" created in the same year to rebuild the Petersburg Committee after the ravages of 1912 and early 1913.

During the war period, cries for unity had abated considerably as mechanical unity found no acceptance in party ranks. In the years which had elapsed since the split in the Duma faction, the existence of the two parties had become so firmly established that there remained little of the simple desire for "unity at any price". In the process of the political struggle the Menshevik social democrats had turned into an adjunct of "public opinion" and sunk to the depth of adapting working-class politics to the requirements of the liberal bourgeoisie. The war had exposed all these features of Menshevism particularly sharply.

The "unifiers" from the Inter-District Committee became a third faction. In the sphere of policy they fully accepted our attitude to the war, even including civil war, and the tasks of the working class in it. This did not prevent them however from dreaming of unity with those against whom they, daily and hourly, conducted agitation and from whom they in every way sought to dissociate themselves. Such an attitude by "non-factional" social democrats presented the worst form of factionalism and lacked even a shadow of principle.

By making use of old acquaintances, the Inter-District Committee was in 1916 attempting to gather comrades under the flag of unity, but this was now out of fashion. The resolution, accompanied as it was by a note on unity, was so vacuous that it did not really require refutation. The Inter-District's itch for unity finally ended up with the Committee speaking simultaneously for Bolsheviks and Mensheviks in its proclamations.

The existence of separate parties with seemingly "identical" programmes was considered by some unifier comrades to be the caprice of individual figures and a manifestation of "impatience", sectarianism and so forth. The enthusiasts for "unity" had overlooked the most important point about the history of the workers' movement in our country, namely, that a section of social-democratic party workers had come forward and although formally recognizing the programme and tactics of "international social democracy" were in essence alien to its revolutionary content. Russian social democracy could now observe the emergence of a purely "liberal workers' party" from its own depths and under the cloak of its own programme. With each day that passed, the war demonstrated the rightness of this view. When discussing the work and proposals of the "unifiers" we did not conceal our negative attitude to "blind unity". But soon even the unifiers began to restrict the circles of social democrats they considered worth unifying with. During the war they proposed to unite just the "internationalists". To that we replied: "Let us get to work and our activity will unite better than any resolutions."

The Food Crisis

The food crisis took the form of a rapid rise in the prices of basic necessities, the periodic disappearance of goods from the market and a swing towards doing business by "knowing the right people", i.e. under-the-counter dealing, and had assumed major proportions by the third year of the war. The proletarian masses of the industrial regions felt this crisis especially harshly. Unrest and strikes over the high cost of living had started in 1915. In 1916 looting of markets occurred in Petersburg. The burden of the food crisis struck above all at working women and workers' wives and mothers who were forced with extremely limited resources to find ways and means of wheedling out hoarded products and became the first to join the fight against emergent speculation.

Sensing a threat from the hungry masses, the Russian bourgeoisie also started a "struggle" against the food crisis. The industrialists grouped together in the Association of Factory and Plant Owners were the first to feel the effects of the troubles in food supply and distribution: workers were starting to table pay claims. The factory and plant owners decided to take advantage of the crisis to intensify the exploitation of the workers by organizing supplies through the plants.

From the very first days of the war, the government had been compelled to adopt a line of intervention and price control. Price control applied however chiefly to small traders. Wholesale merchants and big stores were under no restriction and therefore the controls frequently led simply to the disappearance of items from small shops.

All the patriotic landowners stood out against the regulation of grain prices. The tsarist government passed the business of supplying cereal products directly into the hands of the landowners themselves or their agents. The landowners were hardly likely to object to that, and through various bodies (in particular, the congress of food supply commissioners' delegates held in 1916) set exceedingly high minimum prices for grain products. This policy of minimum prices greatly assisted profiteering and prompted grain producers to hoard grain in anticipation of yet higher prices to come.

Provincial governors were also brought into the struggle against the food crisis and special commissioners were appointed. The divergence of interest between the different groups of exploiters in the business of supplying food to the populace and army, and the industrialists' struggle against the landowners and their minimum prices, led every governor and provincial commissioner to ban the export of grain from his province, yet without any overall plan. Very often the industrial centres found themselves short of the most essential items. We received reports from workers like the one below:

> In Bryansk county, Orel province, there is no rye flour, salt, paraffin or sugar. In Bryansk a pound of sugar costs from one to one ruble fifty. Discontent is rife and more than once there have been strikes in the factories and plants with the demand for "flour and sugar". There is in Bryansk county a village called Star, where there is in the village a factory making glass products which belongs to the Maltsov company and is engaged on war contracts. Workers there struck on 8 October because they had not eaten bread for two weeks, having only potatoes: they selected two spokesmen and sent them to the factory manager with a demand for flour and sugar (for the company had undertaken to procure the items at pre-war prices as it kept wages also at peacetime levels). The manager could not give an answer but just made promises. But the following day the two spokesmen were arrested as unreliable elements and held under emergency regulations; two days later the workers went back but still did not get the bread. There is no organization at the factory.
>
> Lyudinovo village, Zhizdra county, Kaluga province. There is an engineering and mining works in the village belonging to the Maltsov company. There are some 5,000 workers at the plant and a social-democratic organization. The organization consists of twenty people but it has no contacts or literature. The plant works for the defence industry. On the occasion of a shortage of food products and because of the high prices, the workers in September went on strike demanding a rise of 75 per cent. The strike lasted two days; they settled at 50 per cent. In October (during the last two days) an acute shortage of flour and sugar was experienced there as well. Flour had reached five rubles a pood. The workers struck again, putting forward the demand "bread and sugar" and pay rises from 25 per cent to 100 per cent, depending on the particular worker's rate. They were out for a day and a half. Flour was obtained and ten pounds each was distributed together with a pound and a half of sugar, and wages were increased by up to 75 per cent. From 13 to 16 November I stayed in the town of Zhizdra, Kaluga province. There was an acute shortage of domestic items; at all times there was no flour, sugar or paraffin at all. No commodities other than hay were being brought in

from the villages. I then travelled round the villages: grumbling, discontent and a vague apprehension all around.

While the prices of the means of subsistence were relentlessly rising, the wages of the majority of workers lagged far behind the cost of living. In many sectors of industry male adult labour was being supplanted by cheap female and child labour. The employers succeeded in splitting along grade lines, separating off the highly skilled, paying good money on certain machines while keeping the remaining mass on low rates. Thus, even at the beginning of 1916 for example, milling-machine operators, turners, fitters and pattern-makers were earning from five to ten rubles while labourers were on average receiving fifteen kopeks an hour. This did not however stop the patriotic bourgeoisie, which had prospered from the war, moaning about the excessively high pay for workers and their mood for exorbitant "unpatriotic" demands and so on.

The liberal bourgeoisie, organized in the Union of Zemstvos and the Union of Towns, under pressure from the mounting movement in the country against high prices, formed a special body in Moscow for watching over the food question, with the title of "Central Public Organizations' Food Committee". The institution was soon to become the focus of the "civic struggle" against the food breakdown. The whole struggle of these organizations and their centre consisted of correcting the defects of tsarist food policy and finding a line that would reconcile the industrialists and landowners at the expense, of course, of the mass consumers.

The same two political lines which had hitherto existed among the mass of workers conflicted also over the question of the struggle against the food crisis: that of proletarian revolutionary social democracy (communism) and that of the liberal opportunism pursued by defensists of every tendency. All the social-patriotic defensist elements of social democracy (the Mensheviks) and the Socialist-Revolutionaries formed their centre for the "struggle against the food crisis" under the aegis of the War Industries Committees. In February 1916 at the Second Congress of Representatives of the War Industries Committees a special food section was formed.

Our liberal politicians evaded the fundamental cause of both the food supply crisis and the high cost of living as well as the material hardships of the working class arising from it, namely, the war. This was not through ignorance or immaturity on the part of the Labour Group representatives. This evasion of the fundamental cause of all the people's ills was the nub of the defensists' politics. Even the "war industries socialists" could not help understanding this: once having accepted the war, they had to carry their betrayal of the working class through to the end and endeavour to conceal all the consequences of the war.

The bourgeoisie took advantage of the "labour representatives" to divert the proletarian struggle into all sorts of hollow trivialities like co-operatives, public canteens and other such half-measures. The factory and plant owners would gladly meet workers' wishes halfway when it was a matter of organizing canteens inside the factories and plants.

The Labour Group of the Central War Industries Committee sent a delegation to the Petersburg City Duma to try and impress on the Petersburg Fathers of Speculation the need to organize public canteens for the capital's working population. After rather a long period of waiting the City Duma allotted 250,000 rubles to the city guardians of the poor for the organization of public canteens. With this money it was proposed to open some nine canteens with a daily capacity of 8,000 people. That was what the city's "aid" in the fight against the food supply breakdown was limited to.

Differences between the War Industries socialists and the War Industries capitalists then arose over the question of the organization of the canteens. In September 1916 the Labour Group convened a conference of representatives of hospital funds and certain co-operatives representing defensist elements grouped around those institutions.

As a result of this conference, a "Canteen Centre" was created, consisting of fifteen representatives (the Provisional Central Workers' Commission for the Organization of Workers' Canteens). Agitation for the opening of canteens was conducted around Petersburg's factories and plants. The most "astute" and forward-looking manufacturers and plant-owners quickly came forward to meet these demands, as they had an interest in forestalling claims for higher wages, and provided funds to rent premises and equip the canteens. The "movement" undertaken by the defensists in favour of democratizing the guardian-ship of the poor and organizing "self-managing" canteens effectively resulted in feeding only an insignificant number of workers employed in the Petersburg war industries.

Our underground organizations produced their own assessment of both the food supply crisis and the campaign to fight the food crisis conducted by the bourgeoisie and the representatives of the liberals in the workers' movement. Our party's Petersburg Committee proposed the following motion to the district and plant committees on the subject of fighting the food crisis:

> We, workers of the . . . . . works, having discussed the question of the sharpening food crisis, recognize that:
> (1) the food crisis observable in all countries is an inevitable conse-

THE BEGINNING OF THE END

quence of the current war which has latterly acquired the character of a war of attrition;

(2) the continuance of the war will entail a deepening of the food crisis, famine, poverty and the degeneration of the mass of the people;

(3) in Russia the food crisis is complicated by the continued rule of the tsarist monarchy which places the country's whole economy in a state of complete dislocation, surrendering it to the whim of rapacious capital and ruthlessly suppressing any initiative by the mass of the people;

(4) all piecemeal means of fighting the food crisis (e.g. co-operatives, wage rises, canteens etc.) can only marginally mitigate the effects of the crisis and not eliminate the causes;

(5) the only effective means of struggle against the crisis is a struggle against the causes producing it, i.e. a struggle against the war and the ruling classes which plotted it; in taking all this into account, we call upon the Russian working class and all democrats to take the road of a revolutionary struggle against the tsarist monarchy and the ruling classes behind the slogan of "Down with the war!"

This motion was adopted at general works meetings in many major enterprises. The assessment of the struggle and likewise the causes of the current food crisis were given out by our various organizations in the form of special sets of study notes, theses or abridged articles, and distributed around works committees as guidelines for their work. A characteristic feature of all the articles and documents was the theme of "broad democratism" in the organization of provisioning the urban population. The Association of Factory and Plant Owners, having a vested interest in stable wage-rates, declared itself in favour of dividing workers by making special food supply arrangements for certain categories. Nor was the government opposed to such an approach, and partly implemented similar measures in state-owned plants. The remainder of the population was thus incited against these workers. A split between "private" and "state" industry would even penetrate within a single proletarian family. Workers sensed this danger and reacted negatively. Their origin aroused the proletarians' class caution.

All energies of the Unions of Zemstvos and Towns and the co-operatives were directed towards the struggle against the food crisis; but all their efforts proved fruitless. Bread increasingly often disappeared from sale. Many basic necessities had entirely left the "open market", moving voluntarily over to the "under-the-counter" sector.

The working population suffered great hardships. Unrest over the shortage of food products rolled across from one city district to another, embracing ever wider circles of working women, workers' wives and housewives. Quite often unrest took on a turbulent nature like the looting of shops and the beating-up of traders, police and others, but it was still powerless to bring down prices or reduce the scale of the mounting speculation. The tsarist government and bourgeois organizations could not and would not fight the predatory interests of merchant capital and the landowners, industrialists and grain buyers-up. All of this eased our underground work of explaining the causes of the approaching famine. In our fight against the food crisis we concentrated workers' attention on the fundamental cause — the war — and called workers to an organized struggle against the war and our country's ruling classes.

The Food Question in the State Duma

The question of the state of food supply was put down for discussion in the Duma for the end of November, on the 24th. The acting head of the Ministry of Agriculture, Rittich, spoke on behalf of the "renewed" government. In his speech he expressed his readiness to work with the Duma, and stated that because of his short period in office he was unable to give a reply concerning the government's programme. At the same time, Rittich made a typical reservation: "I consider that only measures of a gradual evolutionary nature are possible in the complex sphere of economic relations. I reject any abrupt break."

Many speakers came forward on questions of food policy. At this sitting too, the leading role fell to the Cadets, whose representative, Shingarev, delivered a most instructive speech. He pointed to the symptomatic emptiness on the government bench and compared this with the emptiness within the Council of Ministers itself, where "neither knowledge, plan nor system" could be located. "During the war four ministers of agriculture and six ministers of the interior had succeeded one another, with the result that none of them knew what to do or what his predecessor had done." He went on to give the example of the announcement of a recruitment campaign timed for 15 July, at the very height of the grain harvest. It had only been with enormous effort that Duma members managed in a special sitting to obtain the repeal of the order. Because of this mix-up "the harvest in a whole number of areas had to be brought in by non-Russian manpower". And even then the government did not fail to create a shambles:

> Stürmer's telegram arrives in both Turkestan and the Kirghiz regions and conscription of non-Russians begins during working hours. Result: grave and substantial disorder in those districts and consequent loss of manpower for the farms. Minister Naumov managed with some difficulty in putting prisoner-of-war labour to use; but here too the government swiftly disrupted the plan by insisting that prisoners-of-war be taken off

farm work. The same Naumov now tackles the question of fixed prices and then Naumov resigns. The United Nobility candidate, Count A.A. Bobrinsky, who succeeds him, becomes gradually convinced of the need to set fixed prices and, after a titanic struggle, fixed prices are passed at a special conference. A procurement organization is only just off the ground when all of a sudden Count Bobrinsky has the bright idea that the fixed prices perhaps after all should be revised. A new Minister of the Interior appears on the scene [he is referring to Protopopov — A.S.] and a curious stage fight starts up between him and Count Bobrinsky. Count Bobrinsky really wants to give up his job [i.e. to hand food matters from the Ministry of Agriculture over to the Ministry of the Interior — A.S.] and it was only his own organization, his own ministry and a majority on the Council of Ministers which, confronted by Protopopov's rising star, denied him the chance of winding up his business. . . . Protopopov dreams of pulling the banks into the procurement organization and would like to approach provincial governors while Bobrinsky puts on a show of fighting Protopopov!

Shingarev then passed on to describe the attempts made to hold a special conference on food supply; but Stürmer overshadowed the conference and pushed through "his own policy". Meanwhile the Ministry of Agriculture was putting a plan together for a food supply organization with the involvement of local interests. The plan was published in the form of a mandatory regulation in a bulletin of statutes and government orders. A few days later, however, Count Bobrinsky, terrified that Protopopov would organize a revolution with the aid of the county and rural committees, demanded in a secret circular in the form of a coded telegram that the operation of the organization's rules newly promulgated by the senate be everywhere rescinded.

According to Shingarev's statement, in Russia grain surplus to demand amounted to 440 million poods. "But," he asked, "what if the country is caught in the grip of a crop failure? What if earlier chaos and that earlier worthless piece of business that Mr Prime Minister has been calling upon us to undertake, remains as before? What then? Isn't it abundantly clear that our main practical piece of business is the removal of an administration that is unable to work?"

Thus the Cadets once again posed the question of "businesslike" administration, stressing that the government was "incapable" of working in a way necessary and beneficial to the liberal industrial bourgeoisie. Touching on the question of the war, Shingarev declared that "it must be carried through to the end whatever the price . . . The government at war is living off your resolve, for you have many times eschewed faintheartedness, government incompetence and, at times, even treacherous thoughts. It is precisely the Duma that has formed a focus for the people's thoughts and the people's will which despite worthless bureaucrats will continue to wage the war and wage it unto the end."

Passing on to the question of feeding the civilian population and army, Shingarev stated that "the moment has come to tell the people from this seat: the state demands your grain but it will give away that grain as it has given away its children." It is self-evident that this matter was a direct obligation of the Duma for, in the Cadets' opinion, it had the "moral authority". The food policy had been conceived by them as a policy for fixed prices and a state trading monopoly: "Fixed prices are but the beginning of an enormous duty to the state. A grain monopoly may have to be introduced after the example of France and Germany. One thing we do know: an organized country is invincible but a disorganized country is powerless to deal with even its own bureaucrats."

Shingarev described Russia's domestic and external situation, drawing a historical parallel between Russia's position and the state of France at the end of the eighteenth century. "Are those not our own days, is not that our chaos, is not that our crazy blind administration, are not those our own domestic problems, are not those our own failures in the fight against the external foe, are not those our own ominous, evil rumours of betrayal?" So this Cadet leader had now to spell out that, there being "no other way out, the abolition of this régime, the dispersal of that rabble and replacement of that worthless administration" was indispensable.

The debate on the food question lasted several days, but all the representatives of the various parties who spoke only reiterated Shingarev's basic thoughts. Among the socialist speakers was Tulyakov, who maintained:

> The food crisis is essentially a political crisis, and although it has been previously possible to allay the catastrophe at hand by mutual concessions by the government and society, swift and decisive action is now vital. The old régime has arrived too late with its concessions and the road to bread is now only possible over the head of the old régime and the government embodying it. The food crisis is insoluble not because the administration is without talent, lazy and dissolute, but because an administration that in normal times sees the source of its well-being in the enslavement of the mass of the people has at the height of the food crisis been handed over to landowners who dream of turning Russia into a nobleman's estate. The working class will gain nothing by handing over food matters to local authorities as local government organs are in their present form alien and inimical to the population.

On the model of all opportunists as well as all defensists, the representative of Chkheidze's faction diplomatically avoided the fundamental question of the food crisis, the war. Nor did Rusanov, speaking for the Narodniks (Socialist-Revolutionaries) utter a single word about the root cause of the food supply breakdown. Both the social-democrats (Chkheidze's faction) and the Narodniks on the food question were acting as "outriders" to the progressive bloc, thus in no way reflecting the views of our country's revolutionary proletariat. The debates ended on 5 December. In the end, the motion of the progressive bloc was adopted (114 votes for, with 17 against and 87 abstentions), which contained a series of political details and put forward the need to establish a fixed price system, the involvement of local bodies in the apportionment of food products and the withdrawal of the government from such administration, a firm and systematic state and public regulation of the prices and production of principal industrial products of mass consumption, the drafting of a plan for 1917, a census and classification of the workforce and so on. The implementation of such measures would be dependent on "co-operation between the government and public bodies". Both sides had been striving for this lovers' pact.

Organizing Working-Class Action

The campaign by the organized bourgeoisie against the tsarist government demonstrated to the broadest and even the most backward circles of workers that "parliamentary" methods of toppling tsarist autocracy would not achieve their objectives. The stronghold of tsarism was not rocking before the speeches of representatives of the progressive bloc, Narodniks and Mensheviks. The government replied by steering a rightward course and, in full understanding of the true soul of Russian liberalism, felt confident that it would find a way to a working agreement.

In response to all the fearful "formulas for the transition to urgent tasks" adopted by the State Duma, the State Council and even the Congress of the United Nobility, the tsar bestowed honours upon Metropolitan Pitirim, General Voeikov and others. The court camarilla sustained one victory after another, sowing disintegration in the ranks of the aristocratic world associated with the struggle in the Duma and public organizations.

The widespread illegal literature carrying speeches in the Duma and the State Council, letters from leading liberal figures and resolutions from all sorts of congresses all exercised a decomposing effect upon the foundations of the tsar's throne. During the autumn of 1916 the tsarist monarchy had lost even the small credit that, backed up by the Press, police and Church, it had formerly held among backward superstitious sectors of the population. All these reports, rumours, speeches, appeals and so forth made a profound impression on the war-weary representatives of the countryside now dressed in grey greatcoats. We were by now receiving vague tales of how Duma deputies' speeches about traitors and turncoats within the court and the government were making a big impact on the mass of the soldiers. In those speeches and the accompanying talk about the corruption of the tsarist government the mass of soldiers were able to find some explanation for the army's monstrous defeats. Persistent rumours circulating round Petersburg at the end of 1916 had it that on the northern front soldiers of several regiments had refused to go over to the offensive as they suspected that their offensive and the entire military operation would be betrayed by the traitors inside the government. At the time it was not possible to verify the rumours but subsequently, during the revolution, the incidents were confirmed by members of the command themselves.

The objective growth of revolutionary moods and with it the crystallization in the country of a struggle against the tsarist government, the rise of the strike movement and revolutionary flare-ups posed before us as leaders of social-democratic work in Russia (the Central Committee Bureau and the Petersburg Committee) the question of mass street demonstrations. Sporadic disparate actions, strikes in individual enterprises or even individual working-class districts were not achieving the political objectives for which they had been launched, and were satisfying neither the masses in the party nor broader circles of non-party working masses. The rising class struggle now required new, more decisive methods than strikes. Our conviction at that time was that a suitable method of struggle would be on the streets. Our aim to translate the struggle from the confines of the workplace and bring it out on to the streets in the form of demonstrations beyond the bounds of the working class met with the liveliest response among workers. We had envisaged demonstrations also as the only means of attracting the wider mass of soldiers into political struggle. From November onwards, we discussed concrete forms of such action with representatives of the Petersburg Committee. The round-up of our party workers which began in November had not hindered wide discussion of our tactic of street demonstrations.

During wartime, or, more exactly, ever since the July days of 1914, the Petersburg proletariat had not tested out its strength in street demonstrations. Party organizations had, moreover, lost the habit of preparing such actions, although the tradition of a "procession into the city", to the Nevsky Prospekt, was re-awakened among the mass of workers during nearly every strike.

When considering this question, the Central Committee Bureau took stock of the changed situation from the "peaceful era" of 1914 and was well aware that calls for street demonstrations would invariably finish up with fighting and bloody clashes. The Petersburg Committee, with party workers like K.I. Shutko, G. Evdokimov, V. Schmidt, N. Antipov, N. Tolmachev and others, appreciated the responsibility entailed in embarking on such tactics and decided to undertake preparatory work in that direction, timing street demonstrations for the traditional 9 January celebrations. The directive to prepare for street demonstrations was also given to Moscow, and it was proposed that I travel there to co-ordinate the tactical details of the change-over to street demonstrations throughout the Moscow industrial belt.

The loss of the "machinery" (i.e. the underground printshop) put the Petersburg Committee in an extremely difficult position. In December we had to prepare the leaflets for 9 January. Copy was collected for the fourth issue of *Proletarskii Golos*, but there was no chance of it being printed by the Petersburg Committee. Solving this problem and in particular the business of printing *Proletarskii Golos* no. 4 was undertaken by comrade Antipov, who had been in charge of organizing the Petersburg Committee's "machinery". Comrade Antipov came to an arrangement with some printers in the party and placed his own man at Altschuler's press with the object of using it for the Petersburg Committee's illegal requirements. The publication of the fourth issue of *Proletarskii Golos* in December was one of the Petersburg Committee's major jobs in preparation for the January demonstrations.

Under the leadership of comrade Antipov, our printers evolved a plan for using Altshculer's printing press. "Our man" working at the printshop would work out all the operating procedures, study the layout of the premises and all the peculiarities of the shop. Antipov picked twelve or thirteen bold and determined printers from each trade and on the night of 17 December they carried out an armed seizure of the printshop. Having gained control of the press, the printer comrades locked up the night shift working there and with their own resources set up and rolled off several thousand copies of *Proletarskii Golos*, fourth issue. The first stage of the operation succeeded brilliantly but the ending was unfortunate. People bringing the papers out were arrested at the exit. But some were able to get the literature to the rendezvous point, though further arrests were made on the spot.

At first we had imagined that the fiasco had come about through a random raid by the police who were on the alert throughout the district following Rasputin's assassination. However, the whole series of losses that ensued as well as the hunches of Antipov and others inclined us towards the theory of a betrayal. A number of incriminating facts confirmed these suspicions and also afforded opportunities to pinpoint the person concerned. Suspicion fell upon the printer, Mikhailov (alias Vanya the printer), to be confirmed later by documents after the February revolution.

I had planned my trip to Moscow for 16 December and for greater security I devoted days on end to erasing all traces of the intensive surveillance placed on myself. I succeeded in breaking free and found my way to the train with a valid ticket quite unnoticed. I was in Moscow the next day. I had a reliable refuge in Moscow at R.V. Obolensky's flat in Teply Pereulok, which very usefully had two entrances. The sleuths of Moscow did not know me, so things were considerably easier for me there. I made contact with the party organization through P.G. Smidovich, V.P. Nogin, I.I. Skvortsev, M.S. Olminsky and a number of other comrades whose names I do not recall. I had a meeting with a whole number of "rank-and-file" party workers in the Zamoskvorechie district, and went to a rendezvous at the College of Commerce. I established complete solidarity with the Moscow comrades on all the problems of intensifying street demonstrations. Moscow party workers (the Moscow Regional Bureau of the Central Committee) had also decided to carry out their first trial of street demonstrations on 9 January 1917. Workers in the industrial districts were being prepared for these demonstrations and it was decided to run off a leaflet.

The mood of Moscow workers and of the "democratic" circles of the population was akin to that of Petersburg. My visit to Moscow coincided with Rasputin's assassination and Moscow newspapers, which on this question proved to be free of censorship, were full of relish for this palace "mystery". They attempted to turn the murder of that devout debauchee into a most colossal political event, if not the forerunner of a palace coup. This zeal of the bourgeois papers did bring certain benefits by discrediting the tsarist bigwigs, and dealt a final blow to the "divine" provenance of the tsar's power. Alongside newspaper sensations about Rasputin a great wave of rumours about the inside life of the court, which outdid all "the secrets of the court of Madrid", swept through the newspapers.

At the end of 1916 party work in Moscow itself was taking shape in a very characteristic way: social-democratic work was carried out in nearly all working-class districts but all efforts by Moscow comrades to unify work on a city-wide scale were wrecked by provocational activity which had woven a sturdy nest inside the organization. Owing to these provocations and the intensive internal and external surveillance by the gendarmerie, we could not fully use some very long-established and important party workers who were living in Moscow at that time. And on account of shortage of funds, the Central Committee Bureau was unable to utilize the available forces of the

THE BEGINNING OF THE END

Moscow party intelligentsia to reinforce other districts. We could use a number of comrades from time to time only, despite the crying need for party workers at the centre and in the localities.

Lack of financial resources greatly constrained the activity of the Central Committee Bureau. Contributions from the organizations were extremely modest. What was left of the money I had raised from the material on the pogroms that I had sold in America had quickly dried up. The huge job of securing material resources fell to myself on top of all the other work. The high cost of living weighed heavily on our operations. The necessity of setting up "machinery" for the Central Committee Bureau, organizing regular tours of the organizations and the conference of party organization that we had proposed, in short, the whole plan of work we had mapped out, at once confronted us with a need for substantial funds. The Bureau's treasury was in no position to meet these requirements. To defray our outgoings we had recourse to a number of measures like a proposed 10 per cent regular levy on contributions from local organizations, sale of postcards and portraits of the convicted deputies and also collections around "former" social-democratic figures. In this field we were rendered important services by A.M. Gorky and I.I. Ladyzhnikov who came to our aid. However, all our efforts to obtain financial support from "former" social democrats — people by then occupying key posts in capitalist undertakings and public organizations or working as technicians and managers with leading firms and earning tens of thousands of rubles — suffered failure. I personally sent people out to see some of these gentlemen (who are today "comrades" and members of our Russian Communist Party) and sounded out the ground, but without success. Once, when discussing the problems of our financial policy, A.M. Gorky defined these "has-beens" most aptly: "They'd sooner pay you for a binge at the Cuba than for underground work." And how right he was. Very few responded to our appeal, and they were comrades with unimportant positions in "society" at that time. The Central Committee Bureau also imposed an obligation on Moscow comrades to find resources for strengthening all-Russian work, but financial matters were not too brilliant there either. This lack of means inhibited our work in the extreme. Relations with abroad and the transport of literature consignments required ample resources. Organization of political action throughout Russia likewise required a great deal of money, but as we did not have it, all contacts with the provinces took place spasmodically.

We assumed that if we concentrated our work of organizing demonstrations in Petersburg, Moscow and Ivanovo-Voznesensk, our tactic would in various ways and through direct contact between Petersburg and Moscow workers and workers from other areas become generally familiar and be adopted by advanced proletarians from factories in all the other industrial regions.

The Underground and the International and Tsarist Okhrana

Political surveillance and provocation during the war acquired a scale unknown in the period of "peace". Governments and army General Staffs of all the belligerent and neutral countries sought to exploit the political activity of parties and the revolutionary workers' movement to the advantage of one or other bloc of warring world powers. Politicians and strategists of the belligerent countries did not shun any methods in their aim to weaken their adversaries. Speculation on unrest, strikes and even revolution and the overthrow of monarchies and tsarism formed part of the strategic and military plans of many belligerent countries.

International military and police surveillance and provocation gave us Bolsheviks no respite even while abroad. Our anti-war slogans and anti-tsarist revolutionary activity could not avoid attracting the attention of the governments of those countries at war with Russia and the Entente. German imperialism was the first to reckon on the possibility of using our revolutionary anti-war work in Russia for its own ends. We had foreseen such intentions. The collapse and betrayal of the social-democratic parties of the Second International made schemes for espionage and political adventuring easier for governments and their General Staffs. The militaristic designs of the German and Austrian imperialists did not, however, trouble us, but merely obliged us to be cautious even when abroad not to fall into the clutches of the secret services. Already in the first months of the war there had been attempts by the Austro-German secret services to infiltrate our ranks. But the first agents of the imperialists were "social democrats". We were familiar with the desire of Parvus, a German social-patriot and businessman, to "assist" our revolutionary work. But the least hint of such things would be sufficient for our comrades abroad to break off all relations with anyone who had any links with Parvus or other such gentlemen.

I was personally to stumble upon a number of attempts by the secret service to move among us, give us assistance and obtain "information". The first "top-grade" agent whom I had any dealings with was Troelstra, the Dutch socialist and a leader of the Second International, who in October 1914 had travelled to Sweden as an emissary of the Central Committee of German social democracy. It was from him that I, having just arrived from Petersburg, first heard the statement that the Central Committee of German social democracy was backing its government's war because of the dangers of tsarism and that the Central Committee of German social democracy was also prepared to give us help in our struggle. Troelstra was (or at least appeared to be) quite taken aback by my refusal of the offer and my annoyance at the idea of our struggle being backed up with sixteen-inch shells, and he asked me to convey my views on the Central Committee's proposal to him in writing. I wrote down my reply to the proposal and handed it to Troelstra while he was still in Stockholm.

Also in Stockholm there came first to comrade A.M. Kollontai and then to myself Kesküla, an Estonian social democrat. When we met he tried to make play of his contacts and acquaintance with comrades Lenin, Zinoviev and other members of our foreign centres. Kesküla behaved in a very odd way, declaring himself in favour of a German orientation to our policy, finally offering me his good offices if we required his help in obtaining arms, a printing press and other means of struggle against tsarism. His conduct seemed most suspicious to us and we at once felt him to be an agent of the German General Staff and not only turned down his offer but also broke off all relations with him. His connections in Sweden were considerable. He had contacts with Finnish "activists", friends inside the Russian embassy and also in Russian banking and insurance circles.

Our refusal to have dealings with Kesküla did not preclude further attempts by him to penetrate our midst through other individuals. At the end of 1915, we uncovered a link between Bogrovsky, the secretary of the Stockholm group of the RSDLP(B) and Kesküla. An investigation established that the former had received money from Kesküla, although he had used it for personal purposes only. For infringing the resolution on the inadmissibility of relations with Kesküla, Bogrovsky was expelled from the party and the incident forced us to be even more prudent in drawing people in to assist our revolutionary work.

The investigation of Bogrovsky's activity and his dealings with Kesküla was conducted by comrades N. Bukharin and G. Pyatakov. We soon managed to fall on fresh clues to a ring of espionage surrounding our Stockholm group of Bolsheviks. We succeeded in finding evidence of Kesküla's connection with the Danish left socialist, Kruse, who had been deported from Norway.

In 1915 or 1916 I had an encounter with Kruse at the Danish "Hotel Dagmar" in Petersburg. His arrival in Russia seemed to me highly suspicious and his explanation, a very muddled one, only confirmed my creeping distrust of him. When at N.M. Bukharina's in Moscow in 1916, I received even more pointers which justified my suspicions with regard to the nature of Kruse's activity. Evidently not anticipating any suspicion falling on himself, Kruse had in Moscow offered all those same facilities that Kesküla himself had thrust upon us back in 1914. At the same time he was seeking to make use of our contacts, and in particular N.M. Bukharina's address, given to him by N. Bukharin, to get in touch with Kesküla's friends resident in Moscow. I shared my suspicions with N.M. Bukharina and later received from her a letter written in English of a very odd nature which contained a request that she go and meet some Estonian and convey him a message from Kesküla. I proposed right away to have several photocopies taken of Kruse's letter; this would thus implicate the "left" socialist in direct contacts with the secret service.

During my stay in Russia in the winter of 1915-1916 comrades Bukharin and Pyatakov developed their revolutionary counter-intelligence skills so extensively that the entire espionage service was thrown into alarm. Military and police espionage in Sweden were closely interlinked. German espionage found protectors in Sweden's top governmental circles. French and British intelligence were also at work, relying partly upon top commercial circles and the sympathy of the "democracies" of the Scandinavian countries. Our counter-intelligence so perturbed Swedish police circles that the Stockholm authorities hastened to pick up comrades Bukharin and Pyatakov and concocted some absurd charge to deport them from Swedish territory. Branting and his party majority took no steps to uncover any of these intrigues.

With regard to the offers from Kesküla and his agents, I personally by that time, 1916, had brought them to Branting's notice; but the bosses of Swedish social democracy did nothing to unmask the work of the spy network. The work of anti-war socialist groups in even the neutral countries was subjected to persecution and fell beneath the watchful eye of all sorts of police; it quite often reminded us of tsarist procedures. During our stay in Sweden we did not conceal our identity of views or our contacts with the left groups in the socialist parties of Scandinavia. The addresses of these organizations were a help to us in maintaining relations with both Russia and our centres abroad. We would receive literature at Swedish social democrats' addresses to be ferried over to Russia. This link was discovered by the Swedish police and once (in 1916) they made a raid on the premises of the left groups in the Folkets Hus (people's house) of a south Stockholm working-class district and a certain quantity of our literature was impounded. Correspondence received by our comrades was opened and inspected by sleuths. My rules on illegal work, not to have any party material addressed to myself, safeguarded me however from losing correspondence so that throughout the period of my work

THE BEGINNING OF THE END

there I had no instances of lost documents or letters.

The most reactionary war required the adoption of all sorts of stratagems to fight the workers' movement. The Western "democracies", which had given their blessing to the imperialist slaughter of peoples, and duped the working class about the war's "liberating" mission, took over all the tricks of the tsarist Okhrana in relation to the left social-democratic groups.

The work of the Okhrana did not relax during the war. Wartime conditions gave the gendarmerie unlimited possibilities for rooting out sedition. To the usual peacetime "punishments", prison, hard labour and exile, a new one was added: posting to front-line positions. And many advanced workers were despatched to forward positions as a punishment for holding strikes, protesting against exploitation, or political activity.

Our underground organizations in the big industrial centres lay not just under the untiring watch of external observation, planted agents and other manifestations of spying. For underground organizations the most dangerous form of espionage was provocation, the so-called "inner light". The Petersburg, Moscow and other major organizations could sense at every step the hand of the "internal agency" at work. It was only by means of provocation that the Petersburg Okhrana succeeded in discovering the printshop and arresting Petersburg Committee members and other leading party workers. The standard average duration of a party worker's illegal activity was for Petersburg set at three months. Our organizations geared themselves to this standard. There were of course quite a few exceptions to this rule, but those exceptional cases were regarded by our underground as work "in excess of the norm". After such a three-month term the work of the internal agency and external observation, in the form of shadowing, would culminate in arrests. There were very few instances of street arrests. The Okhrana preferred to uncover a party worker's refuge for the night and make the arrest at the house. Skilled professionals therefore tried above all to arrange their lodgings and flats secretly, that is if they had any.

On my last trip from Stockholm to Petersburg in October 1916 I noticed relatively quickly intensive external observation upon myself. Evading the sleuths trailing me proved fairly easy. I had developed a particularly keen sense and my eyes readily spotted among passers-by the sleuth marching along on my heels. In order to evade arrest I did not use either passports or a permanent flat, although I had both. One passport carnet bearing the name of Mavritsky had been obtained for me by "trusties" and through the "private" means of V. Shurkanov (a provocateur), and I obtained another passport bearing the name of a Finnish national when passing through Helsinki. But both of these I used only for railway travel, though I carried one of them, the Finnish one mainly, as a document in event of any street incident. I did not present them to obtain a residence permit but used the visas obtained by the holders.

In the course of my work I had developed certain "rules". I would never walk twice along the same road. I would never stop over at one flat for more than one night at a time. The locations of the different lodgings permitted me to cover my tracks. Thus by the end of 1916 I had the use of three flats beyond the Neva Gate, two on the Vyborg side, one at Lesny, one on the Grazhdanka and one at Galernaya Gavan. In the event of intensive observation I would hide in one of my flats for a couple of days, which would upset the sleuths' arrangements. I hid the whereabouts of my night-time flats from all comrades most diligently.

Fighting the internal agency, i.e. provocations, was immeasurably harder. The presence of provocations would be finely reflected in the whole work of the organization. During wartime charges of provocation, lurking suspicions and hints were expressed about very many comrades. Many of these suspicions were themselves in the nature of provocations: it was most important to the Okhrana to introduce the maximum suspicion and demoralization into our ranks. We had to check the rumours and suspicions very meticulously, but verification would nearly always falter at the lack of "concrete" facts. A considerable share of the suspicions were founded upon mistrust or the private hunches of individual comrades. It was difficult to establish the grounds for mistrust and to investigate and check the suspect member by gaining a closer acquaintance with his activity outside party circles. Yet this very sensitivity of individual comrades and the ability to "sniff out" the enemy was from my personal experience and the reactions of a number of underground workers very seldom mistaken. It was on the basis of a number of private convictions that we declared the well-known Miron Chernomazov to be a provocateur.

Individual comrades had suspected Chernomazov of scheming and careerism as long ago as 1914. When I came across Chernomazov's activities in Petersburg in 1915 I was greatly struck by its disruptive anti-party nature. At the end of 1915 I was to hear many personal statements concerning Chernomazov's work in the hospital and insurance funds. Chernomazov made use of his position as secretary of the hospital funds of the biggest undertakings on the Vyborg side, the Lessner plants, and planned to create a leading centre for insurance work around his own personality. He worked stubbornly towards this end; by using the Vyborg district party committee, he proved able to secure a majority of the then Petersburg Committee behind him.

Grouping around him young secretaries of several factory hospital funds he worked against our legal journal *Voprosy Strakhovaniya* and opposed it with the idea of a new "non-factional" journal, *Bolnichnaya Kassa*. Simultaneously he began a cunning campaign of intrigue against our Workers' Group of the Insurance Council. Chernomazov and company sought to cloak their work against our insurance organizations with principled differences, charging the Workers' Group of the Insurance Council and the editorial board of *Voprosy Strakhovaniya* with opportunism and accusing them of reluctance to work in step with the Petersburg Committee. This accusation was seconded in the Petersburg Committee by L. Starck and S. Bagdatiev (alias Narvsky). We had to open an investigation into the whole affair, and in the autumn of 1915 we made an examination of these differences of "principle".

Suspicions of intriguing, lust for power, careerism and even suggestions of Chernomazov's and his friends' links with the Okhrana were expressed by the following comrades: G. Osipov (a member of the Workers' Group of the Insurance Council speaking on its behalf), Vinokurov, Gladnev, Faberkevich, Podvoisky, Shvedchikov, Olminsky and Eremeev. Several of them also expressed suspicions about L. Starck and S. Bagdatiev. As evidence against them there was only the "work" of Chernomazov and Co., and so I directed all my attention towards checking it.

I managed to arrange a joint meeting of representatives of the Workers' Group and the editorial board of the journal with the "young" insurance workers organized by the Petersburg Committee on the then very acute problem of the activity of our workers' insurance group and the editorial board of *Voprosy Strakhovaniya*. This joint meeting took place at the flat of the engineer Faberkevich, a former member of the editorial board of *Voprosy Strakhovaniya*. At this meeting we succeeded in proving the complete baselessness of the charges of opportunism and all the reproaches of lack of co-ordination of work with the Petersburg Committee. At the end of the debate the "young" insurance workers (supporters of Chernomazov and Starck) moved a practical proposal on a "coalition" structure for the editorial board of *Voprosy Strakhovaniya* which would reserve half the seats for themselves as "representatives" of the Petersburg Committee. Fully expressed in this proposal was Chernomazov's ambition to penetrate the centre of the insurance work, the very place into which he was not allowed access and where none of the old comrades wanted to work jointly with him or his candidates. We rejected the proposal for a coalition structure for the editorial board as contrary to party statutes and practice on the management of party central organs, for *Voprosy Strakhovaniya* and the Workers' Group of the Insurance Council were all-Russian institutions. On behalf of the Central Committee I declared the "coalition" proposal to be unacceptable; but bearing in mind the importance of the issue and of involving new forces in collaborating I proposed to present a list of people to the Central Committee Bureau whom the "young" insurance workers might like included on the editorial board of the all-Russian organ guiding insurance work. My proposal was accepted by the entire editorial board and by the representatives of the insurance organizations, but caused some confusion in the ranks of the Chernomazovites.

Chernomazov, Starck and Co. were quick to realize against whom the proposal to submit candidates to the Central Committee Bureau was aimed: they did not propose any candidates but made a vigorous attack on myself in person, trying to discredit both myself and the Central Committee as "foreigners" and party bosses divorced from the work. As it was then composed, the Petersburg Committee was under the thumb of Chernomazov, Starck and Co. and had adopted the motion proposed by those gentlemen against *Voprosy Strakhovaniya* and a further one directed against myself personally. It took a lot of trouble to compel the Petersburg Committee to reverse its resolution. But the insurance workers carried a contrary motion which once again refuted all the charges made against them. However, I then managed to get the agreement of the Petersburg Committee's Executive Commission to the expulsion of Chernomazov and Starck from its ranks. However, owing to the duplicity of certain Petersburg Committee members, this was not implemented until the autumn of 1916 when a firm resolution against those gentlemen's intrigues was adopted.

Although without meeting Chernomazov himself, I, on looking into the affair, had become increasingly convinced by his behaviour that we had there a fairly smart Okhrana agent. The suspicions that I had expressed to one or two members of the Petersburg Committee had provided a pretext to the Executive Commission (Bagdatiev, Schmidt and Starck) to demand "more concrete" data from me on his work as a provocateur. The evidence provided by the whole of Chernomazov's activity proved insufficient for these comrades. It was impossible for me to meet this demand and submit concrete data on Chernomazov's function as a provocateur in the form of material proof. Contact with the Okhrana itself would be necessary for that, and I had none. So, by exploiting this alibi, the said Petersburg Committee workers retained links with the Chernomazovites. Only in the autumn of 1916 was a halt called both to Chernomazov's intrigues and to the slap-happy attitude of some Petersburg Committee workers by a resolution from the Central Committee Bureau. All party workers were forbidden to have anything to do with him.

THE BEGINNING OF THE END

At the beginning of the winter of 1915, during one of my habitual tours of Petersburg Committee rendezvous points I met on the Vyborg side, a worker acquaintance, Aleksei Gorin, a turner by trade, who was a member of our underground organization at that time active in Petersburg. As old comrades from working in Paris we got into conversation. When he heard that the Petersburg Committee had fixed up a rendezvous at V.E. Shurkanov's flat where in fact I was then heading, he warned me to be careful with contacts made at that flat. "That flat is a beacon for the Okhrana," he said. Workers from Eiwas whom we knew then came up to us, preventing our continuing the conversation. We had arranged to meet again, but that same evening he and others imprudently gathered at a restaurant on the Petersburg side and were arrested. I was therefore unable to find out whom Gorin suspected when I mentioned the flat of former Third Duma deputy Shurkanov. The remark did, however, put me on the alert and prompted me not to bring Shurkanov into our work. By asking leading questions, I tried repeatedly to ascertain whether anyone else under suspicion had a flat on the Vyborg side but without success.

Petersburg Committee workers would use Shurkanov's flat both as a rendezvous and for overnight lodgings, and for several it was a permanent abode. I too had sometimes to call in there to meet one or another member of the Petersburg Committee. I had not hitherto been acquainted with Shurkanov, and on our first meeting he gave the impression of a rather dim and fairly uneducated worker. From the outset he exhibited great interest in my nomadic life in Petersburg, and made a number of offers which would in his opinion spare me a dog's life of roaming around the city. At that time Shurkanov was working at the Eiwas works. My brief observation of Shurkanov, his way of life and also snippets of information from various Eiwass workers yielded no information that enhanced my suspicions about him. Illegal party workers were to be found living in his flat. In his life he in no way stood out from an average metalworker of the Petersburg district. He was prized among comrades for his hospitality and it was said that he was no fool at drinking. Many old comrades would gather round at his flat for a drink and to reminisce about the old days — for example Poletaev, Afanasiev, Klimanov, Pavlov and others.

Shurkanov's part in party work was an extremely modest one. It was only his history as a deputy that had afforded him the opportunity to maintain his contacts and to render "services" to the organization by making his flat available. He did not have any influence on party work, but by having the contacts and comrades around him at his own place he was well involved in highly clandestine business. At the rendezvous arranged by Petersburg Committee workers at Shurkanov's everything would be talked over in his immediate presence.

Shurkanov showed special solicitude towards myself. My homeless existence worried him particularly and he suggested many time that I take one of his spare rooms. I considered, however, that all these offers were inappropriate and directly violated my precautions on underground work. And for reasons of a similar nature, founded moreover upon a certain secret distrust that I still retained for Shurkanov following A. Gorin's comments, I made various polite excuses and turned down all his offers of lodgings and resting places.

In my struggle against Chernomazov, Shurkanov stood wholly on my side, thereby confirming all the doubts and conclusions I had expressed over the provocateur nature of Chernomazov's activity.

Before 9 January 1917

After the conferences with Moscow party comrades at the end of December 1916 I managed to make a trip to Nizhni-Novgorod. In view, however, of the arrests and searches taking place in Kanavino and Sormovo, I was able to stop only three days there. Since the time of my first visit in 1915 the Nizhegorod organization had grown considerably stronger. Circles were active at the Sormovo works; the party enjoyed influence among workers at the plant. A struggle against the defensist elements within the Mensheviks and Socialist-Revolutionaries was under way. The former found support in the hospital fund and were engaged in seeking "legal" paths for the workers' movement even if that meant working within the 1903 act on factory and works stewards. Discontent was at that time mounting among workers over the high cost of living and the shortage of food supplies which was especially acute for the purely proletarian masses having no ties with the land.

Local party workers did not harbour any special hopes for the chance of movement in connection with 9 January. They did not, however, rule out the possibility of strikes if the capital undertook strong action on those days.

By the end of 1916 the idea of "war to the end", to "the final victory", was largely undermined. Anti-war feelings were rampant not only among the working masses but also embraced wide circles of "city-dwellers". In the army itself, both at the front and the rear, patriotic fever had long since burnt itself out and no artificial efforts could fan it up again. Despair and hatred gripped the labouring masses and only a small push was needed for it to overflow into protest.

The government, landlords and bourgeoisie understood and took stock of the growth of discontent and anti-war feelings, and stepped up their repressive methods of fighting isolated manifestations of protest. Intensive agitation was conducted against us, both in the press and through the various organizations working for "the organization of defence". Every resource was set in motion: accusations of provocation, of German intrigues and bribes. But slander could not halt the workers' movement either: just like the bourgeoisie's other ploys it proved incapable of rousing the proletariat to a battle for the Dardanelles.

The tsarist government was keenly aware that the first blows of popular indignation would be directed against itself and made ready to repulse a spontaneous popular onslaught. In all major industrial centres the police were given training in armed street fighting. The tsar's government resolved to meet the revolutionary movement, which was developing month by month and threatening the foundations of the tsarist monarchy, with a well-prepared and bloody rebuff. Nor did the government conceal its bloody preparations from the eyes of the people. It had decided to spray 1917 with hot lead. But we had by now grown a little accustomed to the horrors of death after those years of carnage and no longer feared them. The threat of them was clear to everyone, not only at the front but in the rear too.

Our little organizations, scattered around factories, plants and mines, were also preparing for struggle. They did not at that stage have any military know-how at their disposal, nor were they as well armed as the tsar's police detachments; but that did not demoralize our fighters, armed as they were with only a thirst for struggle and victory. Every worker had a vague idea that inside those grey greatcoats, soldiers' hearts were beating in time with his own wishes. The task of the proletariat for 1917 was to draw the army into a revolutionary front against the tsar, the landlords, the bourgeoisie and the war.

Index

Abrosimov, 198
Afanasiev, 223
Aleksandrovich (Pierre Orage), 114, 165, 166
Alekseyev, General, 190
Alexandrov, 142
Alexandrova, 97
Alexandrovsk, 61
Alexeev, 171
All-Russian Constituent Assembly, 75
Altschuler, 213
Amalgamated Society of Engineers, 55, 56, 115, 120
America. *See* United States of America
American Federation of Labor, 119
American Socialist Party, 119
American socialists, 41, 49, 50
Amsterdam, 39
Anderson, 56
Antipov, N., 133, 200, 213
"Anya" (Kostina), 133
Arkhangelsk, 61, 63, 192
Armenia and Armenians, 35, 148, 149
Arzamas, 102
Asquith, H., 149
Association of Factory and Plant Owners, 13, 73, 81, 82, 83, 135, 140, 186, 203, 207
Atlas, 81
Attila, 151

Austria, 34, 35, 36, 43, 216
Austro-Germans, 93, 216
Austro-Hungary, 151
Austro-Serbian frontier, 13
Alexrod, 178

Badayev, 4, 25
Bagdatiev, S. (S. Narvsky), 70, 75, 98, 104, 108, 221
Baku, 39, 185
Baltic provinces, 43
Baranovsky, 81
Batursky, 199
Belenin, A. (Shlyapnikov), 126, 142, 201
Belgium, 17, 29, 33, 34, 40, 46, 49, 50, 57, 90, 93, 157
Beloostrov, 64, 68, 70, 109, 128, 132
Benardak brothers, 102
Bergen, 53, 54, 115
Bergen fjord, 53
Berlin, 32, 68
Berzin, 59
Bethmann, 149
Birzhevka, 21
Black Hundred patriotism, 18, 27
Blum, A., 25
Bobrinsky, A.A., 209
Boden, 31, 63
Bogrovsky, J., 52, 113, 217
Bolnichnaya Kassa, 221
Bolsheviks, 4, 5, 8, 21, 22, 26, 32, 35, 41, 52, 78, 79, 88,

105, 107, 117, 121, 171, 181, 202, 217
Bosch, E.B., 61, 64
Bourne, Gustave, 25
Branting, Hjalmar, 36–7, 42, 44, 47, 50, 52, 122, 218
Breido, 84, 136
Brendin, I.V., 186
Brendin, N., 193
Briand, 149
Britain, 18, 20, 29, 33, 34, 40, 46, 50, 53–61, 90, 93, 115, 148, 149, 151, 157, 177, 218
British Socialist Party, 55, 59
Bryansk county, 204
Bryansk locomotive works, 18
Bulgaria, 151
Bukharin, N.I., 59, 61–2, 64, 112, 113, 114, 120, 121–2, 201, 217, 218
Bukharina, N.M., 59, 217, 218
Bundists, 41
Burtsev, V.L., 18, 157
Butykri, 100
Byulleten Rabochei Gruppy, 178

Cable works, 83
Caucasus, 23, 43, 44
Central Committee (RSDLP), 28, 29, 32, 36, 38, 42, 44, 47, 64, 67, 70, 98–100, 108, 109, 113, 115, 120, 140–45, 146, 159, 164, 166, 181–90, 193, 197, 198, 200–03, 206, 212–16, 217, 222
Central Public Organizations' Food Committee, 205
Central War Industries Committee, 71–2, 74, 77, 79, 84, 145, 165, 178–9, 184, 198
Chelnokov, 171, 189
Chernomazov ("Miron"), 70, 98, 99, 101, 104, 105, 108, 142, 152, 200, 220–21, 222, 224
Chernov, V., 114, 165
Chicherin, G., 59
China, 149
Chkheidze, N.S., 4, 5, 22, 74, 107, 137, 165, 166, 170, 180, 187, 210, 211
Chkhenkeli, A., 74
Christiania (Oslo), 52, 61, 114, 115, 120, 121, 122
Chudnovsky, G.I., 121, 122
Chugurin, 142
Congress of the United Nobility, 168, 171, 190, 211
Constantinople, 170, 172. See also Tsargrad
Copenhagen, 47, 48, 50, 120
Council of Congresses, 78
Czechs, 19

Dalin (Y. Levin), 38, 39, 121
Dan, F.I., 4, 5
Danish Social-Democratic Party, 47, 48–9
D'Annunzio, 149
Dansky, 146
Dardanelles, 23, 40, 225
Defence of the Realm Act, 58
Delo, 165
Den, 19, 88
Denmark, 37, 48, 50, 120, 121
Dmitriev, 6
Dolgolevsky, M.L., 59, 113, 121
Donets Basin, 73, 159, 160, 163, 185, 188
Doshchatoe, 101
Drachevsky, 16
Dubois, 25
Duma faction Social Democrats, 4, 6, 25–30, 37–8, 41, 44, 45, 74, 98, 137, 166, 202

INDEX

Duma State, 20, 21, 25, 63, 71, 75, 91, 101, 109, 143, 147, 156, 157, 161, 165, 166, 167–81, 187, 189, 198, 199, 208–11
Dutch social democrats, 39, 49

Egorov, I.N., 186
Egypt, 149
Eiwas Works, 11, 79, 81, 97, 105, 223
Ekaterinburg, 185
Ekaterinoslav, 145, 161–2
Ekonomicheskoe Obozrenie, 165
Elizarova, A.I., 99, 103
Ellert (N. Nakoryakov), 117
Engels, Frederick, 25
England, 37, 53–60. See also Britain
Eremeev, K.S., 103, 221
Ericssons, 2, 7–8, 17, 26, 97, 186
Erzurum, 88
Estonians, 92, 123
Evdokimov, G., 133, 200, 213

Faberkevich, 221
Fiat, 54
Finland, 32, 35, 37, 41, 61, 62, 64–8, 69, 99, 110, 123, 127–9, 140, 142, 149
Finn, 25
Finn-Epotaevsky, 51
Finnish social democrats, 62, 67, 68
Finnmarken, 63
Fokin, Ignat ("Petr"), 99
Folketing, 48
France, 1, 20, 21, 25, 26, 29, 33, 34, 36, 40, 43, 45, 46, 50, 55, 56, 57, 59, 60, 90, 93, 149, 151, 157, 177, 210, 218
Free Economics Society, 25

Galernaya Gavan, 220
Galicia, 20, 35, 40, 148, 149
Geneva, 35
Georgians, 35
German social democrats, 39, 44, 45, 49
Germany and Germans, 1, 14, 16–17, 18, 20, 23, 25, 29, 31, 32, 33, 34–7 *passim,* 39–41, 43, 45–6, 48, 49, 50, 55, 56, 57, 58, 60, 61, 67, 86, 88, 89, 90, 120, 127, 148–9, 151, 157, 177, 210, 216, 217, 218
Gladnev, 221
Globachev, Colonel, 192
Gnevich, 103
Golos Sotsial-Demokrata, 184
Gompers, Samuel, 119
Gordon, N., 32, 114, 121
Gorin, Aleksei, 105–6, 223, 224
Gorky, A.M., 94, 97, 99, 107, 146, 215
Gorlovka mines, 160, 162
Grazhdanka, 6, 141, 220
Grigoriev, 26
Gromov, M., 103
Guchkov, 71, 73, 78–9, 90, 92, 142, 166, 171, 178
Gulf of Bothnia, 31, 37, 112, 124
Gurko, General, 190
Gvozdev, 71, 77, 78, 79, 84, 107, 166
Gvozdevites, 84, 88, 92, 93, 97, 107, 108, 165, 184, 187, 189

Hague, The, 50
Hälsingborg, 122
Hammerfest, 63
Hangut, battleship, 139, 191, 192, 195

Haparanda, 31, 62, 64, 65, 112, 123
Hardie, Keir, 56
Harrison, 54
Haukipudas, 131
Helsingor, 122
Helsinki, 64, 67–8, 70, 109, 110, 122, 138, 191, 193, 219
Herzen Circle, 57
Höglund, Zeth, 35, 44, 114, 122
Holland, 37, 50, 60
Holmenkollen, 52
Hospital Funds, 156
Hungary, 151
Hyndman, 55–6

Ilyin, N.I., 6
Independent Labour Party (ILP), 55, 56
India, 149
Ingerman, 117
Institute for the Study of the Social Consequences of the War, 47
Insurance Council, 73, 88, 92, 164, 185, 200, 221
Inter-District Organization, 164, 202
International, 21, 39, 44, 49, 50, 177
International Socialist Bureau (ISB), 5, 39, 49–50
International Socialist Congress, 49
International Socialist Labour League, 20
International Workers' League, 20
Ireland, 149
Italian social democrats, 47
Italian Socialist Party, 50
Italy, 149
Ivanovo-Voznesensk, 215

Izhor works, 77
Izvestiya Byuro Tsentralnogo Komiteta, 201

Japan, 18, 20, 40, 149
Jews, 19, 27, 35, 86, 115, 117, 161

Kalinin, M., 97
Kaluga province, 204
Kamenev, L.B., 98
Kanava, 102
Kanavino, 102 103, 224
Kapuskas, 59
Karl Marx People's Club, 57
Karunki, 31, 111, 122
Kautsky, Karl, 39, 93
Kayurov, 26, 97, 142
Kayurova, 97
Kazan, 183
Kemi, 64, 66, 67, 68, 111
Kerensky, A.F., 90, 107, 165, 166, 171, 180
Keskülä, A., 51, 113, 123, 217, 218
Kerzhentsev, 59
Khabalov, 198
Kharkov, 145, 183–4, 185, 189–90
Khaustov, 74, 180
Khavkin, A., 123
Khovrin, N., 193
Khvostov, 78
Kienthal, 178
Kiev, 159, 198
Kilbom, Karl, 36, 122
Kirghiz, 208,
"Kirill' (I.F. Orlov), 97, 140, 193
Kirkenes, 61
Kirkwall, 115, 120
Kiselev, 6
Klassekampen, 53
Klimanov, 223

Klimovich, 197
Knudsen, 50
Kola, 61
Kollontai, Alexandra, 32, 39, 42, 47, 61, 144, 164, 217
Kolomna, 9, 10, 15
Kommunist, 62, 64, 92, 99, 101, 113, 182
Konovalov, 189, 199
Kopeika, 21
Kostina ("Anya"), 133
Kovalenko, I.I., 98, 106
Kozin, G., 102, 103
Kozlovsky, M.Y., 63
Krasikor, 146
Krasin, L.B., 146
Krestinsky, N.N., 25
Kristianiafjörd, 115
Kronstadt, 16, 138, 191–7
Kronstadt Committee, 191, 197
Kropotkin, 18, 157, 158
Krupskaya, N.K., 64
Kruse, A., 123, 217–18
Kudryashev, 75, 77, 78
Kuklina, A., 97
"Kuvaka", General, 190

Labour Leader, 56
Ladyzhnikov, I.I., 215
Landrin, 11
Larin, Yuri (M. Lurie), 32, 38, 39, 41, 45, 46, 51, 107
Latvians, 92
League of Russian Workers, 61
Lena, 1
Lenin, V.I., 2, 26, 32, 45, 64, 92, 113, 185, 217
Lesny, 142, 200, 220
Lessner. *See* New Lessner Works
Letts, 59
Levin, Y. (Dalin), 38, 39, 121
Levin brothers, 38
Levit, 102

Liebknecht, Karl, 41, 170
Lindhagen, Carl, 36
Lindley, Charles, 37
Lisovsky, 117
Liteiny, 27, 165
Lithuania, 23, 41
Lithuanians, 59
Litvinov, 54, 56, 59
Ljakonen, Adam, 68
Lloyd George, 57
Lødingen, 63
Lodz, 23
London, 50, 54–60, 115
Löteberg, 112, 124
Luch, 2, 4
Luleå, 31, 62, 124
Lurie, M. *See* Larin, Y.
Lutovinov ("Yurii"), 105, 108
Lvov, G.E., 172
Lvov, V.N., 171, 189
Lyudinovo, 204

Maisky, V., 59
"Makar" (V.P. Nogin), 100, 215
Maklakov, 170, 176
Maksimovich, Aleksei, 94–5
Maltzov company, 204
Manchuria, 40
Mariupol, 163
Markov, 19
Marseilles, 26
Martins, I.K., 56, 58, 59
Martov, 2, 178
Marxist Building Workers, 104
Maslov, 73, 90
Masurian lakes, 17
Mavritsky, 219
Mechanical and Boiler Works, 83
Mechanics' Union, 1
Medvedev, S., 99
Meller-Zakomelsky, 189
Melnichansky, 117

Mensheviks, 2, 4, 5, 8, 21, 26, 32, 41, 45, 74, 78, 84, 164, 165, 176, 177–8, 180, 184, 198, 199, 202, 205, 211, 224
Menson, 117
Metalworkers' Union, 1
Metal Works, 81
Mikhailov (Vanya), 214
Milyukov, P.N., 142, 143, 148, 149, 150, 169, 170, 174, 176, 189
Milyutin, N.I., 100, 103
Minin, 72
Minkin-Menson, 117
"Miron" (Chernomazov), 70, 98, 99, 101, 104, 105, 108, 142, 152, 200, 220–21, 222, 224
"Mironites", 98
Mokhovaya, 20
Molotov, V. (Skryabin), 141, 142, 164, 200, 201
Morocco, 149
Moscow, 11, 39, 43, 44, 78, 80, 84, 85, 92, 96, 98, 100–02, 103, 156, 158, 159, 165, 171, 181, 185, 190, 201, 205, 213, 214–15, 217–18, 219, 224
Moscow Committee, 100
Moslems, 19
Mostovenko, R.V., 159
Murkin, 6
Murmansk, 114
Myasoedov, 89, 147

Nakoryakov, N., 117
Narodniks (Socialist-Revolutionaries), 5n, 76–7, 93, 171, 180, 211
Narva, 9, 84
Narvik, 61, 63
Narvsky, Sergei (Bagdatiev), 70, 75, 98, 104, 108, 221
Nashe Slovo, 121

Naumov, 208–9
Navashino, 101
Nazarov, N.I., 26, 97, 107, 142
Nepenin, Admiral, 197
Neva Gate, 10, 15, 27, 33, 70, 84, 220
Neva Mechanical, 33
Neva shipyards, 24, 81
Neva Stearin, 33
Nevka, 10
Newcastle, 53, 54, 60
New Lessner Works, 1–4, 7, 9, 10, 17, 75, 81, 96, 98, 104, 108–9, 133, 134–6, 186, 201, 220
New York, 58, 116–20
New York People's News, 119
Nicholas I, 87
Nicholas II, 24, 26, 80, 168, 171, 190
Nikolaev, 185
Nikolaevna, Sofya, 100
Nizhegorod, 224
Nizhni-Novgorod, 72, 97, 102, 103, 158, 159, 182, 224
Nobels, 8, 98
Nogin, V.P. ("Makar"), 100, 215
Norgaard, Osman, 63, 64
Norskenflyammen, 124
Norway, 37, 50, 52, 53, 57, 58, 61–3, 114, 115, 120, 217
Norwegian Social-Democratic Party, 52, 114
Novaya Derevnya, 163
Novy Mir, 117

Obolensky, R.V., 215
Obukh, 100
Obukhov engineering works, 33
Odessa, 35
Okhrana (security service), 1, 6, 52, 72, 73, 78, 79, 80, 82, 86, 89, 90, 95, 100, 105, 106,

110, 138, 185, 191, 196, 200, 219, 220, 221, 222
Oldenburg, Prince, 128
Olminsky, M.S., 100, 101, 215, 221
"On the War", 182
"On the High Cost of Living", 182
Orage, Pierre (Aleksandrovich), 114, 165, 166
Organizing Committee (OC), 38, 39, 45, 46
Orlov, I.F. ("Kirill"), 97, 140, 193
Orlov, K., 192
Osipov, G.I., 6, 99, 103, 185, 221
Oslo, 52. *See also* Christiania
Osvedomitelny Listok, 164
Oulu, 62, 66–8, 110, 124, 127–31
Ozerki, 6
Ozol, 81

Paris, 4, 21, 35, 59, 223
Parviainen Shell Works, 7, 82
Parvus, 47, 120, 216
Pavlov, D.A., 97, 106, 142, 223
Pavlova, M.G., 97, 109, 142, 159
Pechori, 103
Pelicanovites, 35
People's House, 68
Persinen, 68
Peters, 59
Petersburg, 1, 3, 5, 6, 7, 9–10, 13–30 *passim,* 32–5, 37, 38, 39–41, 43, 44, 45, 57, 62, 68, 70–109 *passim,* 110, 128, 130, 133–45 *passim,* 152, 156, 158, 164, 165, 169, 171, 175, 177–92 *passim,* 200, 206, 212–17, 219, 220, 223
Petersburg Committee (of RSDLP), 5, 10, 14, 19–21, 23, 34, 39, 70, 71, 74–80, 84, 86, 94–101, 103–05, 108, 133, 136–44, 146, 163, 164, 165, 173–5, 178, 181, 185, 186, 189, 190, 191–3, 195–7, 200, 201, 202, 206, 212, 213, 219–24 *passim*
Petersburg Initiative Group, 79, 164
Petersburg Railway Organization of RSDLP, 104
"Petr" (I. Fokin), 99
Petrograd. *See* Petersburg
Petrov, 59
Petrovsky, G.I., 4, 5, 25, 38, 45
Phoenix, 81
Piletsky, 121
Pisarev, 193
Pitirim, 150, 190, 211
Plehve, 109
Plekhanov, G.V., 18, 35, 73, 92, 157, 158
Plekhanovites, 22, 41, 164
Podvoisky, N.I., 103, 221
Poincaré, 9, 14
Poland, 23–4, 43, 92
Poles, 19, 92
Poletaev, 223
Polish Social Democracy, 23–4, 41
Polish Socialist Party, 41
Pomor, 63
Potresov, 4, 73, 90
Pozharsky, 72
Pravda 1, 10, 19, 101, 104
Pravda-ists, 92, 99, 107, 108
"Priboi", 105
Proletarskii Golos, 136, 189, 190, 213
"Prosveshchenie", 105
Protopopov, 150, 169, 198, 200, 209

Prussia, 14, 29, 45, 46
Purishkevich, 19, 92
Putilov, 9, 25, 75, 83, 86, 105, 196
Pyatakov, G.L., 61–2, 64, 112, 113–14, 201, 217, 218

Rabochee Utro, 74
Rasputin, 150, 158, 213, 214
Rauma, 37
Rech, 18, 19, 21, 88
Red Cross, 24, 47
Renault works, 136, 186
Rennenkampf, 16
Riga, 39, 44
Riurik, cruiser, 139
Rodzyanko, N.V., 150, 169, 171, 176, 180, 187
Rolland, 149
Romanovs, 150, 168, 171
Rossiya, 186
Rovaniemi, 125
Rovio, K., 68, 110, 132
Rozhdestvensky depot, 85
Rubanovich, 90
Rusanov, 210
Russia, 1–30, 31, 32–5, 36, 37–8, 39–46, 47, 50, 51–2, 56, 57, 59–60, 61, 62, 64, 65, 66, 67, 68, 71, 75, 80, 88–109, 110, 111, 112, 113, 115, 117, 118, 119, 120–21, 123, 124, 125–225
Russian Insurance Society, 113
Russian revolution, 38, 58, 152
Russian Social-Democratic and Labour Party (RSDLP), 21, 23, 30, 39, 42, 98, 113, 137–44, 159–67 *passim,* 173–8, 181–90, 192, 195, 217. See also Central Committee, Petersburg Committee, etc.
Russian socialists, 42
Russkie Vedomosti, 38

Russkoe Znamya, 89
Russo-Japanese War, 18, 24, 39, 40
Ryabinin, A.N., 107
Ryabushinsky, 73, 90

Samoilov, 26
Saveliev, 100, 102
Sazonov-Rozanov, 121
Sbornik Sotsiala-Demokrata, 113
Scandinavia, 31–9, 41–53, 218
Scheidemann, P., 41, 93
Scheld, Hans, 36, 44
Schiemann, 149
Schmidt, V., 6, 70, 104, 133, 192, 213
Second International, 36, 50, 51, 96, 216
Secret Diplomacy, 56
Semenov works, 25, 33
Serbia, 20, 151
"Sergei" (Bagdatiev), 108
Seskarö, 112, 124
Sestroretsk, 77
Seydler, 32
Shary, 146
Shchepkin, 189
Shidlovsky, 150, 189
Shingarev, 189, 209, 210
Shkapin, G.M., 6
Shulygin, 169, 176
Shurkanov, V., 105, 108, 141, 192, 219, 223–4
Shutko, K.I., 200, 213
Shuvalov, 6
Shvedchikov, K.M., 99, 105, 140, 221
Siberia, 24, 92, 181
Siemens-Schuckert, 81
Siemens-Schuckert (Dynamo Works), 82
Skobelev, 180
Skorokhod, 82

Skryabin (V. Molotov), 141, 142, 164, 200, 201
Skvortsev, I.I. (Stepanov), 100, 159, 215
Sladkov, I.D., 26, 186, 193
Smidovich, P.G., 100, 159, 215
Social-Demokraten, 52, 122
Socialist-Revolutionaries, 5, 84, 159, 165, 166, 171, 198, 205, 211, 224
Sokolov, N.D., 25, 63, 107, 137, 164, 166
Sokolov, Stanislav (Volsky), 58–9
Sormovo, 102, 103, 159, 182
Sotsial-Demokrat, 26, 28, 32, 33, 38, 44, 45, 51, 62, 64, 75, 92, 99, 112, 201
Sovremennoe Slovo, 85
Sovremenny Mir, 51
Stakun, M., 193
Star, 204
Starck, L., 70, 98, 104, 105, 108, 200, 221, 222
Stasova, E.D., 164
Stauning, T., 49, 50
Steklov, 146
Steklyanny, 27, 70, 98, 106
Stepanov (I.I. Skvortsev), 100, 159, 215
Stetskevich, M.I., 109
Stockholm, 31, 32, 36, 37, 38, 39, 42, 44, 45, 47, 51, 52, 53, 59, 61, 62, 64, 112, 113, 122, 217, 218, 219
Stormklockan, 114
Straits, 170, 172
Ström, Fredrik, 37, 47, 50, 122
Strukov, A.P., 171
Struve, 73
Stürmer, 137, 143, 147, 165, 169, 170, 174, 180, 187
Stüttgart Congress, 32
Sukhanov, 107
Sukhomlinov, 147
Sundukov, K.M., 103
Sveaborg, 32
Sweden, 31–47, 50, 52, 58, 62, 65, 67, 110, 111, 112, 113–14, 122–3, 127, 216, 218
Swiss social democrats, 47–8
Switzerland, 51, 58, 59, 62, 113, 185

Tallinn, 191
Tartars, 19
Terijoki, 64, 109
Third International, 96
Tikhomirnov, Viktor (Vadim), 99, 140, 142
Tolmachev, N. 213
Tornio, 31, 62, 65, 111, 112, 122, 124
Transcaucasian region, 35
Trades Union Congress (TUC), 56
Trecak, 195, 196
Trepov, 149, 180, 187
Triple Alliance, 13
Triple Entente, 13, 23, 49, 50, 123
Tripolitania, 149
Troelstra, 39, 41, 46, 50, 216, 217
Tromsø, 63
Trondheim, 61
Trotskyites, 41, 164
Trudovik, 33
Tsargrad (Constantinople), 148, 149
Tula, 92, 159
Tulyakov, 210
Tumanov, Prince, 80, 81, 82, 83, 86
Tunisia, 149
Turkestan, 149, 208
Turku, 37, 191
Tver, 181

Tyuterev, I.P., 106

Ukrainians, 35
Ulyanova, Maria I., 99
Ulyantsev, T.I., 186, 193
Union General Electric Company, 183
Union of Towns, 146, 154, 167, 168, 172, 189, 205, 207
Union of Zemstvos, 146, 154, 167, 168, 172, 189, 205, 207
United States (Danish vessel), 120
United States of America, 49–50, 57, 58, 115–19, 149, 215
Uritsky, 32, 121
Uskila, 68, 110, 132

Vadim (V. Tikhomirnov), 99, 140, 142
Vandervelde, Emile, 4, 5, 21, 22, 26, 28, 32, 36, 38, 39, 45
Vanya (Mikhailov), 214
Vardø, 61, 62, 64
Vasiliev Island, 9, 85
Vechernee Vremya, 14, 21
Viden, 52
Viipuri, 64, 191
Vinberg, O., 44
Vinokurov, A.N., 103, 221
Viren, Admiral, 197
"Vladimir" (V. Zalezhsky), 77, 98, 99, 108
Vladimir province,
Voeikov, General, 211
"Voice in the Wilderness", 62, 65, 66, 112
Vokov. *See* Gorin, Aleksei
"Volna", 105
Volodarsky, 117
Volsky (S. Sokolov), 58–9
Voprosy Strakhovaniya, 103, 105, 108, 164, 221, 222
Vorobiev. *See* Gorin, Aleksei

Voronezh, 159
Voronin, Lutsch and Cheshire, 81, 82
Vorstand, 41
Vorwärts, 117
Voskov, 117
Vpered, 164
Vulcan works, 17
Vyborg district, 3, 4, 6, 9, 10, 11, 15, 33, 34, 70, 84, 97, 104, 106, 127, 128, 136, 139, 142, 186, 193, 220
Vyxun, 101

Wagon Works, 82
"War and Socialism", 92
War and the Cost of Living, 187
War Industries Committees, 70, 71, 73–9, 88, 105, 107, 136, 143, 146, 165–6, 167, 168, 172, 176–7, 182, 183, 188, 189, 197–9, 205
War Industry Socialists, 74, 165, 173, 176, 200, 206
Warsaw, 23, 41, 44, 46
Washington, 50
Who Needs the War? (Kollontai), 164, 190
Wiik, K., 68, 69, 110, 132
Wilhelm II, 32, 40, 89
Wilson, 119
Wylie clinic, 11

Yakovleva, 100
Yordansky, N.I., 25, 51
"Yurii" (Lutovinov), 105, 108

Zaitsev, V., 193, 194
Zalezhsky, V. ("Vladimir"), 99, 108, 200
Zalutsky, P., 141, 142, 200
Zamoskvorechie district, 214
Zemshchina, 89
Zhizdra, 204

Zimmerwald, 107, 160, 187- 117, 185, 217
Zimmerwaldists, 137   Zorin, 117
Zinoviev, G.E., 32, 64, 92,   Zurabov, A.G., 121